CRITICAL ISSUES
IN CURRICULUM

CRITICAL ISSUES
IN CURRICULUM

Eighty-seventh Yearbook of the
National Society for the Study of Education

PART I

By

THE YEARBOOK COMMITTEE
and
ASSOCIATED CONTRIBUTORS

Edited by

LAUREL N. TANNER

Editor for the Society

KENNETH J. REHAGE

19 NSSE 88

Distributed by THE UNIVERSITY OF CHICAGO PRESS ● CHICAGO, ILLINOIS

The National Society for the Study of Education

Founded in 1901 as successor to the National Herbart Society, the National Society for the Study of Education has provided a means by which the results of serious study of educational issues could become a basis for informed discussion of those issues. The Society's two-volume yearbooks, now in their eighty-seventh year of publication, reflect the thoughtful attention given to a wide range of educational problems during those years. In 1971 the Society inaugurated a series of substantial publications on Contemporary Educational Issues to supplement the yearbooks. Each year the Society's publications contain contributions to the literature of education from more than a hundred scholars and practitioners who are doing significant work in their respective fields.

An elected Board of Directors selects the subjects with which volumes in the yearbook series are to deal and appoints committees to oversee the preparation of manuscripts. A special committee created by the Board performs similar functions for the series on Contemporary Educational Issues.

The Society's publications are distributed each year without charge to members in the United States, Canada, and elsewhere throughout the world. The Society welcomes as members all individuals who desire to receive its publications. Information about current dues may be found in the back pages of this volume.

This volume, *Critical Issues in Curriculum*, is Part I of the Eighty-seventh Yearbook of the Society. Part II, which is published at the same time, is entitled *Cultural Literacy and the Idea of General Education*.

A listing of the Society's publications still available for purchase may be found in the back pages of this volume.

Library of Congress Catalog Number: 87-062792
ISSN: 0077-5762

Published 1988 by
THE NATIONAL SOCIETY FOR THE STUDY OF EDUCATION

5835 Kimbark Avenue, Chicago, Illinois 60637
© 1988 by the National Society for the Study of Education

First Printing, 6,000 Copies

Printed in the United States of America

iv

v

Acknowledgment

The National Society for the Study of Education is greatly indebted to all who have taken responsibility for the preparation of this timely volume on critical issues in the field of curriculum. We are especially grateful to Professor Laurel N. Tanner. Her prompt and wise responses to queries of all kinds and her meticulous attention to detail mark her as a superb editor.

Professor Tanner has had considerable help from her advisory committee, particularly as the volume was in the planning stage. The substantial contribution made by each of the authors whose chapters comprise the book will be readily apparent to readers.

The Society is proud to include this volume in its series of yearbooks.

Table of Contents

PAGE

THE NATIONAL SOCIETY FOR THE STUDY OF EDUCATION iv

OFFICERS OF THE SOCIETY, 1987-88; THE SOCIETY'S COMMITTEE ON CRITICAL ISSUES IN CURRICULUM; ASSOCIATED CONTRIBUTORS TO THE YEARBOOK v

ACKNOWLEDGMENT vii

Section One
Issues of Professionalism

CHAPTER

I. CURRICULUM ISSUES IN HISTORICAL PERSPECTIVE, *Laurel N. Tanner*   1

II. FADS, FASHIONS, AND RITUALS: THE INSTABILITY OF CURRICULUM CHANGE, *Herbert M. Kliebard* 16

III. UNAPPLIED CURRICULUM KNOWLEDGE, *Henrietta Schwartz* . . 35

IV. POLITICAL PRESSURES ON SUPERVISORS, *Robert H. Anderson* . . 60

Section Two
Issues of Policy

V. THE INFLUENCE OF TESTING ON THE CURRICULUM, *George F. Madaus* 83

VI. THE TEXTBOOK CONTROVERSIES, *Daniel Tanner* 122

VII. ARE WE IMPROVING OR UNDERMINING TEACHING? *Karen K. Zumwalt* 148

VIII. WHO DECIDES? THE BASIC POLICY ISSUE, *Richard W. Clark* . . . 175

IX. ISSUES OF ACCESS TO KNOWLEDGE: GROUPING AND TRACKING, *A. Harry Passow* 205

X. ISSUES OF ACCESS TO KNOWLEDGE: DROPPING OUT OF SCHOOL, *Murry R. Nelson* 226

Section Three
Issues of Leadership

CHAPTER   PAGE

XI. LEADERSHIP FOR CURRICULUM IMPROVEMENT: THE SCHOOL
ADMINISTRATOR'S ROLE, *Gary A. Griffin* 244

XII. PROGRESS IN DEALING WITH CURRICULUM PROBLEMS, *Ralph W. Tyler* 267

NAME INDEX 277

SUBJECT INDEX 281

INFORMATION ABOUT MEMBERSHIP IN THE SOCIETY 285

PUBLICATIONS OF THE SOCIETY 287

Section One
ISSUES OF PROFESSIONALISM

CHAPTER I

Curriculum Issues in Historical Perspective

LAUREL N. TANNER

What do school administrators and supervisors and professors of curriculum and supervision have in common? They are curriculum workers—individuals who have roles in the curriculum field. Curriculum workers develop, implement, and evaluate curriculum, obtain instructional resources and materials, engage in the preparation and supervision of educational personnel. Although they have diverse labels and engage in diverse activities, they share responsibility for the interactive functions of curriculum development and professional development. They are encountering very difficult issues as they go about their work.

This book is about the critical issues facing curriculum workers. It is about problems that are surrounded by intensity of feeling, such as the influence of testing on the curriculum and the censorship of textbooks; it is about problems that are widely recognized and on which there is a great abundance of material. (The dropout problem, which is now receiving a great deal of attention from the lay public and professional educators, is an obvious example.) It is also about problems that are not so well known but are, nonetheless, deeply felt by educators, and we are just beginning to define the nature of some of the less well-known problems. For example, practices that in educators' professional judgment will not help children to realize their possibilities are being imposed upon the schools. The problem takes its sharpest form when the question is: What do we do when pressured to adopt a new school program or policy that we know is not in the best interests of children?

When reforms fly in the face of professional knowledge, the result is not only a lowering of morale but the school system descends into conditions of weakness and ineffectiveness instead of being strengthened as was the reformers' intention.[1] As Robert Anderson points out in his chapter in this yearbook, curriculum workers have a duty to resist many pressures, rather than yielding to them.

Public Policy Issues

Currently, the most difficult issues to solve in the curriculum field are of concern not merely to educators but to the public. These problems are closely related to questions of public policy and the solutions will depend heavily on public decisions. If educators are to take the leadership in helping to determine the answers to these questions of public policy, they will have to be certain of the grounds of their positions. The intent of the authors of chapters in this book is to provide curriculum workers with the best available knowledge on these issues as well as guidance and practical suggestions for dealing with them.

PUBLIC VERSUS PROFESSIONAL PREROGATIVES

Today's pressures on curriculum workers to adopt often ill-advised reforms illuminate the persistence of an older problem: the strain between public and professional prerogatives in education. In theory at least there should be no problem: the public sets policy and the professional staff (supervisors and teachers alike) determine teaching practices. The trouble is that the theory bears little relation to reality. Policies are made at every level including the classroom level, as Richard Clark points out in his chapter. And legislatures and school boards are not reluctant to standardize teaching strategies, or to try to, at any rate. Could there be something wrong with the theory?

Educators do not seem to think so. It is generally accepted that the public prerogative and the professional prerogative should be kept in balance; that is, there should be no infringement on the other's prerogatives.[2] It is assumed that the problem of imposed reforms on schools can be resolved by a balance of decision making between the public and professionals; at present the balance has tilted toward the public.

Yet the problem may be in the concept of balance and separation itself, rather than in its violation. It is all very well that the Constitution of the United States and our state constitutions are based on the principle of the balance and separation of powers, which we owe, of course, to the genius of the Founding Fathers. But this principle addresses a political question: the division of power in government and between governments. It does not address the one pervasive problem of educational decision making: how to get judgments based upon the best evidence available. It would be superfluous to add that the framers of the Constitution were not concerned with the problem of the public and professionals at all. These children of the eighteenth century were concerned with federalism.

Over the years, objections to the concept of balance and separation as a basis for educational decision making have been expressed by Myron Lieberman, who argued that the profession alone should make all policy decisions bearing on education, and by James B. Conant, who insisted that the interests of education would be better served if policy decisions were made by lay persons. Neither view is supported by the discussions in this yearbook. A profession has to have something to say about policy; otherwise it is not a profession. As soon as the professional policy works against the public interest the profession is no longer a profession. It becomes a vested interest. Furthermore, the notion that the public should not be actively concerned with the improvement of teaching is not consistent with our traditions. From colonial days, the public—who supervised the teachers—were concerned that schools be maintained and that teachers improve their methods.

The discussions in this yearbook point to the need, not for "balance," but a synergy—a joint, mutually enhancing relationship based on the best interests of the individual and society. The need is for unity and harmony between the public and professionals. Most important, educational decisions must be made on the best available evidence, not on the basis of who makes them. If we take this principle seriously, we must look more closely than we have at ways of achieving unity and harmony.

PUBLIC OPINION AND PUBLIC POLICY

Too often in recent years educators have used the terms "public" and "politics" synonymously—calling, for example, for some balance between politics and professionals. The chapters that follow indicate clearly that if we are to deal with the issues that confront us, the public should not be confused with politics. Often what we have called the public, when we speak of public versus professional power, is not the public at all but the wheel that squeaks the loudest and gets the attention of the media. (And a new educational movement is born.)

Instead of responding to the public, what curriculum workers are likely to be responding to is the dominant political tide of the moment, which is usually determined by vested interests. Political purposes are one kind of vested interest. Policy experts, such as Paul E. Peterson of the Brookings Institution, have criticized the national education commissions of the 1980s for basing their claims on flimsy evidence, and for having political rather than pedagogical purposes. Many of the public policy recommendations made by national panels and commissions in the 1970s and 1980s represent extremes that do not reflect public opinion. For example, the report of the National Panel on High School and Adolescent Education, *The Education of Adolescents* (1976), recommended that the curriculum be reduced to "essential skills susceptible to school training."[3] Many high schools, particularly those serving disadvantaged youth, followed the retrenchment policy. In the 1980s, a new educational policy emerged in the wake of the federally sponsored report, *A Nation at Risk*. The new policy went to a different extreme: states imposed whole new sets of requirements that students must meet for high school graduation.

The public, as Ralph Tyler has remarked, is centrist. It does not favor extremes such as the child versus the curriculum or vice versa.

It is always easy to mistake policy for the public will, but curriculum workers must keep in mind that public policy does not necessarily reflect public opinion. Indeed, as policy analysts have pointed out, "*the movement of public opinion has been directly opposite to public policy.*"[4] This generalization certainly seems to apply to educational policy. One who reads about the changes in schools mandated by legislatures during the last decade might gain the impression that most people favor eliminating everything from the educational program of the public schools except the basic three R's and academic subjects in the elementary school and the several scholarly disciplines in the secondary school. However, the evidence is just the opposite. Far from wanting a narrower curriculum, as Clark points out in his chapter, parents continually want to include more— in the areas of social and personal development as well as in intellectual and vocational development.

The point is instructive for curriculum workers who, in recent decades, have taken an essentially reactive stance instead of being proactive. The danger is growing that curriculum workers may be permanently constricted by the mistaken impression that public policy always reflects public opinion. Of course, educators must have public support, but this does not come about simply by wishing. Educators can, as Lawrence Cremin once suggested, "lay their case before the public," who, after all, expect educators to take the lead in the improvement of educational programs.

A further consideration is relevant here—not merely relevant but crucial. The major issues confronting curriculum workers do not have to do merely with working out the means (curriculum and instruction) by which schools can carry out their purposes; they have to do with the very purposes themselves. The purposes assigned to American schools concern the realization of individual capacities and of new possibilities by society and go back to the Revolutionary era. *The purposes of schooling affect how we define our problems and the means we select for solving them.* Thus they must be continually reclarified by the public and profession together, and educators must seek out such opportunities.

Professional Issues

Many of the issues now confronting curriculum workers are of long standing, but conditions change: the old problems have new dimensions which must be taken into account if these problems are to be thoughtfully solved. Issues also have become more clearly defined (in some cases, redefined) with our improved understanding of the school. Nowhere is this more evident than in issues in the area of professionalism. For example, there was a time when we thought that knowledge leads to practice: teachers who know desirable teaching methodology will apply what they know. But studies by John Goodlad, Philip Jackson, Frederick McDonald, and others reveal that knowledge itself is no guarantee that it will be put into practice. It is acting on knowledge that counts and many teachers are not using what they recognize, and research reveals, as sound methods of teaching. Be it medicine or teaching, the application of knowledge derived from the study of the problems of a profession is fundamental to a profession.

In her chapter in this yearbook, Henrietta Schwartz asks why teachers do not use research on curriculum and how they might. She looks at such factors as preservice and in-service socialization, the practice part of professional education, teacher conceptions of curriculum, teacher dilemmas, and the relationship of supervision to the problem.

In the Seventieth Yearbook of the National Society for the Study of Education, Sand pointed out that teachers were gaining power and visibility as an organized profession, and that teacher power could and should be marshalled for curriculum improvement. "Teacher power now gives the teacher opportunity to perform truly professional leadership functions," he wrote.[5] This is an idea whose time has come. Gary Griffin writes in this yearbook that the conception of the principal as manager and the teacher as worker is not supported by what we know of the complexities of the teaching act: good teaching depends on teachers making good decisions that they alone can make. A very different concept of school-level leadership is required: the principal as environmental manipulator. Leadership means changing school settings so that teachers as professionals and classroom executives can participate in curriculum development. For example, teachers must have opportunities to think together and make decisions together.

The idea of reflection as a regular part of school practice is not new. As Kliebard observes in his chapter on curriculum fads, faculty meetings at Dewey's Laboratory School (1897-1904) were devoted to discussions of school activities in relation to theoretical principles. During this period, Dewey wrote in the Third Yearbook of the National Society for the Scientific Study of Education: "The tendency of educational development to proceed by reaction from one thing to another, to adopt for one year, or for a term of seven years, this or that new study or method of teaching, and then as abruptly to swing over to some new educational gospel, is a result which would be impossible if teachers were adequately moved by their own independent intelligence."[6] As the century comes to a close, opportunities for reflection are still rare among school faculties. Meanwhile, fads continue to retard educational progress and take their toll in other ways.

We are suddenly becoming aware of a problem of enormous importance: the effect of shifting and often conflicting patterns of curriculum reform on teachers, and on the practice of teaching. One year they are to meet the needs of poor children and the next they are to produce more bright graduates to meet national needs. Teachers become demoralized when the pendulum begins its swing and the intervals between swings are ever shorter. The current wave of reform has bureaucratized teaching practice; state legislatures spell out standards and there is less room for teachers to make professional judgments. Karen Zumwalt looks at the "bureaucratization" of teaching and its impact on professional judgment and how the conception of the teacher as curriculum implementor rather than curriculum maker has affected teachers. And on the other hand, she asks, what local factors counter these national trends? How are teachers encouraged to maintain their active roles in building curriculum? The answers to these questions can help curriculum workers deal with the twin problems of demoralization and bureaucratization. Obviously, also, the answers have a direct bearing on whether we can attract people of great ability into teaching, and whether we will keep—or lose—the very able teachers we have.

Curriculum Issues in Perspective

As these issues are studied, we can discern general characteristics of the issues as a whole. Three characteristics stand out as crucial: (a) curriculum issues are interrelated; (b) curriculum issues are solvable; and (c) curriculum issues are opportunities for improvements.

INTERRELATEDNESS

As curriculum workers attempt to deal with the issues that beset them, it becomes clear that the problems are interrelated, as are their solutions. For example, it is clear that there is a relationship between tracking and dropping out of school and, as Harry Passow and Murry Nelson point out in this volume, both are part of the larger issue of access to knowledge. Less obvious, however, is the relationship between whether teachers apply what they recognize as sound pedagogy and students' access to the curriculum; when teachers do not put their pedagogical knowledge into use, students' access to knowledge is limited. There are other relationships. Daniel Tanner points out in his chapter that the censorship of textbooks results in striking differences in access to knowledge from school to school. The bureaucratization of teaching practice, which puts teachers under constant pressure to follow fixed instructional procedures, makes it less possible for them to utilize their pedagogical knowledge and restricts access to knowledge. Moreover, the new requirements mandated by states for graduation from high school are rarely accompanied by resources to help the less able students, and in some school systems dropout rates have reached epidemic proportions. As George Madaus stresses in his chapter, proficiency tests also restrict access to knowledge. The minimum competency movement has deprived some students of opportunities to do advanced work. In some school systems, able students have done less well. Test scores for these students have gone down, not up.

Although the foregoing is concerned with the relations between the problem of access to knowledge and other issues, one can begin with any major issue discussed in this volume—or some other issue not discussed—and note connections with other issues.

But if the problems are interrelated, so are the solutions. If teachers have the room to function professionally, they have the discretionary power to adapt curriculum to meet emergent needs. How this is to be done in individual cases can never be dictated from afar—as from some state capitol. But professional space is not enough if that space is empty. Supervisors and curriculum workers must act on *their* professional knowledge and construct settings needed for teachers to function as curriculum makers.

When principals are able to see the curriculum holistically—how the parts of the curriculum relate to the whole in terms of the goals and functions of the school—they are more likely to make responsible decisions with the faculty when confronted with ill-advised reforms. Some policies have requirements that can be met without destroying the whole curriculum. The state's requirement for a minimum number of hours in certain subjects does not tell us how the course should be designed. If superintendents and principals are able to relate what the school does to what it aims to do, the prospects are better that teachers will apply what they know, that fewer students will leave school before they graduate, that the public and professional educators together will determine the character and content of the curriculum. As Raymond E. Callahan pointed out some years ago, administrators must be educators not managers. Such an administrator is more likely to educate the school board and the public about curriculum problems, and policies are more likely to reflect public opinion, which is what democracy is about.

In attempting to solve one problem we often make improvements in another area. However, the related solutions should not happen by chance; they should be included in the target.

SOLVABILITY

Knowledge based on human investigations instead of supernatural sanctions, an American high school for all instead of a Latin grammar school for the few, professional preparation at the college or university level for teachers instead of no standards of preparation—all are examples of achievements in the course of 350 years of American education. This is not to say that fundamentalist groups do not continue to try to influence the curriculum, that the high school program meets the needs of all young people, or that the professional conception of teaching continues to go unchallenged. As the discussions in this yearbook indicate the old problems still face us as we approach the year 2000. And yet, as Ralph Tyler points out in his chapter, we must not forget how far we have come—and not by accident. Each development resulted from the individual and organized efforts of scientists, philosophers, educators, and the American public. Instead of leaving problems to fate, they were what Emerson called "causationists."

It is important to recognize that some of the tasks involved in solving problems are never finished, which is right and proper. The problem of curriculum improvement is never "settled," because change of various kinds is always throwing up new problems to be dealt with—and new possibilities. Be that as it may, some curriculum issues have been badly neglected. Although they may receive less attention in a given period, neglected issues do not go away. Causationists are needed. The discussions in this yearbook indicate that enough is known about the issues now facing curriculum workers to do something about them as well as discuss them. We have just not followed through on what we know. Again, the case is one of unapplied knowledge.

For just one example, there is a rich literature dating back to the 1960s on the dropout. Now, as then, the students who quit school do so because of academic (and social) frustration. Now, as then, studies show that achievement is related to interest in school. Now, as then, Brookover, Bloom, and others point out that by manipulating variables in the school environment—including how teachers interact with students—students can have more positive experiences and, thus, the school's "holding power" is increased. Now, as then, we know that students are less likely to leave school if they are helped when they have learning difficulties. Now, as then, the curriculum is seen as a key in dropout prevention. The dropout situation is highly paradoxical: we know enough to make real inroads on the problem but it is growing worse. Reason dictates that we not leave our "vaccine" on the shelf, but use it to wipe out the dropout disease.

Each of the issues facing curriculum workers concerns two contrasting scenarios: what is and what might be. The what might be is determined both by approved educational practices (practices on which recognized authorities agree) *and* by the highest level of practice attained. For example, in some school systems, principals have included teachers in decision making, research, and development.

That some schools as institutions have changed shows that this is possible for all schools.

In some schools teachers have retired within themselves or find themselves wedged in between commercialism and conservatism—the "detail men" who sell instructional materials and a mandated instructional regimen that fails to meet the needs of many children. In other schools, however, teachers not only use the pedagogical knowledge they have, but they try to find even better methods. The second scenario—the highest level of practice attained—shows that curriculum workers do not have to accept the first scenario as a fact of educational life.

In this light, a study by Arthur E. Wise on policy choices for the future of teaching has great significance. One policy alternative is the "professional scenario," which entails both a "rigorous process of (teacher) education and certification" and "the creation of working conditions appropriate to a professional conception of teaching."[7] As the numbers of competent teachers increase, Wise points out, public satisfaction with teaching will increase and bureaucratic supervision of teaching will be viewed as less necessary. Wise's analysis points once again to the interrelationship of curriculum issues: professional teaching—the use of pedagogical knowledge—is part (and no small part either) of the solution to the problem of the bureaucratizing of teaching practice.

The professional scenario is what might be (and what already is, in some places). As Wise has suggested, teachers "would teach students to read for knowledge and enjoyment, not simply to acquire testable reading skills," and "they would teach students to write fluently and effectively, not simply to fill in the blanks. In a word, they would teach *professionally*—as the best teachers have always done, when the system allowed it."[8]

Another policy alternative is a two-tiered approach to teaching, comprised of a permanent cadre of professionals and temporary teachers. A large proportion of the teaching force would be temporary and unprepared for teaching. This choice, warns Wise, can only result in tighter control, greater standardization, more "teacher-proof" programs, more accountability via more tests, more teaching that prevents effective learning. Wise warns: "One scenario or the other will not simply happen. Policymakers will determine the future of teaching by the decisions they make today."[9] However, teacher educators are also policymakers, and many colleges of education have endorsed the two-tiered model. As Wise points out, the quality of teachers would vary, and thus the two-tiered approach serves to challenge seriously the cause of professional teaching.

Curriculum workers should bear in mind, however, that policy decisions are also made at the local level. Policy decisions favoring teaching as a profession good enough to attract and hold bright people are made when school systems appoint only highly qualified teachers, instead of employing those who can not find another job. (Enlightened school districts have always followed this policy.) And they are made when working conditions are created that foster professional teaching. With talented individuals, a school system is not bureaucratic and controlling, that is, not if it expects to retain them. Instead, the policy is to provide the conditions under which talent can be used and continue to develop, such as classes that are small enough to permit teachers to meet the needs of individual students and opportunities to come into contact with professionals from outside the school.

Parents who value education want professionals to teach their children, for they know that professional teaching opens access to knowledge and life opportunities. Indeed, parents make their own policy decision by moving out of neighborhoods where schools are staffed by unqualified teachers and the curriculum is delimited to mechanical exercises. In one large city, a group of parents filed suit against the school system demanding that a program organized around "sequential" subskills be abandoned as malpractice because pupils' reading scores on standardized tests fell considerably while the program was in progress. The program required teachers "to substitute procedure-following for the enhancement of learning as their primary goal."[10] Such parents—and their numbers are growing—can provide support for policy choices favoring professional teaching at the local, state, and national levels. As Wise has written: "If most education-minded parents remained committed to the public schools, *they would constitute a political force that would insure sufficient financial support to sustain professional teaching.*"[11]

If parents are to remain committed to the public schools, curriculum workers with supervisory responsibility must themselves follow a policy of professional supervision; there must be full communication with teachers instead of top-down communication and the supervisory mode must be consultative rather than bureaucratic. What must be borne in mind is that problems are solved by the decisions that are made now. Curriculum workers can do much to foster professional working conditions and need not, indeed must not, wait until decisions are made at another level. Curriculum workers are causationists.

Despite the bureaucratic pressures swirling around them, curriculum workers should be aware that not all policy decisions at the state level are on the side of rote learning. Some are clearly on the side of teachers assuming responsibility for real learning. For example, in the fall of 1986, California rejected all of the elementary school mathematics textbooks submitted for approval on the ground that they teach by proclaiming rules without helping pupils to understand. The California policy is based on the body of research in curriculum and instruction under the concept of approved practices, and represents the highest level of (state) practice attained.

Like all of the issues in this book, the problem of the influence of testing on the curriculum has two scenarios. In the situation that has come to prevail as a result of state-mandated testing programs, teachers spend an enormous amount of time preparing students for tests, and neglect curriculum areas not tested. The effect is a reshaping of the curriculum in accord with political, not pedagogical interests. But in the second scenario, standardized tests are used properly, that is, to identify the learning needs of individuals and educational problems at the local level. They do not mitigate against a rich and balanced curriculum. Students engage in projects in music, art, and creative writing, and so on, despite the fact that such activities are not evaluated by standardized tests. Once again, such schools represent the highest level of practice attained.

Clearly, externally mandated testing programs are not the only factor determining which scenario is in evidence in a given school. In the last analysis, the curriculum is determined by what goes on in the school, and curriculum workers, administrators, and the school faculty must assume the responsibility for curriculum determination and development or lose it by default. In some schools, external mandates are seized upon as an excuse for avoiding the problem of providing a balanced curriculum. In such schools, the curriculum is made by default.

Although it may be rationalized as such, this is not in the public interest. In his study of schooling, Goodlad found that proficiency tests limit the curriculum in ways that parents do not want.[12] As in the case of professional teaching, parents are a potential political force on the side of sound educational policy.

Needless to say, there are implications here that curriculum workers ignore at their peril. First, external mandates must be subjected to critical examination by administrators, curriculum workers, and school faculties. Second, they must carry out their responsibility to see that the curriculum best serves students in view of the wider public interest, not vested interests. And always it must be remembered that policy does not necessarily reflect public opinion.

Finally, harrassed though they may be by their problems, curriculum workers must bear in mind that each issue has another scenario, that is indeed reality in some schools, and is in their grasp, if they will only act on the best available knowledge. Although curriculum workers only see their own situation, and it may be a troublesome one, there is another reality and it did not just happen by chance.

Many curriculum workers are not the adventurous type. They find security in easy conformity to external mandates and comfort in routines such as delivering prepackaged programs to teachers. When issues confront them, the problem solvers move out ahead. This is because, in their attack on problems, they are forced to become aware of the approaches that have been employed by others. Problems are opportunities for improvements.

When curriculum issues are viewed as obstacles to effective educational programs, the fact that their solution leads to more effective programs is often overlooked. At bottom, these issues are opportunities for progress and they should be considered as such. We can take each of the issues dealt with in this book and see how this is so. As Kliebard points out in his chapter, a serious problem in education is the adoption of "new" ideas that have been tried and discarded. Schools can counter cycles and fashions in the curriculum if curriculum reform efforts begin as an attempt to solve a problem, rather than as a reaction to a previous era of reform. Not only is the problem of fads dealt with but education is helped to move ahead in a desirable direction.

Clearly, dealing with the problem of unapplied pedagogical knowledge leads to more effective educational programs. Better educational programs are also by-products of solutions to problems like censorship of textbooks, the influence of testing on the curriculum, dropping out of school, and political pressures on supervisors. The important generalization that should be borne in mind is that problem solving leads to better ways of doing things than was the case before the problems became evident. Problem solving is a means of development in any field—medicine, engineering, or education.

Finally, as this book makes clear, curriculum workers are still discovering their problems, and still seeking the terms for discussing them. These are signs that the field is alive and well.

Organization of This Yearbook

Section One examines the issues confronting curriculum workers in their striking interrelationships, considers the problem of educational fads, and an issue that we are just beginning to understand: unapplied professional knowledge. The final chapter in this section deals with political pressures on supervisors.

Section Two deals with the vital question of who makes curriculum policy for the American classroom and with issues stemming from this question, such as the effects of external mandates on the curriculum and on the practice of teaching, the content of textbooks and their use, and the influence of testing on the curriculum. The last two chapters in this section deal with the problem of the marked differences in children's access to knowledge. Tracking, traditionally viewed as an administrative device, is treated in this book as the curriculum problem that it is, as is the dropout problem.

Section Three is concerned with the problems affecting the administrator as a curriculum leader and the question of whether there has been progress in dealing with the issues that have confronted curriculum workers over time. It is of very great import because progress in the future depends on knowing how far we have come and what yet needs to be done.

FOOTNOTES

1. J. Myron Atkin, "Changing Our Thinking about Educational Change," *Challenge to American Schools*, ed. John H. Bunzel (New York: Oxford University Press, 1985), pp. 47-62.

2. Lawrence A. Cremin, *The Genius of American Education* (New York: Vintage Books, 1965), pp. 90-91. See also, Charles Frankel, *The Democratic Prospect* (New York: Harper and Row, 1962), pp. 82-83.

3. National Panel on High School and Adolescent Education, *The Education of Adolescents* (Washington, D.C.: U.S. Office of Education, 1976), pp. 13-14.

4. Thomas Ferguson and Joel Rogers, "The Myth of America's Turn to the Right," *The Atlantic* 257 (May 1986): 46.

5. Ole Sand, "Curriculum Change," in *The Curriculum: Retrospect and Prospect*, ed. Robert M. McClure, Seventieth Yearbook of the National Society for the Study of Education, Part 1 (Chicago: University of Chicago Press, 1971), p. 220.

6. John Dewey, "The Relation of Theory to Practice in Education," in *The Relation of Theory to Practice in the Education of Teachers*, ed. Charles A. McMurry, Third Yearbook of the National Society for the Scientific Study of Education, Part 1 (Bloomington, Ill.: Public School Publishing Co., 1904), p. 16.

7. Arthur E. Wise, "Three Scenarios for the Future of Teaching," *Phi Delta Kappan* 67 (May 1986): 652.

8. Ibid.

9. Ibid.

10. Linda Darling-Hammond, "The Over-Regulated Curriculum and the Press for Teacher Professionalism," *NASSP Bulletin* 71 (April 1987): pp. 28-29.

11. Wise, "Three Scenarios for the Future of Teaching." Emphasis added.

12. John I. Goodlad, *A Place Called School* (New York: McGraw-Hill, 1984), pp. 33-60.

CHAPTER II

Fads, Fashions, and Rituals: The Instability of Curriculum Change

HERBERT M. KLIEBARD

The history of education is a chronicle of fads.
W. W. CHARTERS[1]

It has become commonplace for observers of the educational landscape, particularly in the field of curriculum, to take note (sometimes with alarm) of the short life span of many of the so-called reforms. Allusions to the phenomenon of "pendulum swings" abound, but relatively little has been adduced as to the reasons for that phenomenon. Cycles occur, of course, in other areas such as politics and clothing fashions, but critics claim that the fads in the curriculum world occur with greater rapidity and that they are often substitutes for genuine and needed change in the system. Moreover, a sense of pessimism often accompanies the articulation of the phenomenon, since there seems to be little point in working for reform when the inevitable result is a return to the status quo ante. When these cycles become habitual, it is difficult to maintain even the illusion of progress.

I should like to offer four hypotheses that could account for the occurrence of cyclical change in curriculum affairs as it is commonly observed. The first has to do with a boundless expansion of the scope of the curriculum in conjunction with direct and immediate utility as the supreme criterion of success. Practically speaking, there are no boundaries to what can be included in the curriculum, and, therefore, any contender for admission is legitimate. Second, because the rhetoric of reform is usually more powerful than the opposition, a reform is inaugurated without the accompanying structural changes in the system that are needed in order to make it succeed. When this occurs, the life span of the reform is almost bound to be short. Third, the changes themselves do not so much take the form of one curriculum ideology actually replacing another as they do a resurfacing of a

16

temporarily submerged position in the light of favorable social and political conditions. Since curriculum ideologies are obviously not independent of the social and political climate, the changes become a function of the interaction of a given social and political climate with certain familiar ideas as to how the curriculum should be selected and organized. And finally, rapid changes in curriculum fashion are related to the rise of a professional class of school administrators whose professional status and perhaps even their survival depend simply on being at least as up-to-date as the school system down the road. In other words, change itself is perceived as desirable rather than change in a particular direction, and, therefore, change tends to be more for the purpose of public display than the result of firmly held pedagogical beliefs. These four hypotheses are not meant to exhaust the possibilities for explaining the phenomenon of curriculum instability, but they may offer a starting point for a serious investigation of its persistence.

Beyond Academics: Building a Curriculum for "Life"

> In olden days a glimpse of stocking
> Was looked on as something shocking,
> But now, God knows,
> Anything goes.[2]

One phenomenon of particular significance regarding the course of study has been its almost infinite expansion over the course of the twentieth century. In high schools, for example, it is not uncommon for as many as 400 subjects to be offered,[3] with additional programs added as critical problems such as adolescent suicide become matters of public concern. Compared to the four sedately academic programs of study recommended by the Committee of Ten in 1893[4] (which itself sanctioned the admission of relatively new subjects, such as modern foreign languages), the modern high school curriculum simply has no boundaries. Covering the span of the entire educational ladder, state departments of education, school boards, and school administrators are continually responding to public outcry, media attention, and pressure from interest groups to include this or that in the curriculum. Moreover, this expansion of the course of study has proceeded at such a pace that it has become almost impossible to speak about *the* American curriculum except in very general terms. As Robert Hampel has pointed out, two major new reports on the state of education in the United States independently called one of their sections, "We Want It All."[5] The curriculum has become everything but also nothing that can be easily characterized except in those all-inclusive terms. The fine art of *exclusion* in curriculum matters has fallen into wide disfavor.

While this state of affairs is to some extent dictated simply by the absence of purpose in curriculum matters, it is also the culmination of a concerted and self-conscious drive to break down what were considered to be artificial barriers between school and life. With the arrival of mass public education, the academic curricula of the nineteenth century were considered to be simply beyond the mental capacities of or irrelevant to the interests of the new population of students entering schools, particularly at the high school level. The basic response to mass public education was to adapt the curriculum to the "needs" of the majority of students allegedly incapable of profiting from the standard curriculum. Therefore, in the early twentieth century, we begin to see the curriculum modified in an effort to tie the subjects of study more closely to the actual activities that human beings perform. Typical of the reaction to the traditional curriculum was that of the superintendent of schools in the small city of Eau Claire, Wisconsin, one of a new breed of professional school administrators, who declared in 1911 that the "most marked defect" of the curriculum was that it was simply "too bookish and too little related to life and the actual needs of those entering upon the duties of citizenship."[6] And, in fact, he was able to fashion a curriculum by 1915 that was substantially in tune with that sentiment.

Within a relatively few years after the Committee of Ten report was issued, major leaders in the newly emerging curriculum field were urging that traditional academic subjects be restricted to a particular group destined for college with the majority of students engaged in studying subjects that were directly related to their functioning as citizens, as family members, and as workers. One notable example of such an effort was the work of Franklin Bobbitt in bringing such new curriculum ideas to the city of Los Angeles. As a professor on the education faculty of the University of Chicago, Bobbitt was in a position not simply to issue pronouncements on what the curriculum should be like, but to influence practice in cities like Cleveland and San Antonio through his consulting work and through the increasingly fashionable school survey as an instrument for changing the curriculum.

In the case of Los Angeles, Bobbitt was actually employed by the school system for a period of three months in order to initiate the curriculum reform project, and it continued, practically speaking, for the entire 1922-23 school year. As a first step, Bobbitt undertook to draw up "a comprehensive list of human abilities and characteristics which appear to be generally needed by the citizens of Los Angeles."[7] In other words, the curriculum as Bobbitt envisioned it was not a collection of subjects deemed to be representative of intellectual culture (as was at least implicitly assumed by the Committee of Ten), but a scientifically determined catalog of actual activities performed by citizens in a given locale. This meant essentially that there simply were no limits to the curriculum except insofar as it coincided with life as it was actually lived. Bobbitt arranged the activities that would form the basis of the curriculum according to his own system of classification:

    I. Social Intercommunication, Mainly Language
    II. The Development and Maintenance of One's Physical Power
    III. Unspecialized Practical Labors
    IV. The Labors of One's Calling
    V. The Activities of the Efficient Citizen
    VI. The Activities Involved in One's General Social Relationships and Behavior
    VII. Leisure Occupations, Recreations, Amusements
    VIII. Development and Maintenance of One's Mental Efficiency
    IX. Religious Activities
    X. Parental Activities, the Upbringing of Children, the Maintenance of the Home Life[8]

As Bobbitt himself recognized, "There are probably few desirable human activities which will not fall within one or another of these several categories."[9] Moreover, these activities were set forth in minute detail. Included were items like the following:

535. Shaving.
551. The boxing, crating, or otherwise making up packages for parcel post or express.
630. Ability and disposition to earn the equivalent of what one consumes and to share effectively in a public opinion that makes this demand of all. A sense of personal independence that will not permit one to be an economic parasite upon others, and which demands that others be not parasitic upon him.

Whatever may be the objections raised to Bobbitt's ultimately quixotic attempt to catalog all of human activity or to his smuggling in his own values under the guise of scientifically observed activities, his abiding conviction that the curriculum should be geared to *life* and not mere intellectual mastery remained not only a persistent but a dominant theme in curriculum thinking.

Although the contemporary American curriculum obviously does not reflect precisely the tenets that Bobbitt set forth, it has moved sufficiently in that direction so that there is little sense among school people that a line can be drawn between what is appropriate to include in the curriculum and what is inappropriate. For all intents and purposes, anything goes, and the sheer inclusiveness of what passes for the curriculum in modern times may have a great deal to do with its apparent instability. If the curriculum is to be substantially tied to those things that human beings need to know in order to perform their daily tasks successfully, then as those activities and as the perception of the problems of living change, the curriculum must change correspondingly. Curriculum reform, in this sense, represents a never-ending process of making room for an emerging and presumably urgent kind of activity that needs to be performed.

Cast in its most positive light, fads and fashions in curriculum represent merely a process by which the curriculum responds to changing needs and times. But what has been lost in that process is any sense of what a school is for. As John Goodlad reported on statements of purpose prepared by the fifty states: "There is something for everyone in the material prepared by the states. But because the documents range over such a variety of topics . . ., one gets little sense of what is essential and what is secondary."[10] Aims stated in terms such as "self-realization" and "worthy home membership" function primarily as slogan systems, ritualistic statements which can possibly enlist public support, but in no sense set limits on or give direction to what should be included in the curriculum. If anything, they are a license to do anything. Rather than attempting to state the purposes of schooling in terms of laundry lists of high-sounding aims, those statements of purposes ought to convey some sense of priorities in relation to the institutional setting where those purposes are to be accomplished. In part at least, this means a reconsideration of the school as an all-encompassing institution ready and able to accomplish almost anything. It requires hard decisions about the distinctive role of formal schooling in relation to the roles of other social institutions.

Such a reconsideration does not mean simply abandoning all other roles; it does mean seeing them as subsidiary to a central one.

Intellectual mastery of the modern world has never been formally rejected as the central purpose of schooling, but in practical terms, it has waxed and waned in terms of both professional and public consciousness. Americans have always had a supreme faith in the power of formal schooling to do many things besides initiating youth into the intellectual resources of our culture. Rarely has that faith been examined in realistic terms, and the rise and fall of many so-called innovations may simply be a result of the school's inability to function successfully in terms of such amorphous curriculum boundaries as well as the kind of direct and concrete payoff that certain curriculum leaders, such as Bobbitt, envisioned. A more appropriate starting point than a catalog of human activity would be to examine seriously and honestly the nature of schooling, not only what it should accomplish in terms of its central task, but what it *can* realistically be expected to do. We would then be in a position to use that conception of schooling as a filter to screen out trivial or chimerical proposals for curriculum change as well as those that are best essayed in another setting. Without disciplined attention to what should be excluded from the curriculum, a revolving door in curriculum matters becomes almost inevitable.

Curriculum Change versus Organizational Structure

> *You say eether*
> *And I say eyether,*
> *You say neether*
> *And I say nyther;*
> *Eether, eyether, neether, nyther,*
> *Let's call the whole thing off.*[11]

Just as the twentieth century was dawning, John Dewey may have hit upon one of the most significant reasons why curriculum innovations were failing with such monotonous regularity. A change in curriculum is more than it appears. It involves not simply the substitution of one element of a course of study for another; that new element frequently requires for its survival a compatible organizational structure. In other words, when a curriculum change is introduced without due regard for a modification of the context in which the change is to take place, that innovation is almost surely doomed to a short life. Referring to educational reformers like Horace Mann and Pestalozzi, Dewey argued that their progressive reforms had become commonplace in terms of "pedagogic writing and of the gatherings where teachers meet for inspiration and admonition."[12] The catch was that while the domain of "preaching" had been secured by the reformer, "the conservative, so far as the course of study was concerned, was holding his own pretty obstinately in the region of practice."[13]

Under these circumstances, Dewey pointed out, the reforms when instituted create "a congestion in the curriculum," which weakens their strength and leads to their being characterized as "fads and frills."[14] When financial troubles occur or when the simple efficiency of the school is somehow impaired, the "insertions and additions" get cast out precisely because they have not become part of the educational whole.[15] While the reform has the advantage in terms of rhetoric, it becomes inserted into a system that draws its criteria of success from exisiting standards, a situation that almost insures that the reform will be temporary. The fact is, as Dewey pointed out, "we have no conscious educational standard by which to test and place each aspiring claimant. We have hundreds of reasons for and against this or that study, but no reason."[16] An obvious case in point is the persistence of scores on achievement tests as the ultimate criterion of success in curriculum ventures. Certain kinds of success are amenable to that kind of measurement, but others are not. As Dewey expressed it:

The things of the spirit do not lend themselves easily to that kind of external inspection which goes by the name of examination. They do not lend themselves easily to exact quantitative measurement. Technical proficiency, acquisition of skill and information present much less difficulty. So again emphasis is thrown upon those traditional subjects of the school curriculum which permit most readily of a mechanical treatment—upon the three R's and upon the facts of external classification in history and science, matters of formal technique in music, drawing, and manual training.[17]

Thus, as long as criteria of success that are incompatible with the survival of the reform remain in place, the new program's place in the school curriculum is bound to be short-lived.

Dewey distinguished between two sorts of studies: The first represents "the symbols of intellectual life, which are the tools of civilization itself." These are the traditional subjects of study. The other group aims at "the direct and present expression of power on the

part of one undergoing education, and for the present and direct
enrichment of his life-experience,"[18] and it is the conflict between
these two conceptions of the course of study that leads to much of the
backing and filling in curriculum affairs. Dewey offered the following
proposition as his key to unlocking this conflict:

The studies of the symbolic and formal sort represented the aims and material
of education for a sufficiently long time to call into existence a machinery of
administration and of instruction thoroly adapted to themselves. This
machinery constituted the actual working scheme of administration and
instruction. The conditions thus constituted persist long after the studies to
which they are well adapted have lost their theoretical supremacy. The
conflict, the confusion, the compromise, is not intrinsically between the older
group of studies and the newer, but between the external conditions in which
the former were realized and the aims and standards represented by the
newer.[19]

Seen in this light, the curriculum reform exists in a school culture
which is basically antagonistic to it. The administrative structure of
the school and the modes of teaching that prevail are drawn from
another theoretical framework, and the persistence of this "machinery" ultimately crushes the curriculum reform. We sometimes fall into
the trap, Dewey implied, of thinking of such things as sorting children
by grade levels and the system of selecting teachers as "matters of
mere practical convenience and expediency." Quite the contrary,
Dewey argued, "it is precisely such things as these that really control
the whole system, even on its distinctively educational side."[20]
    Thus, if reformers were to undertake to teach critical or creative or
imaginative thinking, for example, they would have to fit that change
into an administrative and structural machinery that had already
imbedded in it the conditions for its downfall as a reform. It is most
likely to be taught as a series of discrete skills, much like reading is, in
a setting requiring order and regimentation. And the teachers will, in
all likelihood, be instructed merely to carry forward a curriculum in
which they have no stake and which they had no part in creating. The
teacher, in Dewey's day and in ours, will, by virtue of training and
working conditions, have no conception of what the curriculum
means as a whole, and, as Dewey pointed out, "it is certain beyond
controversy that the success of the teacher in teaching, and of the pupil
in learning, will depend on the intellectual equipment of the
teacher."[21] Thus, as long as the structural conditions conducive to
their success are absent and, as long as reformers retain the upper hand

in terms of public argument, the familiar ebb and flow of curriculum fashions will continue. In a spirit of exaggerated optimism, or perhaps just wishful thinking, Dewey predicted "that we are now nearing the close of the time of tentative, blind empirical experimentation; that we are close to the opportunity of planning our work on the basis of a coherent philosophy of experience and of the relation of school studies to that experience; that we can accordingly take up steadily and widely the effort of changing school conditions so as to make real the aims that command the assent of intelligence."[22] The persistence of cycles of curriculum change is testimony to the fact that the day has not arrived.

It should be no source of comfort to curriculum reformers that, seven decades after Dewey presented his analysis of the phenomenon, Seymour Sarason arrived at essentially the same explanation. The only way a process of change that takes the form of "delivery of the curriculum" can be successful, Sarason argued, is if the characteristics of the school culture do not adversely affect it. Take, for example, the common observation that "the relation between teacher and pupil is characteristically one in which the teacher asks questions and the pupil gives an answer."[23] When the role of the student is essentially restricted to that form of verbal intercourse, a reform like the teaching of critical thinking is almost necessarily doomed. In that case, the basic framework of classroom discourse is simply not congenial to the way intellectual or critical inquiry proceeds, and the result is a return to the previous state of affairs. As Sarason expressed it, "any attempt to change a curriculum independent of changing some characteristic institutional feature runs the risk of partial or complete failure."[24]

Perhaps not coincidentally, Sarason took Dewey's own Laboratory School as an example of how the structural features of a school can be modified in order to support educational reform. Of great significance to the operation of Dewey's school was the fact that it was founded on certain pedagogical principles which served as the basis not only for the selection of subject matter but also for the way in which the school was organized and for how the teachers and other school personnel saw their roles within the organizational structure. There was a continuity between what the school was trying to accomplish and the day-to-day work of the school personnel. This did not mean, however, that strict rules were set forth for defining what was proper or improper within its confines. Quite the reverse. As Dewey himself expressed this point, "The principles of the school's plan were not intended as definite rules for what was done in school. . . . [T]he 'principles' formed a kind of working hypothesis rather than a fixed program and schedule. Their application was in the hands of the teachers, and this application was in fact equivalent to their development and modification by the teachers."[25]

Additionally, there were weekly meetings with teachers, not to discuss administrative issues or discipline problems, but to review the prior week's work. Significantly, the emphasis was not upon projection of activities in terms of the next week's lesson plans or on statements of objectives for the future, but upon *reflection*. Specifically, there were frequent discussions on the workaday operation of the school in relation to the theoretical principles that were supposed to guide it. (Obviously, since hardly any schools have guiding theoretical principles—only statements of mushy slogans— this would not be possible on a widespread basis in schools today.) Moreover, a cooperative social reorganization was deliberately fostered, and teachers were encouraged to visit the classrooms of other teachers. Even formal seminar groups were initiated. As Dewey recalled this emphasis on the sharing of experiences, "there was daily and hourly exchange of results of classroom experience,"[26] exchanges that could only be possible with the conscious modification of the traditional school structure that isolates teachers not only physically by classroom but often by department and by subject.

Reports by the teachers formed the basis of the weekly informal conferences as well as formal seminar groups. Teachers were encouraged to share their experiences with one another, their successes as well as their failures. At one teachers' meeting led by Dewey in 1899, a typical question raised was the following:

Is there any common denominator in the teaching process? Here, are people teaching children of different ages, different subjects; one is teaching music, another art, another cooking, Latin, etc. Now is there any common end which can be stated which is common to all? This is meant in an intellectual rather than a moral way. Is there any intellectual result which ought to be obtained in all these different studies and at these different ages?[27]

The weekly meetings on *pedagogical* questions was one element of an organizational structure designed to be consistent with the working hypothesis that was the theoretical basis of the school. The professional isolation that tends to be fostered by conventional school structures makes a cooperative effort in behalf of a school reform a virtual impossibility, and this perpetuates the cycles of reform and counterreform.

As Sarason pointed out, "John Dewey created a school; he did not have to change an ongoing one."[28] It may be, oddly enough, a less formidable a task to create a new institution than to effect structural changes in an existing one. Dewey's followers in his own day, as well as many modern reformers, set out to carry forward the ideals that guided the Laboratory School to a wider spectrum of schools. But ideals and "missionary zeal" are not sufficient conditions to bring real change about.[29] As Dewey observed at the turn of the century, the rhetorical battle may be won under those circumstances, but lasting reform can not. The machinery of the organization and its internal dynamics must be changed accordingly if the innovation is to have any chance of succeeding. This requires an intimate understanding of the particular institutional culture involved, not a putative generalized formula for how to succeed.

Curriculum Change, the Political Mood, and Social Progress

> It's progress,
> Where every man can be a king.
> Why next to progress,
> Love's a juvenile thing.[30]

Americans have such an abiding faith in the power of education to effect both fundamental social change and alterations in basic human values that they need to be reminded every now and then that formal education does not exist independently of its relationship to the larger social order and to other sources of human action. Their belief in education is so strong that it is widely regarded as the most efficacious instrument of social progress. When a major problem arises of almost any sort, ranging from an AIDS epidemic to large-scale unemployment, Americans characteristically look to schools as the way to address it. As Henry Steele Commager once put it, "In the past we required our schools to do what in the Old World the family, the church, apprenticeship and the guilds did; now we ask them to do what their modern equivalents, plus a hundred voluntary organizations, fail or refuse to do."[31] This exaggerated faith in the power of one social institution to accomplish almost anything, especially without due regard for other social forces and institutions, may itself be one contributing factor to the parade of curriculum fashions. When schools blithely undertake, or have thrust upon them, a function for which they are unsuited, then the program collapses of its own weight only to be replaced by another one when the national mood changes.

This is not to say that schools and programs of study in schools are mere reflections of larger social forces over which the schools have no control. It does mean that ideas about what should be taught in school, rather than being independent of those forces, are in constant interaction with social trends. But it is not the actual events or trends themselves that are the sources of the curriculum cycles. It is the events or trends as filtered through certain fundamental beliefs about the nature and function of the curriculum that pervade our consciousness. Robert Nisbet expressed the basic idea most cogently: "We may think we are responding directly to events and changes in the history of institutions, but we aren't; we are responding to these events and changes as they are made real or assimilable to us by ideas already in our heads."[32] If some kind of understanding of the cycles of curriculum fashion is to be achieved, then, it is likely that we would have to come to grips with the question of how events in the larger social and political sphere interact with fundamental ideas we have about what should be taught in schools.

Perhaps a couple of examples can illustrate this point. As World War II was drawing to a close, there was a natural tendency for Americans to yearn for "normalcy." The reaction to the disruption and turmoil that the war effort had created made the appeal of a society that ran smoothly and where people adjusted contentedly to their roles in the social order particularly potent. That national mood interacted with the curriculum doctrine that held out the most promise for achieving that state of normalcy, social efficiency. Ever since that doctrine emerged in a coherent form just after the turn of the century, its appeal had been to a stable social order that simply worked efficiently. The postwar national mood in interaction with social efficiency as a curriculum idea emerged in the mid-1940s as life adjustment education. The enormous appeal of life adjustment education to educational leaders and school personnel across the country was its promise of the harmonious adjustment of American citizens to what life had in store for them. When conflict reemerged only a few years later in the form of the Cold War, life adjustment education quickly fell out of fashion. The new national mood was one of fierce competition with the Soviet Union, especially in the areas of science and technology. Interacting with that national mood were curriculum ideas that stressed tough academics and strenuous mental activity. What emerged, especially after Sputnik punctuated the process that was already taking place, was a radically different curriculum doctrine whose major emphasis was on the structure of the various academic disciplines. That "cycle," then, moved from a "soft" education emphasizing learning the everyday tasks of life as the route to happy adjustment to a "hard" education emphasizing academic rigor as a way of coming to grips with a serious external threat. But it was dictated neither by a social trend nor a curriculum doctrine alone; it was the result of a perceived problem interacting with an extant curriculum doctrine. In Nisbet's terms, these events were made real by ideas that were already floating around in our heads.

If we pursue further, however, the case of the public reaction to Sputnik, it is also illustrative of the peculiarly American tendency to look to schools as the corrective for major social or political or even technological deficiencies. Although the "soft" American curriculum provided a convenient and perhaps even publicly plausible way of explaining the Soviet Union's accomplishment in space technology, the actual reasons for their success in sending a satellite into orbit in 1957 were undoubtedly much more complex than and perhaps even irrelevant to the question of whether schools in America taught less of this or more of that than Soviet schools did. It is in this sense that the Sputnik experience is also illustrative of the characteristic tendency of Americans to exaggerate the power of formal schooling to correct social deficiencies and to act as a direct instrument of progress. The relationship, then, between national trends as they affect curriculum policy on one hand and the supreme faith of Americans in the sheer power of education as a force for progress on the other makes changes in curriculum fashion a naturally recurring phenomenon. As long as public concern about various social tendencies continues to shift and as long as schooling is seen as the way to alleviate that concern, then curriculum doctrine will shift as well.

Although this state of affairs may be inevitable under present conditions, it cannot be a source of satisfaction either with respect to the conduct of schooling or as a way of achieving social progress. No one can be against progress, but genuine progress can actually be impeded when it is equated with mere change and especially when it is only the appearance of change. In the first place, change alone can be regressive as well as progressive. This is imbedded in the "pendulum swing" metaphor commonly used to describe the phenomenon. Secondly, as Commager's felicitous characterization, "the school as surrogate conscience," implies,[33] attributing critical social responsibilities to schools may simply turn out to be a way of avoiding the stark realities of the situation. Merely assigning schools the responsibility for addressing problems not only in the case of a perceived space race, but of alcoholism, drug addiction, teenage pregnancy, or poverty may serve to salve the public conscience; in the long run, however, it may also serve to impair genuine attempts to address those issues with all the seriousness they deserve.

Changing Fashions and the Culture of Professional School Administration

Ev'rythin's up to date in Kansas City.
They've gone about as fur as they c'n go![34]

Just as one can speak of an institution having a distinctive culture, so may one at least raise the question of whether a professional field can also be so characterized. Tyack and Hansot, for example, have argued that a temper of millennialism and a crusading spirit drawn from an early nineteenth-century Protestant ethic continued to animate the work of school administrators even after the industrial revolution transformed the material conditions of schooling.[35] But while some residue of that spirit may have survived into the twentieth century, there was also developing a new culture of educational administration that was more closely tied to professional expertise than traditional Protestant values.

Beginning roughly in the 1890s, the model for the aspiring as well as the established school administrator shifted from Protestant revivalism to bureaucratic efficiency. In effect, this new professional-ism ultimately evolved into what Tyack and Hansot call an "educational trust."[36] This means that a federation of tightly knit networks not only dominated the day-to-day operations of public schools for at least most of the twentieth century, but spread the gospel of the new management practices that were to provide America's public schools with the metaphors and the standards of success that set the tone for what constituted an up-to-date curriculum.[37] Typical of the new way of thinking about schooling in general and the curriculum in particular was the following from the work of one of the key members of the school administration trust, Ellwood P. Cubberley of Stanford University:

Every manufacturing establishment that turns out a standard product or a series of products of any kind maintains a force of efficiency experts to study methods of procedure and to measure and test the output of its works. Such men ultimately bring the manufacturing establishment large returns by introducing improvements in processes and procedure, and in training the workmen to produce larger and better output. Our schools are, in a sense, factories in which the raw products (children) are to be shaped and fashioned into products to meet the various demands of life. The specifications for manufacturing come from the demands of twentieth-century civilization, and it is the business of the school to build its pupils according to the specifications laid down. This demands good tools, specialized machinery, continuous measurement of production to see if it is according to specifications, and a large variety in the output.[38]

Given the power and influence of the school administration trust, intellectual credentials were quickly being replaced as the basis for heading a school or a school system by professional credentials that included not only a degree in administration but an ideology drawn from the world of business and manufacture.

Two powerful mechanisms helped spread the message of a needed change in school practices. One was the school survey, of which Cubberley's Portland survey is a prime example. Typically, a school system would invite a member of the trust such as Cubberley or George Strayer of Teachers College to conduct a survey of the school system's program of studies. Almost invariably, the survey report would include recommendations for needed changes, and to demonstrate that the school system was in step with the latest trends local school officials had almost no recourse but to try to implement those recommendations. The second mechanism comprised a system of private networks established by prominent leaders in the burgeoning field of school administration which insured that only those with the right ideas occupied key superintendencies. Perhaps the most natural network consisted simply of the students trained by one of the leaders. According to Tyack and Hansot, for example, Strayer's influence was not only significant in terms of what he taught in his courses at Teachers College, but "in his role as a placement baron" as well.[39] As they explained the relationship,

The relation between sponsor and alumnus was one of mutual advantage. In return for assistance in moving ahead on the chessboard of superintendencies, the alumnus helped the professor recruit students, invited the sponsor to consult or survey his district, notified him of vacancies, helped place his graduates, and kept him in touch with his field. The graduate turned to the sponsor for advice and help in getting ahead. His advancement often depended on pleasing his sponsor as well as the local school board (of course the two were connected).[40]

It was not long before these mutually advantageous networks began to exhibit their own norms and behavioral regularities.

Apart from a generalized business orientation, however, the ideologies were neither well defined nor internally consistent. According to Tyack and Hansot, the new breed of school administrators "tended to have prefabricated solutions to preconceived problems. One reason for this was that they did not inquire in any fundamental or open-minded way into the conflicting goals of education."[41] The overarching motive for instituting any change was to demonstrate that one's own school system was at least as innovative as others in the vicinity. Without any sense of purpose or deeply held commitments to a particular course of action (except perhaps to hard efficiency), change itself became a predominant factor in the emerging culture of school administration. No administrator could really afford to stand pat. And when change occurs simply for the sake of change, it is no great mystery as to why changes in schools occur and reoccur with such monotonous regularity. Survival, or at least status, for the school administrator came to depend on change alone, not on change in a particular direction.

Conclusion

There can be no single-factor explanation for so broad and widespread a phenomenon as the constant ebb and flow of curriculum fashions. It is likely that such a persistent pattern is an outgrowth of plural causes and tendencies. Among some of the more plausible of these are the four factors outlined here.

The first relates to the absence of purpose in curriculum decision making, a lack that has opened the door for virtually any candidate for admission to the course of study. In an age when an academic curriculum prevailed, for example, certain subjects were out of bounds or at least subsidiary. In an age of a "shopping mall" curriculum, nothing can be excluded, and this dictates the perennial shifting of what the curriculum is in any given time and place. As long as the boundaries of the curriculum are coterminous with the boundaries of life, then "social skills" can enjoy equal status with biology as a school subject.

The second, is a function of a basic incompatibility between the rhetoric of school reform and the way in which schools are organized. Under these circumstances, innovations that win the battle of words prove indigestible within the supremely stable structure of schooling and are ultimately regurgitated. Only when the significance of the institutional culture is recognized as a vital factor in curriculum reform can change be sustained.

Thirdly, the combination of a supreme faith in the power of schooling and the interactive relationship between curriculum ideas and political and social trends also contributes to the pattern of cycles. As new social tendencies emerge, they become real (in school terms) by filtering them through certain fundamental ideas about curriculum, and as different social tendencies resonate with different curriculum ideologies, one curriculum fashion supplants another. Unfortunately, this process takes place almost unconsciously and without due cognizance of the implications of those fundamental ideas.

The fourth hypothesis is related to the fact that day-to-day decision making in the schools of America is, by and large, in the hands of a professional breed of school administrators who have been socialized into a particular way of thinking and acting. Over the course of the twentieth century, the culture of school administration has drawn extensively from the norms and canons of the business world. Without an articulated sense of inquiry into the nature and purposes of schooling, that professional culture encourages, not change in a purposive direction, but change itself.

FOOTNOTES

1. W. W. Charters, "Regulating the Project," *Journal of Educational Research* 5 (March 1922): 245.

2. "Anything Goes," from *Anything Goes*. Music and lyrics by Cole Porter. Copyright 1934 by Harms, Inc.

3. Arthur G. Powell, Eleanor Farrar, and David K. Cohen, *The Shopping Mall High School: Winners and Losers in the Educational Marketplace* (Boston: Houghton Mifflin, 1985), pp. 11-12.

4. National Education Association, *Report of the Committee on Secondary School Studies* (Washington, D.C.: United States Government Printing Office, 1893).

5. Robert M. Hampel, *The Last Little Citadel: American High Schools Since 1940* (Boston: Houghton Mifflin, 1986), p. 147. The two studies are Ernest Boyer, *High School* (New York: Harper, 1983) and John I. Goodlad, *A Place Called School* (New York: McGraw-Hill, 1984).

6. Roger Tlusty, "Curricular Transformation as Social History: Eau Claire High School, 1890-1915" (Ph.D. diss., University of Wisconsin-Madison, 1986), p. 218.

7. Franklin Bobbitt, *Curriculum-Making in Los Angeles* (Chicago: The University of Chicago, 1922), p. 4.

8. Ibid., p. 7.

9. Ibid.

10. John I. Goodlad, *A Place Called School*, p. 48.

11. "Let's Call the Whole Thing Off," from *Shall we Dance*, a RKO Production. Lyrics by Ira Gershwin. Music by George Gershwin. Copyright 1937 by Gershwin Publishing Corporation.

12. John Dewey, "The Situation as Regards the Course of Study," *Journal of Proceedings and Addresses* (Washington, D.C.: National Education Association, 1901), p. 332.

13. Ibid.

14. Ibid., p. 333.

15. Ibid., p. 334.

16. Ibid., p. 335.

17. Ibid., p. 340.

18. Ibid., p. 337.

19. Ibid.

20. Ibid., p. 338.

21. Ibid., p. 342.

22. Ibid., p. 348.

23. Seymour B. Sarason, *The Culture of the School and the Problem of Change* (Boston: Allyn and Bacon, 1971), p. 35.

24. Ibid., p. 36.

25. Katherine Camp Mayhew and Anna Camp Edwards, *The Dewey School: The University School of the University of Chicago 1896-1903* (New York: D. Appleton Century, 1936), pp. 365-66.

26. Ibid., p. 375.

27. Ibid., p. 368.

28. Sarason, *The Culture of the School and the Problem of Change*, p. 212.

29. Ibid., p. 213.

30. "Progress," from *Love Life*. Lyrics by Alan Jay Lerner. Music by Kurt Weill. Copyright 1948 by Alan Jay Lerner and Kurt Weill.

31. Henry Steele Commager, "The School as Surrogate Conscience," *Saturday Review* (11 January 1975), p. 55.

32. Robert Nisbet, *History of the Idea of Progress* (New York: Basic Books, 1980), p. 4.

33. Commager, "The School as Surrogate Conscience," p. 54.

34. "Kansas City," from *Oklahoma!* Music by Richard Rodgers. Book and lyrics by Oscar Hammerstein, 2nd. Copyright 1943 by Williamson Music Inc.

35. David Tyack and Elizabeth Hansot, *Managers of Virtue: Public School Leadership in America, 1820-1980* (New York: Basic Books, 1982).

36. Ibid., p. 106.

37. Raymond E. Callahan, *Education and the Cult of Efficiency: A Study of the Social Forces that Have Shaped the Administration of the Public Schools* (Chicago: University of Chicago Press, 1962).

38. Ellwood P. Cubberley, *Public School Administration* (Boston: Houghton Mifflin, 1916), p. 338.

39. Tyack and Hansot, *Managers of Virtue*, p. 135.

40. Ibid., p. 142.

41. Ibid., p. 153.

CHAPTER III

Unapplied Curriculum Knowledge

HENRIETTA SCHWARTZ

Common sense dictates that when one has professional knowledge it will be applied; theory into practice is the sine qua non of a profession. Applying knowledge requires theory, strategies, and practices determined to be effective by research, time, and leadership. Education has a body of theory. In the literature there are approved educational practices found by research to be effective. Indeed, Goodlad's recommendations in his studies of schooling were based on the effective educational practices found in the literature.[1] According to Berliner, existing data on best practices in education are as comprehensive as those in the "hard sciences."[2] Professionals know what these practices are; for example, giving students time to respond to questions has been found to be significantly related to gains in achievement. There is nothing secret about them. Jackson has written:

[G]ood schools, unlike the manufacturers of perfumes or other exotic concoctions, have few, if any, secrets to divulge. What their teachers and administrators know about how to educate, most other educators know as well. The determination to act on that knowledge is another matter entirely, of course, and is surely one of the major qualities distinguishing truly outstanding schools from those that are less so.[3]

Research has found that the quality Jackson writes about—acting on knowledge—is missing in many classrooms. Teachers are not implementing what they know and recognize as sound pedagogy. Goodlad found, for example, that teachers tend to stay with a single method; they do not vary their teaching methods in accord with their purposes and the demands of the subject matter. The curriculum knowledge is there but they are not using it. The codified body of research is being developed; the knowledge base is large and growing. But the commitment and conditions necessary to use the knowledge base in education still elude us. Goodlad's study provides evidence of this:

[L]earning appears to be enhanced when students understand what is expected of them, get recognition for their work, learn quickly about their errors, and receive guidance in improving their performance. These pedagogical practices are very much within the control of teachers, and it has been my experience that teachers recognize them as desirable pedagogy. But our data suggest a paucity of most of them. About 57 percent of the students in the early elementary grades answered "yes" when asked whether they understood what their teachers wanted them to do. Forty percent answered "sometimes." . . . Almost [20 percent] at all levels perceived themselves as not being informed of their mistakes and corrected in their performance.[4]

Anthropologists call the time lag between the creation of new knowledge and its application to improve the human condition "a cultural gap." Others call the gap between research and practice "engineering." We in education call the unapplied knowledge we have managed to accumulate about teaching, learning, and schools the "implementation problem." This chapter is concerned with the implementation problem in pedagogy. Why is it that teachers are not putting their pedagogical knowledge into practice? The answer to this question has important implications for both the in-service and preservice education of teachers. Assuming that preservice programs in teacher education do provide students with the best possible evidence for given practices, what prevents teachers from using this pedagogical knowledge in classrooms? How can the problem be dealt with? This chapter will explore these issues.

All professions, including teaching, are questioning the basic assumption that those who know desirable practices will employ them. Knowing does not mean doing, whether we are talking about medicine, law, or education. Professionalism, or research-based practice, is a much more complex problem than was first recognized.

Pedagogical Knowledge: Questioning the Assumptions

One may have "pedagogical knowledge" from having read about it. But in no sense can this passing acquaintance with practice be equated with preparation for practice. One may have studied about and may clearly *recognize* approved educational practices without knowing how to implement them. Eisner maintains that knowledge is not power until it is applied and that most teachers do not know what they know and have no way of finding out because they get so little feedback on their teaching.[5] The isolation of the classroom inhibits the discovery of behavior that is inconsistent with knowledge.

THE PRACTICE PART OF PROFESSIONAL EDUCATION

Do prospective teachers actually have the preparation for practice—experiences rather than simply reading the lore? As Tanner and Tanner remind us in their work on supervision, "If you are prepared to do something, you see it as your area of competence and responsibility, and consequently it becomes a professional responsibility."[6] Unfortunately, however, this belief is not widely held by policymakers, and teaching, perhaps more than any other profession, is regulated by nonprofessionals—by legislators, commissions, lay boards, and public opinion. Recent studies indicate that the quality of teacher education programs and certification criteria are both infinitely variable. Some states such as New Jersey, California, and Texas have approved alternative routes to certification that include no pedagogy or professional preparation and are based on on-the-job training as the means of acquiring a teaching credential. These credentialing procedures reflect unbelief in a knowledge base in teaching and a lack of respect for schools of education by legislators and/or the governor and mitigate against professional teaching. Obviously, the portion of the teaching force whose preparation includes no pedagogy and no knowledge of the research is unprepared to implement theoretical knowledge in their classrooms.[7]

The situation is that of a vicious circle: because so many teachers are unprepared, stylized teaching methods are mandated and supervision becomes more bureaucratic. The nonpecuniary rewards of teaching have been dwindling as teachers are increasingly viewed as bureaucratic functionaries rather than as practicing professionals. As Darling-Hammond observes, lack of input into professional decision making, overly restrictive bureaucratic controls, and inadequate administrative supports for teaching contribute to teacher dissatisfaction and attrition, particularly among the most highly qualified members of the teaching force.[8] The ultimate result is that the implementation gap widens.

In a profession, the practitioner uses codified knowledge and the wisdom of best practice in his intervention with clients. Before this behavior becomes part of the standard operating style of teachers the teaching force, in collaboration with teacher educators and scholars and researchers in teaching, must deal with some basic dilemmas in the profession. For example, does the profession seek *equity* or *excellence* in its professional preparation programs? Most of the major reform reports of the 1980s recommend raising entry standards for teachers, but teaching has historically had relatively flexible admission standards and has been the road to upward social and professional mobility for those previously excluded from the mainstream. How can the profession combine equity and excellence?

Another dilemma: one of the core assumptions of teaching is "a teacher is a teacher is a teacher" and one teacher's opinions and contributions are as good as any other's. But it is clear that some teachers apply pedagogical knowledge more than do others, and the reform reports have called for differentiation among the teaching ranks in status and salary. How will the profession reconcile the tradition of *egalitarianism* with the calls for *differentiation?* More importantly, is differentiation actually acceptance of a situation where some teachers are not expected to apply pedagogical knowledge?

The third dilemma is a bit like the nature/nurture paradox. Are artists born or trained? The literature is replete with examples of what good teachers are and do. But is it an *art* or a *science?* Can students be trained to do what good teachers do and be what good teachers are or must some basic aptitudes be present before training?

A fourth dilemma arises as recent reports and state legislators call for more standardization in the content and delivery of curriculum. Teachers and university faculty have a long-standing tradition of academic freedom: the right of the professor and teacher to teach without restraints, to develop curriculum, and to structure the delivery as he wishes within peer-determined limits. The dilemma is: How can the curriculum of teacher preparation programs, in-service activities, and the classroom accommodate *standardization and individualization?* (The standardization of in-service activities has driven many a teacher from the profession.)

Finally, what shall be the focus of the professional preparation program, the *curriculum* or the *child?* At the university level, the content of the curriculum takes precedence over the student as an individual. In the kindergarten class, the reverse is true. Although Dewey counseled in 1902 that the child and the curriculum are part of the same process, they continue to be pitted against one another. Consider, for example, alternative routes to certification that include no pedagogy. How do teachers and teacher educators strike a balance and try to integrate both dimensions?

These five dilemmas are not insoluble. Dualisms can be resolved with a "both/and" approach used by most other professions. Above all, the dilemmas must be approached with an understanding of, and admiration for, the centrality of the role of the teacher in any reform movement. The reform movement of the 1980s has been a mixed affair, including both teacher-proof prescriptions and cries for professionalism. If we expect teachers to use the knowledge that is available, we must carefully supervise the induction period, point out pedagogical methods that have proven helpful, and teach teachers how to incorporate them in their own teaching practices. Offering feedback and advice is essential. However, all this will come to nought unless the system allows teachers to use their pedagogical knowledge.

The national reports on education and various commissions on teacher education (including the Holmes Group and the Carnegie Task Force on Teaching as a Profession) agree that teachers need to be well educated, sensitive, intelligent, capable of learning from theory and example, action researchers, and amateur actors who like children, working with people and with ideas. They should be familiar with the principles of learning and other pedagogical theory, possess skills in analysis, synthesis, and presentation, and knowledge in the subject area, as well as knowledge of the major studies in education bearing on their field or subject area. They should have the opportunity—vast opportunities—to apply their knowledge and skills under the supervision of a variety of masters as well as under the tutelage of an experienced university faculty person who can communicate with the student and the faculty in the school and show practical application of the cumulative body of knowledge in teaching. Some scholars feel that the reason why teachers are not using curriculum knowledge in the classroom is their lack of pedagogical knowledge. Others feel that not understanding the subject matter is the barrier to the application of knowledge to practice. Goodlad feels that subject matter preparation is an individual rather than a general problem in teacher education.[9] Shulman maintains that more emphasis should be given to content.[10]

Regardless of the subject area or the grade level taught, fully three-quarters of the teachers in Goodlad's study indicated that they were greatly influenced in what they taught by two sources—their own background and their own and the students' interests and experiences. They gained better and more applicable training on their own and through their students than from formal instruction; teachers' initial encounters with curriculum frequently took place on paper rather than in the classroom. Drawing upon content knowledge and transforming it for use in the classroom is a critical problem for the novice teacher, as Shulman pointed out.

Our work does not intend to denigrate the importance of pedagogical understanding or skill in the development of a teacher or in enhancing the effectiveness of instruction. Mere content knowledge is likely to be as useless pedagogically as content-free skill. But to blend properly the two aspects of a teacher's capacities requires that we pay as much attention to the content aspects of teaching as we have recently devoted to the elements of teaching process.[11]

Clearly, new teachers do not come into the classroom as full-blown masters of curriculum. The processes of acquiring the knowledge, skills, attitudes, and relationships to be a good teacher are developmental, and not unlike the five stages of implementation of a curricular change proposed by Hall and Loucks. First, the teacher is concerned with mastery of the subject matter and materials; second, with the organizational structure of the material; and third, with his role and performance as a teacher and the expectations others have for him. The fourth stage is characterized by an understanding of the principles of curriculum development and of how to engage students in learning. Finally, in the last stage the teacher values his ability to know, think, and teach. This last stage of value internalization is the mark of the professional. The last two stages are difficult to achieve because they require a philosophy of curriculum and reflection on one's behavior in light of that philosophy.

The artificial separation of content and pedagogy in most teacher preparation programs does not facilitate the integration of curriculum and instruction. In fact, before beginning an effort to design or change the curriculum it is essential that teachers' conceptions of curriculum be made explicit, discussed, accepted, or modified. Like the dedicated scientist, teachers using their curriculum knowledge must be tireless masters of delayed gratification.

If the new teacher's conception of curriculum is simply to assign discrete learning tasks, give students some feedback, make corrections, and give a test, then some reeducation of the teacher is in order. If the master teacher's most sophisticated advice to the student teacher is "don't smile until Christmas," some attention needs to be given to the modeling function of supervising teachers. Teachers' conceptions of curriculum are strongly influenced by where they work and with whom they work. Working conditions and peer interactions in the school must foster reflective thinking about curriculum and instruction. Without these supports, curriculum innovation will likely fail.

Novice teachers and budding administrators do not get enough practice in various, real situations before assuming the role of a full-fledged professional. In medicine, the prospective doctor spends at least five years in supervised practice before becoming a recognized professional. If the doctor is specializing, another three years of supervised practice may be required. In nursing, at least three years are spent in supervised practice, with a year added for each specialization. These prolonged practice periods are called internships or residencies, or in law, apprenticeships, and are concurrent with and extend beyond a good university education including graduate school. There are a few model programs in teacher education that systematically build in early field-based pedagogical experiences. The California State University requires, prior to student teaching, a semester of observation and participation in schools preceded by an early field experience—all under university faculty supervision.[12] The experience should include acting on curriculum knowledge.

The state of Illinois requires 100 clinical hours in classrooms supervised by a university faculty member before formal student teaching. Whether prospective teachers have the understanding needed for making the most of these experiences is a nagging question. Do they know what they are looking for when they go into classrooms? Interns in medicine who observe in an operating room know whether they are viewing an appendectomy, a lobotomy, or the delivery of a baby, and because they talk with their peers and supervisors they can make some judgments about whether the operation they have observed fits the model described in the textbook as "best practice."

Shulman maintains that the knowledge base for teachers is a complex configuration consisting of propositional knowledge—principles, maxims, and norms, case knowledge of specific, well-documented events in the form of prototypes, incidents, and parables, and strategic knowledge or professional judgment based on experience and reflection. Most of the current reform reports say little about content transformation or the essentials of pedagogy.[13]

Little is said about the essential procedures a new teacher must have at least observed in schools and classrooms and less is said about what a new teacher should have practiced with children. Take, for example, the problem of grouping in a classroom. Before a new teacher is allowed to take on a classroom, should theory-backed experiences be given with large groups, small groups, triads, cross-age groups, homogeneous groups, mixed groups, mainstreamed classes,

classes segregated by sex, race, and social class, or integrated along the same variables? What happens in physical education when a teacher allows groups to self-select and how much does a teacher have to know about individual children before assigning them to a classroom group?

UNAPPLIED CURRICULUM KNOWLEDGE AND CURRICULUM CONCEPTS

There is an old Chinese proverb that says: "One sees what is behind one's eyes." Basic to any curricular reform or implementation effort is information about the teacher's conceptions of curriculum. Eisner speaks of curriculum as a "mind-altering device"; Posner views curriculum as something that is product-oriented, comes before instruction, and is descriptive.[14] Schwab's definition, below, is much broader and holistic and is the bias of this chapter. Over the last forty years theorists have tried to move away from the common assumption of curriculum as a program of studies or what was listed in the college catalog. In spite of these heroic efforts, the concept of curriculum as subject matter packaged in courses or units or lesson plans persists to this day and is the basis of most efforts in curriculum design. This concept mitigates against the application of curriculum workers' knowledge.

Another factor in the problem of unapplied curriculum knowledge is the teacher's concept of curriculum. The curriculum encompasses what is to be taught as well as how it is to be taught, yet for many teachers, their job has absolutely nothing to do with curriculum adaptation or change: they view themselves as an instructional delivery system. And such a view makes impossible the implementation of professional knowledge, which includes adapting the curriculum to the motivational and achievement levels of individual students. Professional teaching absolutely depends on such adaptation, as this definition of curriculum by Schwab makes clear:

Curriculum is *what is successfully conveyed* to differing degrees to different students *by committed teachers using appropriate materials and actions*, of *legitimated bodies of knowledge*, skill, taste, and propensity to act and react, *which are chosen* for instruction *after serious reflection* and communal decision by representatives *of those involved in the teaching of a specified group of students* who are known to the decision makers.[15]

This statement reflects what Goodlad, Brophy, and others have concluded based on extensive studies of schooling and classrooms: There is no "American public school system," no uniform curriculum. Each school is a unique culture sharing only some common elements with all other schools. "Curriculum is not necessarily the same for all students of a given age and standing. Nor does it differ necessarily in all respects for each and every student or school."[16]

And yet, although each school and each classroom is unique there are principles and practices which will serve them all. As Dewey pointed out, the acts in teaching are too complex to be reduced to a formula.[17] Principles are not formulas, but guiding ideas. And therein lies a problem. Supervision provided teachers at the preservice—and in-service—level tends to treat teaching as a mechanical formula. Little wonder that so many teachers behave as mechanical dolls—and thus fail to vary their methods and meet the needs of individuals. For professional behavior depends on teachers being able to draw upon theory as needed to meet emergent situations. Thus although teachers *may* know theory from having read about it, current methods of supervision (which are mandated in some states) do not allow that theory to be put into practice. Robert Anderson discusses this problem in some detail in this yearbook.

Major reform reports, such as *A Nation at Risk* and the Carnegie Commission Report, have called for reform in teacher education as a means of getting at the problem of teachers' weaknesses. It is assumed by such commissions that problems like that of unapplied knowledge can be attributed to the poor quality of teacher education programs. Yet as Cornbleth has noted, teachers in the United States have on the average thirteen years of teaching experience and, further, "those years of classroom experience have likely had considerably more impact on what teachers do or do not do than the one or two years of teacher education they experienced more than a decade ago. Yet school reform reports say little or nothing about the conditions of teaching in elementary and secondary schools. This does not mean that teacher education is without problems."[18] The point is that to look at the problem of unapplied knowledge segmentally, and as residing primarily in preservice teacher education, is to doom it to remain forever unresolved. There are factors in the school setting that promote or prevent the utilization of professional knowledge. Applying knowledge requires a theory, strategies, skills, and time for implementation. The teacher must be a student of teaching. Moreover, implementation depends on great leadership skills and curriculum knowledge on the part of the supervisor. In some schools teachers *are* using approved educational practice and growing in their ability to relate theory to practice. In these schools educational leaders have provided a setting that makes these things possible—and, indeed, they will tolerate no other state of affairs.

For the most part, the principal of a school is too busy managing the enterprise to engage in sustained and continuous watch over the curriculum; another agency is required. Schwab and others recommend that the other agency be a curriculum group which will address the question of what should be taught, how, to whom, by whom, and for how long. The group would provide new knowledge for the experienced practitioner and encourage teachers' use of curriculum knowledge and the sharing of the results of their efforts with others. This process is what other professions do when they document individual experiments and case studies of a new treatment. To be responsible and effective, the group needs a particular membership. The teachers are the most important members of such a group; for they know the students and the classrooms best. University faculty from the teacher preparation programs with expertise in pedagogy should be members of such a group and curricular experts should be participants on an on-call basis. In forming the group, the principal needs to understand that the political system of the school will change as teachers are involved with university faculty in real decision making about curriculum.

Like supervision of preservice teachers, the supervision of in-service teachers has, in the main, been conducted mechanically and without regard for the teacher's role in solving curriculum problems. For the teacher has a role; if indeed these problems are to be solved, the "buck" ends at the teacher's door, no matter what policies are adopted at other levels, as will be discussed shortly.

Teacher conceptions of the curriculum are also an enormously important factor in whether teachers implement curriculum knowledge. As Goodlad observed:

Teachers at all levels of education are predominantly content-centered: They depend heavily on what is to be taught to carry the burden of instruction. This remains true in spite of the concern expressed in recent decades for learners and learning. . . . Content is organized into subjects to preserve knowledge and to expedite the accretion of new knowledge. To serve education, content must be organized for instructional purposes. The most significant organization for teaching is that which exists at a given moment in a teacher's mind. The teacher must be both a student of content organized for preservation and an organizer of content for instruction.[19]

Curriculum was conceived of as a plan of instruction in the Eight-Year Study and later refined by Tyler in his famous *Basic Principles of Curriculum and Instruction* (1949). The processes for developing curriculum and delivering instruction were seen in terms of outcomes, experiences, organizing activities, and evaluation. There have been many adaptations of Tyler's model, including some by Herrick, Taba, and Goodlad. Although criticized in later years, the model did turn attention away from the separation of content and method and set the stage for more integrated views. The problem is intensifying, for it is the almost inevitable result of certification procedures that include no pedagogy.

CYCLES AND FADS AND PEDAGOGICAL KNOWLEDGE

The problem of ahistoricism in curriculum development is dealt with by Herbert Kliebard in his chapter in this yearbook. It is considered here as it affects the utilization of knowledge. Supervisors and curriculum workers have an unfortunate tendency to move from one trendy fad to the next. What is deemed appropriate one year is deemed inappropriate the next. This generates confusion and blurs sound educational principles such as the need to see learner, learning processes, and content interrelatedly. Curriculum workers must maintain a clear vision of a balanced curriculum, or teachers are unlikely to use their professional knowledge. One cannot keep one's head above water when one typhoon follows on the heels of another. While the curriculum fashions may change from year to year, the culture of the school has great cultural ballast and changes little.

Socialization as a Teacher

The prospective teacher is socialized into the profession at the university in ways that have little to do with the culture of the schools. In most programs the fifteen-week student teaching experience is a sheltered and mentored one, even in internship programs which are longer and provide more variety and realism. The first years of teaching are so powerful that they frequently wipe out what was learned about curriculum and pedagogy at the university.

Research indicates that teachers come out of their preparation programs filled with professional ideals. Then what happens to them? Some writers say that ideals are doomed to destruction; it seems wiser to say that whether the ideals remain alive and well depends on the school setting. Teachers have always been asked to do more than teach the three Rs. Ravitch traces the school's role in social reform over the last forty years and the attendant expansion of the role of teacher from transmitter of knowledge, skills, and mainstream beliefs and behaviors to one of social change agent. Schools and teachers are not able to cure society's ills, "responsibilities for which they were entirely unsuited. When they have failed, it was usually because their leaders and their public alike had forgotten their real limitations as well as their real strengths."[20]

As if the above factors were not enough, schools are difficult places in which to work; they were built for children, with few accommodations for adults and adult interaction. Lortie writes about the isolation of the teacher and the lack of a career ladder.[21] Kerr describes the bone-freezing boredom of teaching, because teaching, as it is presently structured, does not allow an adult to change functions or settings from time to time.[22] Finally, Schwartz, Little, and others looking at the stressful working conditions found in urban schools, point to a system that does not provide necessary rewards in status, security, and sociability.[23] Teachers suffer from the "Rodney Dangerfield syndrome" in that they get little respect from a negative press and public, their jobs frequently put them in positions of fiscal (and physical!) jeopardy, and they have little time or opportunity to make friends and interact with other adults during the course of the school day. From the perspective of intellectual stimulation, self-respect, economic security, and friendship, it would be irrational for the more able student to choose teaching as a career. Yet sound education depends on bright and energetic teachers staying in the classroom and remaining bright, energetic, enthused, and stimulating. When excitement dies, learning dies with it.

As Victor F. Weisskopf, a professor emeritus of physics at Massachusetts Institute of Technology, tells mathematics and science teachers, science is not a collection of facts and correct answers. It is curiosity, discovering things, and asking why is it so. The teacher's curiosity must stay alive if students' excitement is to stay alive. The same may be said about any domain of knowledge, not just science.

The teacher's curiosity and excitement does not always stay alive, however. Once the teacher has developed a style and set of responses that seem to work in the classroom and seem to be accepted in the school culture, making changes is a difficult process. New teachers coming into a system may know their subject, understand and have practiced good classroom and instructional techniques, but the socialization forces of the school are very powerful. Joyce has suggested that these powerful factors affect the quality and effectiveness of staff development programs and attempts to change the curriculum.[24] He identifies eight factors that inhibit the incorporation of research findings into successful curriculum and instructional programs:

1. Privatism, or what Lortie calls the Robinson Crusoe syndrome; once the classroom door is closed, the teacher does as she pleases[25]
2. Cynicism—reactions to terms and assumptions used in reform literature that teachers perceive as derogatory such as "teacher-proof curriculum," "teachers come from the least academically qualified groups," "change agent"
3. Lack of experience with powerful teaching and training options and lack of clarity about what behaviors teachers are expected to perform
4. Not developing collaborative problem-solving approaches
5. Poor initial training and lack of experience
6. Pressures toward normative teaching by school culture
7. Low self-esteem
8. Lack of reward for innovation

What, then, can curriculum workers do to deal with these pressures? This statement by Unruh is enormously constructive and on target: "To overcome these and other negative factors, every teacher and school administrator should be a student of teaching. They should constantly study the profession, polishing their skills, developing new ones, rethinking the curriculum of the school, and making the learning environment more challenging and effective."[26]

As Dewey frequently counseled, knowledge from the behavioral sciences must be brought to bear on problems in the educational situation. The analytical tools of the anthropologist can provide insights into the problem of unapplied curriculum knowledge. The nine universal cultural patterns, as described by the anthropologist, Melville J. Herskovits, seem particularly useful, for all schools and classrooms have these cultural patterns.[27] For example, all cultures and subcultures have a *value system*, which indicates the preferred ways of doing things or specifying what is good and what is bad. All have a cosmology or *world view*, which specifies the beliefs concerning the position of man in the cosmos, the limits individuals must adhere to in the school, the community, the church, or the classroom. Each cultural unit has some form of *social organization*, which governs individual and group relationships even to the point of determining forms of verbal address. Each system has a *technology*, a body of knowledge and skills used to perform the tasks necessary for the system to function and survive. There is an *economic system*, which regulates the allocation of goods and services in the school and the classroom. Furthermore, there is a form of governance or a *political system* regulating individual and institutional behavior which specifies how decisions are made, how power, authority, and influence are acquired and used, and who participates in what decisions. Typically, there is a special *language* uniquely suited to the educational process or the subject matter of the classroom. There is an *aesthetic system* which defines what is beautiful, creative, and artistic. Finally, there is a *socialization process* or educational process that regularizes the transmission of knowledge to the neophytes.

But the important thing is this. The teacher finds that he or she must live up to the norms of behavior or expectations, which are determined by the ways the school culture has developed to tend to these nine areas. For example, if prevailing school values embrace professional improvement, new teachers will be socialized to accept this value. And if the social organization favors teachers engaging in professional collaboration with one another, application of pedagogical knowledge may be the direct outcome. If the political system is such that principals and teachers are colleagues in professional activity, teachers are more likely to focus on their educational function (as opposed to their custodial function). Each of the cultural universals, and the unique pattern of interaction among universals, affects teachers' utilization of pedagogical knowledge. And each provides a lens for viewing the problem of unapplied knowledge in a given school or classroom. The cultural universals model is only one of many conceptual frameworks that anthropologists use to look at the world but it serves a useful purpose here as an analytical tool, particularly when considered in the context of Schwab's four "commonplaces."

In Schwab's view of the school as an organization, curriculum delivery is a negotiated process between the four commonplaces or universals of education: the teacher, the student, what is taught, and the milieux of teaching/learning. While each of the four commonplaces is theoretically important, at any given time one may become more important than the others, as in the case of the current emphasis by the federal government on the need to correct (upgrade) the high school curriculum. The emphasis today is on *what is taught*, with a hue and cry to eliminate the electives introduced in response to the demands of the 1960s and 1970s to meet the student's individual needs; we are urged now to go back to a discipline-centered curriculum for all, to combat the twin evils of Japanese markets and Soviet missiles. Schwab, by contrast, calls for a "diversity of curricula." He would have schools attend to Herskovits's universals, while also accommodating the uniqueness of local needs, attending to the practical and fulfilling the need for localism in curricula; he would have curriculum workers attend to the theoretical—as well as to the specifics of a curriculum. Most of all, he would have university professors be involved with the practical aspects of curriculum change.

OVERT COMPLIANCE AND COVERT RESISTANCE

Teachers will not accept and cannot be told what to do. Throughout the history of public education, all who have tried it have failed. Teachers are not assembly line operators and will not behave so. Furthermore, they have no need, except in rare instances, to fall back on defiance as a way of not heeding. There are a thousand ingenious ways in which commands on what and how to teach can, will, and must be modified or circumvented in the actual moments of teaching. Teachers practice an art:

Teachers must be involved in *debate, deliberation,* and *decision* about what and how to teach. Such involvement constitutes the only language in which knowledge adequate to an art can arise. Without such a language, teachers not only feel decisions as impositions, they find that intelligence cannot traverse the gap between the generalities of merely expounded instructions and the particularities of teaching moments. Participation in debate, deliberation, and choice are required for learning what is needed as well as a willingness to do it. There is an obvious moral here for teacher-training.[28]

Schwab's emphasis on willing participation by teachers is supported by a three-year study conducted at Roosevelt University in Chicago and San Francisco State University on dysfunctional stress (burnout) among teachers in urban schools. Researchers tried to identify the working conditions related to absenteeism, nonparticipation, apathy, negativism about the job, the school, the children, and, most of all, one's self. These problems tended to be characteristic of highly stressed faculties in schools with poor achievement scores, or in schools with low productivity. The cosmology of high-stress schools revealed that the teachers no longer believed anything they did would make a difference in students' learning. The three major factors which seemed related to high-stress situations were teachers' feelings of lack of:

1. *status* (feelings of being a worthwhile professional, that is, consulted on curriculum decisions rather than constantly being "put down" by the principal, the media, the central office, and so forth);
2. *security* (fiscal and physical safety and job security);
3. *sociability* (the time and opportunity to interact with other adults and discuss personal and professional issues in an atmosphere of trust and respect).

Teachers cite barriers to teaching as a factor in "burnout." Barriers are anything that interferes with what they see as their proper role and behavior in the classroom, and anything they are asked to do without consultation, discussion, and choice.[29] A typical comment is, "The lack of power to change the situation for the better makes the job stressful." Teachers perceive that directives forced upon them from above clearly affect the performance of their job. At the same time, they see that they have little input into the decision-making process, that little opportunity is given to them to express ideas to policymakers, and that administrators manipulate them and can be either too authoritarian or too nondirective. In addition, principals expect teachers to do a variety of nonteaching functions—patrolling halls, lunchroom duty, taking attendance in a homeroom—and teachers resent having to function as security personnel to bolster safety inside schools. Boards of education commonly demand copious and often repetitive paperwork, whether it be new forms or daily lesson plans.

Without feelings of status, security, and sociability, teachers "burned out," "dropped out," or were "carried out." The survivors were certainly not interested in curriculum-change projects mandated from above without consulting them. The social organization and political systems in highly stressed schools robbed teachers of their opportunities for collegiality, innovation, and the creativity of peer interaction. Significant here is that these systems also robbed teachers of a voice in curriculum decisions, the voice which is at the core of their professional identity. It is clear from this and other studies that dealing with the issue of unapplied knowledge will require creation of working conditions that are appropriate to a professional conception of teaching.

THE CURRICULUM WORKER

The curriculum worker must have—and act on—curriculum knowledge. He or she must be a reader of scholarly journals, a teacher, a learner, an applied researcher, and have a knowledge of past practices in curriculum. In addition, he or she must be capable of working well with individuals and groups—teachers, parents, the school principal, professors, school board members, in often touchy curriculum matters. According to Schwab, curriculum leaders "must be capable of skillful use of rhetorics of persuasion and elicitation."[30]

Seemingly, however, most curriculum workers are not given sufficient preparation, including well-supervised internships, to deal with these responsibilities in the field. A study by Pitner, asking field people how useful their graduate work was in preparing them for their current role, generated the following responses:

1. The curriculum worker's day is characterized by brief, disjointed, verbal encounters with a wide range of people seeking immediate solutions to problems, while academic programs ask graduate students to spend long hours reading, writing, and weighing alternative solutions to problems.

2. The supervisory role requires skill in conflict resolution, and the graduate student typically learns to avoid conflict and to accept the authority of expertise.

3. Supervisors depend on their skills in face-to-face communications to accomplish their work, while graduate students function in an atmosphere that emphasizes written communication.

4. The workplace is highly charged with eruptions and rare periods of calm, but with the expectation that supervisors will be calm and rational. University training programs particularly at the graduate level, value ideas and reasoning, and downplay the practical use of feelings.[31]

The above responses point to serious discontinuities between professional programs and practitioners' responsibilities. They point to the need for laboratory experiences for prospective curriculum workers where solutions to educational problems are guided by educational principles. Curriculum workers, like all professionals, must have an excellent education at the graduate level. Such an education requires that the laboratory experiences make real the principles of education learned in coursework, not that they be kept in separate boxes. We have learned this from the experience of other professions.

For a long time the difficulty in talking about the kind of individual and role needed to assist with curriculum revision programs in schools was that of insufficient knowledge: the ordinary organizational life and tasks of people in schools were not described adequately. Empirical and ethnographic studies over the last decade with their "thick" descriptions (for example, studies by Goodlad and Sarason) have partially remedied this situation and we now have some answers to the questions: What knowledge, skills, and abilities do the curriculum change agents require? What structures must support individual efforts to install curriculum change? How long will it take? Who must be involved? Studies conducted over the last two decades have much to contribute toward making graduate programs more useful.

Theory Into Practice: Narrowing the Gap

The climate of the school is a crucial factor in whether or not teachers act on their knowledge. Since the late 1930s, studies on social climates have given powerful evidence in support of open communication, a great degree of teacher autonomy and administrative trust, democratic-collaborative working relationships focused on solving problems. These characteristics keep recurring in the research associated with climate and outcomes. Over the years, it has become clear that whether or not teachers improve the curriculum, individually and as a school faculty, depends on the ethos of the school and on the nature of curriculum leadership. Teachers behave differently from school to school. In the introductory chapter of this yearbook it was pointed out that curriculum issues are inextricably intertwined. Certainly whether or not teachers act on their knowledge rests substantially on whether curriculum workers act on theirs. University faculty who are educated in curriculum improvement and research can bring to bear the best available knowledge on teachers' classroom problems. The trouble is that involvement in practical field-based curriculum projects is not often regarded by the university as serious scholarly activity and is unrewarded.

The best curriculum utilization projects and plans can fall prey to the vagaries of private agendas and public pressures that are part of the lifeway of the public schools. The university can keep faculty members interested and involved in curriculum activities in the schools by making participation as rewarding in deliberations on tenure and promotion as are research and publications. But it is more difficult for the schools to maintain a focus. Changes in the economic system, the expanding or contracting need for teachers, the seniority system, the involuntary transferring of experienced teachers to achieve racial integration, revolving-door principals, and the impact of unionization on the socialization of new teachers have diverted many noble efforts over the last three decades. Initially experimental programs like the Ford Foundation Urban Master of Arts in Teaching in the 1950s and 1960s and the Teacher Corps programs of the late 1970s brought bright, idealistic interns and new teachers into urban schools along with their university mentors. Their missionary zeal was at times overwhelming. Both programs required an extensive field experience and a supervised internship, characteristics which found their way into the ongoing preservice programs of the universities. In the schools, both programs brought experienced teachers into their efforts and frequently renewed their energy and enthusiasm and honed curricular skills that needed reawakening. Experienced teachers were viewed as a resource for new teachers, and new teachers and university supervisors were viewed as sources of new knowledge and skill. Both programs did reasonably good things for about a decade. From the beginning, both programs tried to ignore the bureaucratic static, but the constant bombardment of minutiae, the shifting priorities of large city school systems, and the reduction of funding dampened the zeal of program staff. These nontraditional efforts, involving grass roots participation in curriculum decisions, knowledge, and utilization rather than top-down efforts, were hard work and required high levels of energy and selfless devotion; they were probably too ambitious from the start. Be that as it may, such curriculum reform and utilization efforts were effective when they were focused and when the decisions made by groups and individuals about a particular curriculum strategy were followed by hard sustained work and technical expertise tailored to the individual schools. Both in Teacher Corps and in the Ford Training and Placement Programs some university faculty members left the field when under siege, rightly arguing that working in the public schools was not their job.

The evaluations of these programs over the last twenty years reveal that any program which attempts to change behaviors in public schools ignores the contextual settings of the schools at great risk. Knowing what to expect and what to look for in a local school culture and in the centralized school district are critical skills for the curriculum worker. Most university professors do not wish to deal with the political realities of teachers and principals who are transferred from one school to another in the middle of a project irrespective of their crucial participation in a curricular effort at a particular school. One may not wish to address the realities of the impact of the unions on the values and social organization of a school and the economic consequences for the allocation of faculty time and other instructional resources, but someone must address these issues in any curricular utilization effort. To ignore these external forces is folly. No project is immune from the changing condition of the public schools.

Nevertheless, there are examples of effective university involvement aimed at helping teachers to become more academically effective and thus have a sense of inner control over events in their classroom. Thus they are encouraged to apply their knowledge in the future. Successful school-university programs elicit teacher participation in the identification of curriculum issues and take an aggregate rather than a segmental approach to school problems. There is attention to student characteristics, and an effort to develop promising programs for educational improvement. An example of coordinated school-university effort for curriculum improvement is to be found in San Francisco's Bayview-Hunters Point, the low-income, black area of the city.

The Bayview-Hunters Point Educational Complex was formed in 1978 by a faculty member at San Francisco State University, Fannie W. Preston, and funded for three years by the San Francisco Foundation. The Bayview-Hunters Point Educational Complex was part of Superintendent Robert Alioto's Redesign Plan for the San Francisco Unified School District and part of the Urban Mission program of the university. The overriding goal of the Complex was to upgrade the quality of the curriculum and the instructional program in three geographically and racially isolated elementary schools. The curricular efforts sought chiefly to establish a program that would have a long-term continuing effect on these black schools, such that the program would appeal to whites, Hispanics, Asians. In the words of the proposal, the revised curriculum was to "lead to a voluntary balanced enrollment." The project was to involve the professional preparation programs and faculty at the university in field-based curriculum development and in-service education programs. Finally, the program was to provide enrichment opportunities for students.

While some faculty from the university did place teams of student teachers at one or more of the three schools, it was understood that faculty were to work with the existing staff on curriculum problems which they identified together. When the funding ended, the university adopted one of the Complex elementary schools as a laboratory school and continued to support faculty involvement in curriculum projects; these included the development of a children's literature curriculum with the primary teachers, an oral language program, a global education curriculum, and an English proficiency program.[32]

Although external funding ceased for a year in 1981, both the university and the district continued to support curriculum development and change activities at the laboratory school. Test scores in reading at the school have gone up significantly during the course of the program. This single school project featured tenured university faculty in the field, interacting with classroom teachers involved as colleagues in shared decision making. The project director was able to function as a curriculum leader and had credibility in the school, the district, and the community, as well as at the university. The focus was on curriculum development by individuals who were members in good standing in their respective school cultures and by university faculty members who understood and were accepted by the school culture and who knew the points of entry into the system.

The program was reconstructed by the university and the school district in 1983 and became the Institute for the School Improvement Process. At present, the staff works with three schools each year in three-year cycles, but the total number of schools worked with is five at any given time. An important part of the program is the action plan developed by each school-based group during a summer workshop. This plan is viewed as a commitment to accomplish specific professional responsibilities designed to improve curriculum and instruction. Each action plan serves as an evaluation document for the second summer workshop and as a starting point for the second- and third-year activities of the group. The program is viewed by teachers and curriculum workers as most successful and has been adopted by the school district.[33]

Effective school-university programs exhibit the following characteristics, summarized in a Carnegie Foundation Report.[34] When planning for a productive program:

1. a common action agenda must be acknowledged;

2. a true spirit of collaboration must emerge;
3. a single project must be identified;
4. those involved must be adequately rewarded;
5. the focus must be on activities, not machinery; and
6. there must be commitment to doing and knowing why.

There is a tendency for schools to look inward, which prevents ideas
and insights from coming in. That is why involvement with the
university is so important—the very meaning of "university" is wide
and global: ideas and actions from various sources, not just one.

Curriculum workers can work with the problem of applied
knowledge by looking outside—at the highest level of practice—the
settings where teachers, experienced and new, do use research-based
strategies. Typically, these adaptations occur in school systems with
administrators who encourage, identify, and reward professionalism
and innovation. There are several factors that seem to foster teacher
use of research in curriculum and instruction. Among these are: the
need to be explicit about expectations and resources, the involvement
of teachers and university faculty in debate, dialogue, and discussion
about the proposed change, the commitment to action and the strong
and continuous interaction between university and school, between
theory, implementation, and practice. In any form of educational
improvement, "the supervisor and teacher together are a key source
for diagnosing classroom and schoolwide problems concerning the
curriculum, learning, the educative environment, and the relationship
between the school, home, and community. As professional
practitioners, the supervisor and the teacher must be intelligently
informed consumers of research and intelligent investigative
participants. This has been borne out from the Eight-Year Study to
the contemporary research findings on effective schools."[35]

Supervisors, both from the university and the school system, can
help narrow the gap between research and practice. The in-school
supervisor can question the forces of tradition and the comfort of
routines in ways that would lead to the public stoning of an outsider.
The naive outsider can question why some response to a problem is in
the form of a recipe and cite research that might lead to a new
response. The university faculty member can perform another very
important bridging function, and that is relaying to other faculty the
need to study problems that are meaningful to the practitioner rather
than problems that are highly specialized or capable of quantification.
The key point to remember is preparing the novice teacher with the

theory and skills to format curriculum knowledge to fit curriculum needs.

Conclusion

The following ideas can provide guidance to curriculum workers in dealing with the problem of unapplied curriculum knowledge:

1. Curriculum workers cannot assume that all teachers recognize sound pedagogy, particularly in light of alternative teacher certification programs, such as those in New Jersey.

2. Even those who recognize approved educational methods must have peer and administrator support and well-supervised opportunities to practice them.

3. Sound pedagogy is not final; the body of knowledge and skills in teaching is continually expanding. Therefore teachers need continually to search for better methods of teaching students.

4. Dealing with the problem of unapplied knowledge requires the comprehensive and coordinated efforts of university faculty, teachers, supervisors, and administrators.

The gap between research and practice can be narrowed, but not by blaming the victim. As discussed, teachers do not use what they know for various reasons. The systematic application of knowledge to practice requires supportive systems that permit the professional to apply his or her specialized knowledge; it requires practitioner participation in the interpretation and application of research-findings to curriculum problems. Application of research findings proceeds more smoothly and with a greater sense of commitment when the practitioner has participated in the problem-solving process.

Finally, narrowing the gap requires that the initial teacher preparation program has carefully selected, screened, and rigorously trained the new practitioner; it has given the neophyte knowledge, analytical skills, and plenty of opportunities to observe and interact with master practitioners, to engage in supervised practice with ongoing feedback, and the time to correct errors and practice new techniques. The participants in the preparation of professionals and those being prepared trust each other and maintain a working level of trust throughout their professional careers. They trust each other to do what they say they are capable of and what they will do. This is a definition of professional work. When the work and the workplace and the preparation places, the in-service educators, the schools, and the universities resemble the above conditions more closely, teachers will use curricular knowledge in the classroom.

FOOTNOTES

1. John I. Goodlad, *A Place Called School* (New York: McGraw-Hill, 1984).

2. David Berliner, "Making the Right Changes in Preservice Education," *Phi Delta Kappan* 66 (October 1985): 94-96.

3. Philip W. Jackson, "Comprehending a Well-Run Comprehensive: A Report on a Visit to a Large Suburban High School," *Daedalus* 110 (Fall 1981) 94-95.

4. Goodlad, *A Place Called School*, pp. 111-12.

5. Elliot Eisner, in conversation with the author on February 7, 1987.

6. Daniel Tanner and Laurel Tanner, *Supervision in Education: Problems and Practices* (New York: Macmillan, 1987).

7. C.E. Feistritzer, *The Making of a Teacher* (Washington, D.C.: National Center for Educational Information, 1984).

8. Linda Darling-Hammond, *Beyond the Commission Reports: The Coming Crisis in Teaching* (Santa Monica, CA: Rand Corporation, 1984). Ed 248 245.

9. Goodlad, *A Place Called School*.

10. Lee Shulman, "Those Who Understand: Knowledge Growth in Teaching," *Educational Researcher* 15 (February 1986): 4-14.

11. Ibid., p. 8.

12. Ann Reynolds, *In Change Delight* (Denver, CO: American Association of Colleges for Teacher Education, 1985).

13. Judith Warren Little, "Moving toward Continuous School Improvement," in *Making Our Schools More Effective* (San Francisco: Far West Laboratory, 1984). ED 249 590.

14. Elliot Eisner, conversation with author, February 7, 1987; George J. Posner, "Education: Its Components and Constructs" (Paper presented at the Annual Meeting of the American Educational Research Association, Chicago, 1972).

15. Joseph Schwab, "The Practical 4: Something for Curriculum Professors To Do," *Curriculum Inquiry* 13 (Fall 1983): 240. Emphasis added.

16. Ibid.

17. John Dewey, *Democracy and Education* (New York: Macmillan, 1916).

18. Catherine Cornbleth, "Ritual and Rationality in Teacher Education Reform," *Educational Researcher* 15 (April 1986): 4.

19. John Goodlad, *School, Curriculum, and the Individual* (Waltham, MA: Blaisdell Publishing Co., 1966), p. 198.

20. Diane Ravitch, *The Troubled Crusade* (New York: Basic Books, 1984).

21. Dan C. Lortie, *Schoolteacher: A Sociological Study* (Chicago: University of Chicago Press, 1975).

22. Donna H. Kerr, "Teaching Competence and Teacher Education in the United States," *Teachers College Record* 84 (March 1983): 525-552.

23. Henrietta Schwartz, George Olson, Albert Bennett, and Rick Ginsberg, *Schools as a Workplace: The Realities of Stress*, NIE Report 6-80-1011 (Chicago: Roosevelt University, 1983) ED 239 009; Little, *Moving toward Continuous School Improvement*.

24. Bruce Joyce, "A Memorandum for the Future," in *Staff Development/ Organization Development*, ed. Betty Dillon-Peterson, Yearbook of the Association for

Supervision and Curriculum Development (Alexandria, VA: Association for Supervision and Curriculum Development, 1981), pp. 113-127.

25. Lortie, *Schoolteacher*.

26. Glenys G. Unruh and Adolph Unruh, *Curriculum Development: Problems, Processes, and Progress* (Berkeley, CA: McCutchan Publishing Corp., 1984), p. 243.

27. Melville Herskovits, *Man and His Works* (New York: Alfred A. Knopf Publishing Co., 1949).

28. Schwab, "The Practical 4," pp. 245-66.

29. Schwartz et al., *Schools as a Workplace*.

30. Schwab, "The Practical 4," p. 259.

31. Nancy Pitner, "Training of the School Administrator: State of the Art" (Paper presented at the Annual Meeting of the American Educational Research Association, New York, 1972).

32. Fannie W. Preston, *Final Report: Bayview-Hunters Point Educational Complex* (San Francisco: San Francisco Foundation, 1982).

33. John Lynch, *A Proposal to Continue the Institute for the School Improvement Process* (San Francisco: San Francisco State University, 1986).

34. Gene I. Maeroff, "Mending Our Social Fabric," *NASSP Bulletin* 67 (March 1983): 32-33.

35. Tanner and Tanner, *Supervision in Education*, p. 357.

CHAPTER IV

Political Pressures on Supervisors

ROBERT H. ANDERSON

Curriculum workers, supervisors, and others in leadership roles are frequently daunted by essentially political forces and pressures that call for compromise of professional standards or ethics or the diversion of energies intended to benefit children to other and less legitimate activities. In some cases, the pressures take the form of mandates or their equivalent from state governments, state agencies, or other powerful entities seeking to accomplish certain broad social or political goals through the instrument of public education. In other cases, the pressures are more localized and originate with parents, both individually and collectively, with boards of education, or with the administrative officers of the local school district. On occasion the pressures come from prestigious persons, organizations, or other opinion-influencing entities such as the media. Whatever their origins or their merit, such pressures sometimes pose enormous problems for supervisors and eventually dilute, alter, or imperil the overall quality of educational services. In this chapter we examine these pressures and consider how curriculum workers are affected by and deal with them.

The Perennial Public Outcry

One of the constants in public education is that segments of the general public have intense concern about this problem or that, and look to the schools to deal with it. Every year there are pressures to do something much more effectively, or to begin doing something not now on the school agenda, or to cease doing something that is on, but assertedly does not belong on, that agenda. Such pressures have been present since the early nineteenth century; one is able to find in the years between 1820 and 1850 demands for curriculum expansion (geography, government, natural science, and vocational education) as well as demands that the catechism be reestablished as a textbook

60

and nonsectarian books be removed from school libraries.[1] The problem of pressures on supervisors began with the creation of the state superintendency of education. Horace Mann's ideas on method and on discipline were criticized by ministers and theologians.[2] There have been pressures on supervisors as long as there have been professional (as opposed to lay) supervisors. It is a perennial problem. School people are constantly faced with the need to defend existing policies or programs, respond to proposals for add-on services or programs, rework or revise courses and/or procedures, and keep a reasonable peace with their clients and the public at large.

The criticisms and pressures that come from lay groups and individuals, however well motivated such persons may be, often grow out of assumptions, perceptions, and beliefs that are inconsistent with the current knowledge base about children and how they learn. Although few citizens or government officials would feel qualified to define "best practice" for dentists or engineers or air traffic controllers, almost every adult seems comfortable in the role of educational authority and critic. Memories of their own school experience, opinions reinforced by stereotypes in literature, movies, and even comic strips, and an ingenuous tendency to shift all kinds of child-control responsibilities from themselves and other societal institutions to the schools, cause them to prescribe unsuitable approaches. A presumption of overall teacher ineptitude, combined with a simplistic definition of the well-run classroom, tempts many parents and others to insist upon formal, competitive, basics-oriented, teacher-dominated, no-nonsense classrooms. Naive and unjustified confidence in standardized achievement tests, in the conventional A-B-C-D-F marking system, in fear of nonpromotion as a strong motivator, and in textbook coverage as a legitimate delivery system causes parents to press for models of schooling that may or may not have been appropriate earlier in the twentieth century but surely are inappropriate as the twenty-first century approaches.

Perhaps workers in other professions face somewhat similar pressures, but it may well be that educators, including especially those in curriculum work, carry a heavy burden as the public vents its frustrations and voices its needs.

It is of course likely that many of the aforementioned pressures are legitimate when judged by the educational well-being of children. Clearly there is much in the present-day curriculum that is inappropriate, if not actually dangerous, for children, and clearly there are some absent topics or procedures that it is urgent to include. Even more likely is that the curriculum is abundant in topics or procedures that require modification or updating. Also likely is that a fair share of the existing curriculum is appropriate and effective, although sufficient recognition and credit may be lacking; or worse, these excellent components may be the target of critics and special interest groups whose motives or perceptions may reasonably be questioned.

Curriculum workers therefore occupy a sometimes precarious and often complex role, as they seek to deal with criticisms both warranted and unwarranted, with proposals both sensible and preposterous, with statements or allegations both informed and ignorant, and with demands both reasonable and unreasonable. They cannot expect that the mass media will be unbiased and objective in their presentation of education-focused stories, nor can they assume that equivalent attention will be given by the press and/or television to events or data that reflect favorably upon them and their achievements. Other professions doubtless have the same kind of experience with media, but the battle for the minds of young people seems especially fierce and relentless in modern America and curriculum workers engage in that battle at probable disadvantage.   .

Elsewhere in this yearbook will be found discussions of some of the major issues that provoke confrontation and require responses protective of child welfare. Kliebard has examined the problem of the recycling of curriculum ideologies; the present vogue is a "hard" education. Yesterday it was "do your own thing." Madaus addresses the serious policy issues that are involved in testing, the foci and the limitations of which may unduly influence the learning opportunities for children. Other authors refer to the almost unending list of problems the nation faces, such as drug abuse, child abuse, latchkey children, street violence, drunk drivers, one-parent and no-parent families, teenage pregnancy, abortion, high unemployment rates for the unskilled, early-age nicotine addiction, suicide incidence, juvenile crime rates, adult illiteracy and ignorance of world affairs, decline in "patriotism" and appreciation for capitalism, neighborhood deterioration, hunger and malnutrition. The public school system is often identified as the agency that has either contributed to the problem, or failed to respond to it, or both. In addition, there is a long list of problems that an allegedly inadequate school system has either created or heightened: poor discipline among the young, lack of motivation to learn and achieve, abysmal test scores, weak command of necessary skills and information, questionable values, insufficient skills for job success, narrow world view, premature dropouts, and other failures to produce well-rounded, life-long learners out of the school experience.

The cruel predicament for curriculum workers is that most of the problems, stated as failures of the system, are indeed both serious and relevant to the educational enterprise. The failures must absolutely be corrected, and the problems must absolutely be dealt with. It is clearly in the interest of children for them to succeed in acquiring the skills, knowledge, and attitudes that will equip them to function effectively in their adult roles as citizens, parents, neighbors, and workers. The building of self-confidence, responsible self-discipline, good work and study habits, and other "virtuous" behaviors can only be advantageous, especially if one's individuality and unique aspirations are not damaged in the process. It is in fact a legitimate goal in American schools for children to develop pride in country as well as a healthy and informed world view. While "values" is a very open-ended word, it is also arguable that a public school education should reinforce the values upon which the society rests, granted that their exact definition is increasingly difficult and that such reinforcement is truly easier said than done.

Well-intended but potentially harmful criticism of the curriculum derives from differences of value and orientation. For example, there are many who insist that the arts and music are "frills" and should be eliminated from the curriculum. The problems arise when mandated solutions are not perceived by professionals to be in the best interest of children.

Some comments about the critics. Legislators, governors, federal officials, leading citizens who become involved in criticism of education, and media personnel tend to be college or university graduates, many with advanced degrees, who have above-average competitive drive and a positively skewed career experience. This tends also to be true of school board members, although to a lesser extent. Such persons often believe that their success is the result of perseverance and hard work. Only a very few of them came out of disadvantaged backgrounds, and most of them have little understanding of, or sympathy for, persons at the lower end of the educational or socioeconomic spectrum. Hardly any of them had serious learning difficulties or they could not have succeeded in the law schools, journalism schools, or other environments from which they launched their careers. Their views of what can and should be done to prompt greater learning in the schools are therefore oversimplistic and naive. As a result, they tend to recommend tougher tests and other policies

that make school a more demanding experience, without much
thought for the possible negative effects on large blocs of children
who find school much more difficult than they did.

The same is true of proposals to improve the educational work
force. Journalists, whose biases are rarely sympathetic to most public
institutions anyway, find more profit and excitement in stories about
"what's wrong" with teachers than in stories about "what's right."
Politicians find it more profitable to propose quick fixes for alleged
teacher inadequacies than to offer more constructive solutions that are
almost invariably more expensive. All of these people often tend, as
well, to regard teachers and school administrators as ineffectual and
below-average, albeit well-intentioned, persons among the professionals they know. As a result, they are quick to ascribe incompetence
to school people and to endorse or accept proposals that may have
little if any beneficial effect upon the workers at whom they are
directed. Worse, some of their proposals create problems or tensions
among the workers, which can have a negative effect upon the
children with whom they work.

To the extent that the foregoing characterization of certain critics
is reasonably accurate, school people need to be somewhat more
tolerant of the viewpoints the critics express, or at least less unnerved
by being placed on the spot. This does not mean ignoring or
disregarding their messages, which could cause the critics to step up
their attacks. It does mean, however, that educators need on the one
hand to develop "thicker skins," and, on the other hand, to exhibit
patience as they seek to deal with, and wherever possible to educate,
the critics who are leaning on them.

How Are the Pressures Perceived?

Despite the fact that the problem of pressures on supervisors is not
a new problem, and is viewed by many as increasingly serious,
knowledge in this area is deficient. This became evident early in the
preparation of this chapter. It is hoped that the observations,
assertions, interpretations, and recommendations offered here will
stimulate vigorous search for such knowledge.

Information was collected over a period of months from
professional books and journals, newspapers and magazines, radio/
TV programs, and personal conversations. In addition, an ERIC
search was done, university graduate students were canvased, and
central office specialists were interviewed in groups. There was little

system in this approach, and the aggregate of material garnered is neither coherent nor representative of all dimensions of the basic problem of pressures on supervisors. However, at least a first step has been taken, and the seriousness of the problem is now all the more evident.

As was indicated, a search was ordered from the ERIC database on the topic "Politics of Curriculum Planning." Sixty-nine items were produced, out of which came the following list of topics, problems, or themes in connection with which pressures are being or have been generated:

- competency-based education
- conflict between courts and governmental agencies and local authorities regarding curriculum
- conflict between school boards and administrators over program leadership and control
- redirecting secondary programs toward career education and employment requirements
- peace education; international education; understanding the Soviets
- health and physical education programs; sex education issues; death and dying
- nuclear weaponry and disarmament as curricular themes; nuclear-age education
- environmental pollution; environmental studies
- equity in results as contrasted with equity in opportunity
- bilingual education versus English-only policies
- new information technologies and skills
- multicultural education and cultural pluralism
- secular humanism
- creationism versus evolution in the school curriculum: religion-science conflict
- controversial social issues; teacher neutrality vs. commitment
- the role of the federal government in school curriculum development
- family life education; moral and spiritual development; character education
- differential curriculum and unequal opportunity in socioeconomic classes

- influence upon curriculum of political and religious extremists
- religious content, religious practices in schools
- arts, aesthetics, and affective education as program elements
- balance, accuracy, and depth in the history/social studies curriculum
- financial cutbacks requiring deletions of programs or services
- home instruction in lieu of compulsory attendance
- legal aspects of pupil evaluation
- futures education: forecasting; decision making; options
- teachers' methods of classroom control and their control of the flow of knowledge in discussion
- policy control over instructional program: state; school board; the profession
- sexism, racism, and other forms of bias in educational opportunity.

The items on this list, which are in random order, could be both refined and expanded. The listed topics are not of equivalent importance or sensitivity. Material on all the items was published between 1980 and 1985. As an aggregate the items provide clues to the enormous variety of concerns being expressed by the citizenry, by special interest groups, and by educators as schools and their offerings come under scrutiny. Each concern presents a challenge sufficient by itself to require a significant response effort on the part of schools and teachers. Moreover, they often call for conflicting responses: obviously the public is not of one mind about what should go on in the public schools. In responding to one concern, curriculum workers are likely to be criticized by advocates of some of the others. More importantly, curriculum workers are led to view the curriculum and its improvement piecemeal. Yet as Cremin pointed out, "someone must look at the curriculum whole and raise insistent questions of priority and relationship."[3] If not the curriculum worker, who?

SUPERVISORS' VIEWS

In extensive collective interviews with central office curriculum and supervisor specialists, it was learned that pressures from outside the school system are seen as a mixture of the welcome and the unwelcome. There is sympathy, for example, for the efforts of state agencies to define minimum standards in ways that broaden opportunities for children and render them less helpless against poor curriculum leadership and inadequate programs at the local district levels. Many school districts, it was pointed out, operate at or below the margin because of insufficient resources, unenlightened leadership, or a combination thereof. Pressures of various sorts from the state, and guidelines or even mandates to be followed, can result in upgrading of offerings. On the other side of the coin, however, can be aggressive or rigid guidelines and mandates that limit local initiative and reduce flexibility to meet the special needs of students.

Among the more welcome actions at the state level is the emergence of performance measurement standards, both for the professional staff and for school children. Most supervisors and curriculum workers seem to feel that clearer and more challenging guidelines for acceptable performance will help schools to develop stronger and more effective programs. Pressures of this sort benefit learners, and are accepted in good spirit.

When asked whether or not certain pressure groups, especially those who would censor textbooks or attack programs regarded as "dangerous" (such as sex education, values clarification, humanistic pedagogy), are disruptive and ultimately damaging to children, these educators tend to indicate that the pressure groups generally fail to reach all of their goals, but small gains are sometimes made and the staff pays a high price, in time and energy lost, in the course of negotiation and confrontation. A problem is that although the pressure groups come after the school people one at a time, there are so many such groups that the school people often feel besieged by an alliance of powerful forces in a massive effort to seize control. These educators perceive that the skill and the motivation of school board members, who as a unit are the appropriate line of defense, make the difference in maintaining the school district's integrity and in protecting the staff from unreasonable demands.

Sometimes, of course, board members themselves are the originators or advocates of unreasonable or unwelcome demands. Against the advice and counsel of their administrative and legal staffs, boards have been known to decree a policy or program or procedure that cannot be defended in terms of child well-being or educational efficacy. Examples in recent history include attempts to evaluate teachers in ways that destroy morale and seem motivated by a punitive rather than a constructive posture toward the staff. One school board supported a policy of using the polygraph (lie-detector) in pupil discipline cases, causing an unprecedented uproar not only locally but across the state, and stuck to its policy well beyond a reasonable time before finally admitting its error. Another example of highly questionable policy is the conduct of strip searches in elementary schools.

Some of the central office people with whom I talked were especially concerned about recently adopted state policies to require seven-period days in the secondary schools, one effect of which is to restrict exposure to a variety of subjects and to make balanced scheduling more difficult. It was noted that reducing fifty-five minute class periods to forty minutes represents a reduction of about twelve to fourteen classes in a year's time, which for some subjects (for example, calculus) calls for compressing material and hastening the pace to a possibly unproductive level. One effect of reducing available time is that teachers resort less often to discussions, pupil work activities, and other pupil-involvement activities, and more often to straight lecturing ("chalk and talk") or other didactic approaches of the very sort that have been criticized and lamented in recent commentaries on the condition of secondary education.

The effects of establishing more rigorous standards for secondary school graduation, and correlated restrictions concerning participation in interscholastic sports or extracurricular activities, probably represent at best a mixed blessing. Complaints by employers, and to some extent parents, about the uncertain meaning of a high school diploma have intensified. That many young people finish high school with poor command of basic skills is obviously a serious and embarrassing problem and much of the blame belongs with educators who fail to meet basic needs, or, as some observers note, negotiate a kind of "truce" with students that prevents protests or disruptions in return for less rigorous classroom expectations. Often the responsibility should be shared by school boards, taxpayers, and others who, whether directly or indirectly, deny schools the resources and support needed to deal with difficult problems and challenges. Often, too, the responsibility goes beyond the school and into the families. Regardless of who is essentially responsible, the fact is that most of the "illiterate graduates" could have been helped to be more successful academically. Higher expectations coupled with resources and support doubtless will be helpful.

That the schools manage to keep large numbers of adolescents from dropping out, and that the retained students sometimes benefit in nonacademic ways from the school's efforts prior to graduation day, are facts that tend to be ignored or unappreciated by the critics who point to "meaningless" diplomas. It is at least possible that some of the students at the bottom of the class have received intelligent and conscientious attention by teachers who worked against the odds and achieved some results. In a more uncompromising atmosphere that threatens the bottom-half students in unreasonable ways, it seems likely that dropouts will increase, fewer salvage operations will be possible for the struggling, and ultimately the schools will have to abandon or neglect the borderline learners—at a cost to them and to society that is disheartening to contemplate.

A related comment was made about exceptional children and how service to them has stimulated new thinking about what is possible for borderline nonexceptional learners. Pressures from the federal government, through various title programs and especially through PL 94-142, to make stronger provisions for disadvantaged and handicapped children have had a very positive effect for the most part. It is probable that PL 94-142, in addition to the benefits it provided for special children previously underserved, has had a remarkable and positive influence upon mainstream children and their teachers. The approaches used with special children have in many cases been adopted for use with regular pupils; the interactions between special and regular children have been educative as well as socially significant; heightened awareness of the power that resides in all children has stimulated fresh thinking about what is possible; and the wisdom of providing additional and special training for teachers of special education classes, along with more varied resources and smaller classes, has not gone unnoticed.

One of the bittersweet consequences of serving all kinds of children, and not only those in college preparatory programs, is that average test scores are affected in ways that some critics consider deplorable. One interesting observation by a central office supervisor is that the best way to get higher test scores is to get rid of the lower-quarter students. It is said that some districts have even fudged on their scores by not including the test packages from classes in the lower tracks. When such ruses or dishonest tactics seem justifiable to administrators, the pressures that lead to such unprofessional behavior are surely having an unintended effect.

VIEWS FROM THE CLASSROOM

Since the role of supervisors is to work with classroom teachers, it is important to know how classroom teachers feel about the political and other pressures to which the schools are subjected, and how they respond to, or cope with, such pressures. In order to get a sample of opinions, classroom teachers enrolled in university graduate courses in four major universities were asked to respond through individual statements and in class discussions. What follows is an approximate summary of their reactions. Incidentally, in all cases the graduate students became intensely involved in the discussions, and seemed grateful for the opportunity to talk about the painful dilemma that confronts them as unwise decisions are forced upon them.

A general impression is that teacher resentment runs very high, and there is strong feeling that children are in fact damaged by the policies in question. On the whole, though, teachers have not devised coping strategies in any systematic way, and teacher frustration is not matched by a concerted effort to fight back. Creative problem solving, especially at the group or organizational level, is relatively absent. Most of the coping strategies mentioned below are only in the minds of individual teachers, and there were virtually no comments about efforts to implement them in some collective manner. For example, despite the frequent mention of teacher union activity, as a political force, no references were made to an actual activity underway.

Another element or factor that emerged from the discussions and the written responses is that many teachers perceive that they are essentially helpless as individuals, and that many school administrators are neither inclined nor able to serve as the leaders and organizers of counterattacks or appropriate public information measures when pressures are felt. In a few cases, however, pride was expressed in a principal or a superintendent who took initiative to "resist a bad directive" or "go to bat for the kids even at risk of job loss." Given the role played by local customs and circumstances, and especially given the weak and uncoordinated roles played by professional organizations, it is hard to assess administrative apathy or silence, as alleged, or the impact of the occasional aggressive response.

Among teachers' responses to the basic question "How do you cope?" there were two actions or approaches mentioned far more often than any others. One was to draw upon research data and expert opinions to provide policymakers with rationales and information to guide them in framing or revising mandates and regulations. Teachers mentioning this approach appeared confident that a sufficient research base exists, and that policymakers are likely to be persuaded by evidence within that base.

The second most-mentioned approach is to involve the teachers union or equivalent representative group. Several teachers mentioned that union protests had in the past proved successful in getting a policy reversed or modified. No mention was made, by contrast, of "good" policies (from the standpoint of pupil well-being) that resulted from a proactive initiative by a union or administrators organization. Perhaps if this possibility had been probed specifically, there might have been a few examples cited. Overall, however, *it does not seem that collective action is used very often by the teaching profession as a mechanism for dealing with pressure groups.*

Some teachers indicated that when an undesirable policy enters the picture, they turn to parent groups, citizens' advisory committees, or other organizations whose mission is to promote child well-being. The formation of study groups was mentioned as a device that has sometimes succeeded in investigating the ramifications of the offending policies and in issuing a protest or position statement to the board of education or agency mandating the policy.

A number of respondents indicated that their response to undesirable policies is to step up their efforts to serve children better, especially those most adversely affected by the policies. This "antidote" approach is perhaps professionally commendable, but in a sense it seems impractical since it puts a heavy load on the teachers without addressing the (presumed) evil that prompts the extra effort.

Not surprisingly, a number of teachers indicated that they try to ignore, as quietly and inconspicuously as possible, questionable mandates. Several justified this response, which is technically a form of insubordination, on grounds that pupil well-being transcends loyalty to a bad policy. Others suggested that policies, like policymakers, come and go, and that therefore a truly bad policy is likely to be changed over a few years' time.

Direct defiance of a policy happens very rarely, but some teachers noted that it is possible to accept and implement a bad policy in small, slow, incremental stages. Go through the motions, they advise, but only as much and as long as necessary to keep out of trouble. One person mentioned that foot-dragging can, unfortunately, also serve as a technique for delaying the implementation of policies that are *good* for children, and that therefore a distinction needs to be made between "good guy" resistance and "bad guy" resistance. Responses of this sort serve as a reminder of how difficult it is to understand the moods and the motives of teachers as they react, or seem to fail to react, to forces around them.

Pressures to Maintain or Reinforce Inappropriate Practices

It is ironic that some of the most damaging pressures that impact upon school children are those to which the education professionals themselves have been most loyal, at least in the past. Many of those pressures have come to be accepted as desirable by the public at large. When parents, legislators, and others talk about "back to the basics," often the alleged "basics" are simply practices and emphases that were, and to some extent still are, highly valued by teachers and administrators. One needs only look at Winslow Homer's famous painting of a country school, within which a stern teacher, front and center, surveys a very subdued group of children, at least one of whom is in tears, to recall how somber an environment has been perceived as typical and appropriate. Practically all general commentary (in novels, plays, monologues, comic strips, cartoons, and ordinary conversation) about school conditions portrays the vulnerability of children to punitive grades, threat of nonpromotion, a competitive learning atmosphere, powerful authority figures, and unyielding complexity in learning tasks. These conditions as an aggregate, some believe, are appropriate if necessary learning is to occur.

The maintenance and reinforcement of most of these practices, it now seems justified to argue, is deleterious to children and can prevent, rather than conduce, the learning that is intended. Examination of several counterproductive practices may be helpful in order to place pressures for their continuation in perspective.

CORPORAL PUNISHMENT

One example of pressure that can be especially harmful to children comes from adults, paradoxically including some parents and even some school administrators, who advocate corporal punishment as a means of achieving better discipline. It has been an embarrassment to the profession that some of its members, either on their own initiative or in response to community approval, resort to spanking, paddling, caning, or other physically abusive activities. Often such measures have been in place for many, many years and they are sufficiently accepted within the culture so that little thought is given to the brutality, as well as ineffectuality, of the abusive practice. Whatever historic or other justification may be used by teachers and administrators for hitting or injuring children in schools, corporal punishment is a cruel, inappropriate, and ugly approach to discipline and its total elimination should be the goal of all educators. Especially given the direct link that can be made between corporal punishment and other forms of child abuse outside the school, failure to adopt such a stance is in effect a signal to other adults that maltreatment of children is, after all, not such an evil thing.

NONPRODUCTIVE COMPETITION

One of the most challenging problems faced by teachers is to inspire enthusiasm for learning and to maintain high levels of focused learning activity in the classroom. A common belief within the culture, doubtless with theological origins, is that children are not inherently motivated to learn and that various forms of coercion must be employed in schools if sufficient effort is to be made by them. As noted above, the hickory stick or rattan, other punishments and restrictions, low marks, and the prospect of failing a course (such as French 1) or of failing an entire grade in an elementary school are among the familiar mechanisms to which teachers have often turned in their efforts to keep children from neglecting their school work. Especially valued, it would seem, is the use of a competitive marking system that rewards high achievers with As, Bs, or equivalent numbers and punishes lower achievers with Ds, Fs, or uncomplimentary numbers.

Nearly all parents, and a distressingly high percentage of teachers, consider it both legitimate and necessary to place children in competition with each other as part of a motivational framework, and there is virtually universal faith in the A as a symbol of complete success, the C as a symbol of average success, and the F as a proof of genuine failure. When seen as locations on the "normal curve" (a misleading practice if there ever was one), these letters permit adults to make comparisons of all sorts (including moral) between children and to "sort them out" on a scale of worthy to unworthy, or intelligent to stupid, or conscientious to slothful. Few seem disturbed by the effects of such comparisons upon the children as they seek to find personal and social meaning in their lives within the school, and few appear to understand how counterproductive and socially dangerous is competitive marking as an aspect of schooling.

In recent years two related strands of theory and research have illuminated this problem and deserve more discussion both inside and outside the school. One strand examines the ways that children learn best, and an overwhelming conclusion is that many if not most children benefit more from working cooperatively than from working in isolation. This conclusion applies equally to adult learning, and derives from much of the newer literature on adult education, including undergraduate and graduate level learning in universities.

Education for the professions, and even efforts to spur worker growth within the business and industrial worlds, are increasingly geared to patterns of team learning, frequent sharing, and cooperative interaction. It seems clear that the predominance of the each-on-his-own pattern of activity in public schools is out of sync with what is going on elsewhere.

A second strand, closely related, examines the element of competition as a factor in human productivity, and finds it far less defensible than nearly all Americans are inclined to perceive it to be. Zeal to do well, eagerness to fulfill one's potential, and pleasure in accomplishment are sufficient spurs to learning in and of themselves, and the notion of succeeding in learning at the expense of someone else is abhorrent rather than attractive. Collaboration is one of the most human needs or drives, and working and learning together are fulfilling activities. This is not to say that competition in all forms is undesirable, since humans everywhere enjoy pitting their skills against others in many contexts, but rather to say that the *pervasive* use of learner-versus-learner in schools is a practice to be eliminated as soon as possible.

UNSUITABLE ORGANIZATIONAL STRUCTURES

Among the worst pressures exerted upon the curriculum and upon children are those that derive from the deeply entrenched system of graded, unit-age, self-contained classrooms within which pupils of presumed equal ability compete against each other for extrinsic symbols of success. In the late 1840s, when the Quincy Grammar School in Boston became the first visible and influential model in America of graded school organization, one of the consequences was a gradual shift from an individualized, tutorial approach within a multiaged context to an arrangement featuring large-group instruction to children of essentially the same age. Corollary developments in teacher education with the growth of normal schools, and in the emerging textbook industry that produced progressively more difficult materials for use within the graded structure, helped to produce an apparently efficient system. No doubt that system facilitated the work of teachers and helped public school systems to cope with ever-increasing enrollments.

Before long, however, several deleterious effects of "lockstep" age-graded schools were being challenged by educators such as W. T. Harris, Francis W. Parker, John Dewey, and others who saw the need for more flexible arrangements responsive to individual needs and differences, especially in light of new information about human development. Eventually such challenges evolved into efforts to implement continuous pupil progress in a variety of forms, particularly although not exclusively at the primary level. These efforts were significantly abetted by the development in the mid-twentieth century of deliberately multigraded (or multiage) pupil groupings within team teaching or other collaborative staffing arrangements. Unfortunately, the age-graded, self-contained, textbook-dominated classroom has been extremely resistant to modification, and even the brief period of enchantment with "open education" associated with British primary schools failed to stimulate enduring changes away from the lockstep.

In the research literature that has been generated since approximately the early 1970s, there seems again to be a ground swell of opinion and information that supports less rigid organizational structures and the provision of more opportunities for each pupil to succeed in learning tasks appropriate to his or her history and readiness. Within that literature is a strong strand favoring cooperative learning, peer tutoring, cross-age groupings, and other arrangements designed to cause mastery of the experienced curriculum. Little if any research supports age-gradedness, and more and more studies suggest that multiage pupil aggregations offer superior prospects for both social and intellectual development. Also growing, as noted previously, is the literature advocating a dramatic reduction in competitiveness as an element in classroom dynamics, and a commensurate increase in opportunities for children to share, to help each other, to tackle problems together, and to pool their intellectual and other resources in pursuit of common goals.

Recently, scholars of pupil grouping practices have become more sensitive to the artificiality, and possibly even the maleficence, of a rigid age-graded organization in the growing up experience of children. What the British aptly called "family grouping," and what in the Little Red Schoolhouse was a natural mixed-age collection of brothers, sisters, cousins, and neighbors, is or was more representative, these scholars note, of the work and play patterns within which children lived and matured over many thousands of years. It seems likely that the educational as well as the social and psychological costs of altering mixed-age child groups in so dramatic a fashion have been heavier than society realizes.[4] Within only a generation or two, as graded schools became more common, children whose ancestors never had much interaction with their literal age-mates found themselves in the exclusive and possibly oppressive company of children born in roughly the same bloc of time. Furthermore, the context of daily interaction with these supposed "equals" was competitive, and the forming of bonds and mutual support systems was inhibited by pressures to succeed, as often as not at the expense of others.

Within such a millennial perspective on pupil grouping, the hypothesis that multiage groups are more natural and therefore more nurturing for children receives further theoretical support. In effect, the understandable nineteenth-century effort to make schooling more efficient and manageable through a graded system has backfired, and the well-being of children has been unintentionally compromised. An unrealistic faith in the graded classification system, a naive acceptance of the standard curriculum as embodied in graded textbook series, a trusting attitude toward competitive marks and fear of nonpromotion as motivational mechanisms, and (perhaps especially) a resolute loyalty to the self-contained classroom as the focus for learning have combined to deprive children of the best possible learning opportunities and in many ways to cause them harm. Were teachers sufficiently aware of the hazards in the conventional structure, and were school leaders and university professors more zealous and articulate in proposing and maintaining more appropriate alternatives, pressures to continue with that conventional structure would be more fiercely resisted, and the twenty-first century might offer a brighter future for school children.

UNSUITABLE LEGISLATIVE MANDATES

Challenging enough for curriculum workers and supervisors is the implementation of mandates that come down from governmental bodies with respect to programmatic additions, emphases, or approaches that the profession perceives to be consistent with its own values and priorities and with the legitimate needs of children. Often the mandate is recognized as a prod or instruction that might not have been necessary had the educators been sufficiently diligent in updating or revising their offerings. Sometimes the mandate is regarded as superfluous or even gratuitous, as in cases where legislators call for more, or a sufficiency, of something to which the educators have in fact been attending. In many such instances, the profession accepts mandates in reasonably good spirit and relatively little effort or emotional adjustment is required to respect and implement them.

At times, however, a bandwagon or a crusade unloads its message on the steps of the state capitol, and soon there is proclaimed the adoption or implementation of a curriculum component, an administrative practice, or an instructional approach for which professional enthusiasm is lacking, or in support of which there is an insufficient theoretical or research base. Some of these practices or approaches have been noted in the lists previously presented, for example, creationism versus evolution, excessive tightening of standards for pupil progress, and tinkering with class scheduling. More recently, there is great concern about the decision of several state legislatures, and legions of school administrators, to adopt what is called the Madeline Hunter model of instruction, and the so-called clinical supervision system recommended to insure its implementation.

Probably there is no historical precedent for the spread of the Hunter approach, nor have educators had much prior experience with so intense an advertising and sales campaign not associated with a conventional commercial organization. Probably, too, it is unique for an instructional/supervisory technology to spread so rapidly in the face of a limited and generally negative research literature and extreme skepticism on the part of the professional community of supervisors and curriculum specialists. Few advocative phenomena have generated as many articles, convention presentations, and debates, and it is almost impossible to find an advocate of the Hunter supervision model outside of the group of Hunter disciples who have assumed responsibility for training and consultation.

Critics acknowledge that the Hunter approach has some merit and can be usefully applied to the advantage of pupil learners in some situations. However, they perceive that it suffers from a highly directive orientation in which there is only one definition of "good" teaching, for the supervision of which there is no need to negotiate ground rules or other understandings in advance of a classroom visit. Especially since research support is extremely thin, these critics are concerned when state officials and others in power proclaim the Hunter approach as mandatory policy. Workers in school systems affected by such mandates need to be especially alert to research information and informed opinion about the model, and then to respond in professionally appropriate ways.

Dimensions of Defense and Response

In the foregoing discussion I have mentioned various means used to respond to pressures or to defend against unwelcome and unfair charges. At least two other aspects of the profession's ability to cope with pressures require attention: (a) protecting the time and energies of supervisors, and (b) strengthening the reaction capability of supervisors through organizational unity.

DIVERSION OF ENERGIES

In a given school district, whatever its size, there exists a distinguishable cadre of professionals whose essential function is to define, to stimulate, and to monitor the instructional program. There are also cadres of other professionals assigned to administration, to provision of special services, and to other categories of maintenance and development. In a puristic sense, the only legitimate function of all of these cadres is to insure the quality and well-being of the instructional cadre, whose members in turn have as their sole purpose the transformation of curriculum goals into student learning. From the perspective of this yearbook, it is the curriculum development/instructional supervision cadre whose influence upon teacher behaviors, and therefore upon pupil benefits or losses, is especially significant, and whose ability to exert beneficial influence is therefore seen as essential.

One of the most vexing problems of the curriculum development/instructional supervision cadre (for whom we use simpler labels such as "curriculum workers") is the discrepancy between time and resources *required* for program leadership and time that proves to be actually *available*. Theoretically, a school district could be staffed adequately (although "adequate" evades accurate definition) and, vis-a-vis curriculum leadership, the entire available time and energy of the curriculum workers could be devoted to that work without distraction, interruption, or diminishment. In the real world, however, adequate staffing is so uncommon that the profession has had virtually no experience with it and has had no opportunity to ascertain its value or its cost-effectiveness. Furthermore, in the real world curriculum workers are almost invariably called upon to assume administrative and other functions, only rarely connected to program development or even to the curriculum/supervision job descriptions, that eat into the time and energy available for their assigned and legitimate tasks.

As often as not, this role reassignment occurs because of various political pressures or related difficulties encountered by the board of education or the central administration, whose resources may be strained and whose perceived ability to cope or even to survive may be in doubt unless their numbers are augmented. Inquiries of curriculum workers, including in-depth interviews, confirm that they are frequently co-opted or conscripted by beleaguered administrators to help them at least on special, "fire fighting" assignments, and often on continuing assignments that tend to make them unofficial members of the administrative team. Of interest is that sometimes the opportunity to work on administrative problems and to consort professionally with the power structure of the school system has enough psychological attraction so that the diversion from curriculum work is not resented. Some even indicate that participating in the battle against hostile or threatening outside forces may be a better way to serve children than to fulfill the curriculum/supervisory functions more completely. Such a rationalization might have some merit, but it seems more logical to protest the disruption of leadership in curriculum activity and to suggest that top-level administrative officers should find other ways of protecting their flanks or managing their workloads.

A related and grievous problem is that the roles occupied by nonadministrative central office personnel are likely to be abolished or downgraded in times of financial crisis or other belt tightening. Most school districts, even those with a relatively strong tax base and good community relations, have experienced pressures to reduce budgets. Loath to cut back on pupil-teacher ratios or on services popular with patrons (for example, interscholastic athletics), budget makers find it convenient to reduce the cadre of curriculum workers. Since their roles have less public visibility, there is less likely to be a protest from teachers or principals than if teaching or administrative ranks are cut, and there is much less guilt at the top budgeting level because (a) the curriculum workers are often regarded as luxury items and (b) the possible short-term losses to the educational program and therefore to children are seen as minimal.

I became painfully aware of such thinking while serving for several years as chairperson for a project funded by the Association for Supervision and Curriculum Development. Known as the Effective Supervisors Project, the effort focused on seeking to learn whether tangible evidence can be collected, or pursued through research by the project committee, to show what difference it makes to have, or not to have, a cadre of centrally based supervisors and curriculum workers. An excellent committee tackled the problem, and through a series of related studies and investigations some useful information about aspects of the problem was obtained. Unfortunately, the committee concluded that the larger question as posed would be extremely difficult and expensive to pursue, and the committee was terminated. Several articles grew out of the committee's various activities, and the continuing scholarship and research of the members and of a few doctoral students supported by the project budget may eventually lead to a clearer view of the curriculum worker's contribution to school effectiveness.

Some of the statements in this chapter (for example, about cooptation and budgetary vulnerability) are supported by the committee's inquiries and interviews. Contacts with hundreds of supervisors, through correspondence and conference sessions, confirmed that curriculum workers are indeed exploited for administrative purposes, are somewhat insecurely tenured in role, and feel rather anonymous and dubiously effective. Most of those with whom the committee interacted were almost unduly appreciative of the attention being paid to them. If, as seems likely, they are representative of their fellow supervisors across the country, one lamentable conclusion is that the energy going into curriculum work in most districts is less than robust. Another is that the curriculum workers as a group are in a relatively weak position to cope with the political and other pressures that descend upon the schools and threaten their programs.

THE IMPORTANCE OF ORGANIZATIONAL UNITY

If it is true that curriculum workers are often vulnerable to role interference, and if it is also true that inappropriate pressures for curriculum changes bombard the schools, it follows that several means must be utilized to strengthen the reaction capability of the several leadership cadres. Among these must be an active and aggressive effort by local, regional, state, and international organizations concerned with curriculum and instructional supervision. The efforts of individual curriculum workers should not be minimized, for in fact there are many examples of strong and articulate curriculum directors, assistant superintendents, and equivalent functionaries who provide skillful leadership in dealing with pressure groups, explaining and defending good school practices, harnessing and implementing worthy new ideas, and rallying the school staff to stand their ground, or move to higher ground, as appropriate. The impressive contributions of such individuals, who unfortunately receive far less acclaim and appreciation than they deserve, need to be more adequately documented and publicized, as encouragement for their fellows under siege.

In the long run, however, public understanding of the relative merits of numerous "causes" will not derive from the isolated efforts of exceptional local leaders. Professional organizations, prime among them the Association for Supervision and Curriculum Development (ASCD), must take the lead through their programs and conferences, their publications, their task forces and committees, and through their officers and staff. The ASCD journal, *Educational Leadership*, its several newsletters, its yearbooks and other occasional publications, have played an important role in making solid information available, in addressing various positions on controversial issues, in clarifying questions raised by critics and others, and overall in providing a substantive basis for the difficult decisions that must be made at state and local levels.

There are other influential organizations, such as those serving school administrators and those representing scholars and practitioners in the various academic disciplines (sciences, mathematics, English, and so on). These groups, too, publish useful information and analyses, assemble members for discussion and debate, and speak out on controversial as well as more routine issues.

Whether these and other groups, including ASCD, have sufficient resources or clout to turn back the forces of ill-conceived or dangerous ideas, a good example being the pell-mell adoption of questionable testing programs or poorly designed teacher evaluation campaigns, has yet to be adequately demonstrated. A generalization supported by my experience over more than forty years as participant and observer is that the professional organizations have made substantial progress toward the goal, but a more focused and aggressive effort will be required. Meanwhile, political pressures remain powerful and promise to increase. In the absence of an authentic national spokesperson, such as federal or state officials can hardly be expected to be and such as few university-based scholars are empowered to be, the associations seem to be the best hope educators have.

If staff development and curriculum improvement, two basic and interrelated functions within school districts, are to be conducted with sufficient skill and intensity to assure the well-being of children, there must be adequate time and support for them. Neither function, however, is acknowledged in most of the recent national commission reports or in state legislation calling for educational reform. That teacher evaluation systems, new or revised program requirements, stricter instructional policies and other activities make additional demands upon administrators and supervisors, as well as teachers, is rarely recognized as a cost factor in the sweeping changes that are proposed. In the business world and in most other professions, major shifts in emphasis or activity are generally facilitated by investments in worker retraining, changed supervisory assistance, necessary resources, and organizational redirection. In education, however, no such investment is usually contemplated, and at best the time and human resources previously devoted to "regular" program maintenance are simply reshuffled as the new expectations take over. Spokespersons for teachers and supervisors must fight to turn this situation around.

FOOTNOTES

1. R. Freeman Butts and Lawrence A. Cremin, *A History of Education in American Culture* (New York: Holt, Rinehart and Winston, 1953), pp. 213-220.

2. Ibid., p. 220.

3. Lawrence A. Cremin, *The Genius of American Education* (New York: Vintage Books, 1965), p. 58.

4. I am indebted to Professor David Pratt of Queens University in Canada for this hypothesis.

Section Two
ISSUES OF POLICY

CHAPTER V

The Influence of Testing on the Curriculum

GEORGE F. MADAUS

For years, students of the senior class were required to read ["Phileopolis"] and answer questions about its meaning, etc. Teachers were not required to do so, but simply marked according to the correct answers supplied by Miss Quist, including: (1) To extend the benefits of civilization and religion to all peoples, (2) No, (3) Plato, and (4) A wilderness cannot satisfy the hunger for beauty and learning, once awakened. The test was the same from year to year, and once the seniors found the answers and passed them to the juniors, nobody read "Phileopolis" anymore.

GARRISON KEILLOR
Lake Wobegon Days

Garrison Keillor's amusing vignette from *Lake Wobegon Days* illustrates what this chapter is about. It is about the effects of testing on the curriculum, teaching, and learning. Its thesis is that testing is fast usurping the role of the curriculum as the mechanism of defining what schooling is about in this country. In recent years, it seems that the aims of education, the business of our schools, and the goals of educational reform are addressed not so much in terms of curriculum—the courses of study that are followed—as they are in terms of standardized tests. It is testing, not the "official" stated curriculum, that is increasingly determining what is taught, how it is taught, what is learned, and how it is learned.

I thank my generous colleagues, Walter Haney, Joseph Pedulla, Martin Rafferty CM, and James Bernauer SJ, for their help, ideas, and reactions. I also thank Rita Comtois and Amelia Kreitzer for their reactions, editorial assistance, and attention to detail.

83

Recently, as a means of documenting the increasing attention to testing, and the concurrent decreasing attention to curriculum concerns, Haney plotted the amount of space devoted over the last fifty years in *Education Index* to citations concerned with testing and curriculum. And while column inches in *Education Index* is admittedly a fairly crude way of charting what is happening in the world of education, his data certainly suggest that standardized testing seems more and more to be the coin of the educational realm. His results reveal that the average annual number of column inches devoted to citations concerning curriculum has increased only modestly over the last half-century: from 50 to 100 inches per year in the 1930s and 1940s, to 100 to 150 inches in recent years. In contrast, attention devoted to testing has increased ten-fold in the last fifty years, rising from only 10 to 30 column inches in the 1930s and 1940s to well over 300 inches in the 1980s.[1]

Proponents of testing argue that the power of testing to influence what is taught, how it is taught, what is learned, and how it is learned is a very beneficial attribute. This view of testing and curriculum is sometimes referred to as measurement-driven instruction. Its advocates hold that if the skills are well chosen, and if the tests truly measure them, then the goals of instruction are explicit; teacher and student efforts are focused on well-defined targets; standards are clear and uniform; accountability at all levels is easier and more objective; and the public has concrete information on how well the schools are doing.

Can measurement really drive instruction and influence the curriculum? How does a test come to exercise power over curriculum and instruction? What is the nature of that power? This chapter explores these issues. However, to anticipate, the lesson of history is clear. Tests can be, have been, and in some places are the engines that drive teaching and learning. Is this a good thing? The answer depends on one's philosophy of instruction, curriculum, education, and testing. There are profound implications in this driving metaphor about the nature of instruction, curriculum, education, teaching, and testing.

At the outset, let me make explicit my bias *against* measurement-driven instruction. It is nothing more than psychometric imperialism. Testing programs should, in my view, be seen as an ancillary tool of curriculum and instruction—albeit, a very necessary, useful, and important one—and nothing else. The long-term negative effects on curriculum, teaching, and learning of using measurement as the engine, or primary motivating power of the educational process, outweigh those positive benefits attributed to it. The tests can become the ferocious master of the educational process, not the compliant servant they should be. Measurement-driven instruction invariably leads to cramming; narrows the curriculum; concentrates attention on those skills most amenable to testing (and today this means skills amenable to the multiple-choice format); constrains the creativity and spontaneity of teachers and students; and finally demeans the professional judgment of teachers.

I shall begin by setting forth some basic definitions and distinctions regarding testing. Second, I shall describe seven principles concerned with the impact of standardized testing on education. Third, the effects of school system testing programs are outlined. Fourth, I examine the effects of state-mandated testing programs. Fifth, the recommendations of the various reform reports regarding testing and the possible consequences of implementing them are discussed. Finally, I examine the implications of the policy use of tests for curriculum development.

Types of Tests and Testing Programs

While standardized tests can be differentiated in a number of ways[2] I shall concentrate on the following four: (a) the variables measured, (b) the referent of the test score, (c) the source of testing, and (d) the influence of rewards or sanctions being associated with test results.

VARIABLES TESTED

A wide range of variables has been the subject of measurement, though the main emphasis has been on the measurement of cognitive rather than affective characteristics. The cognitive variables which have attracted most educational and commercial attention are "intelligence" and achievement in basic skill areas of the curriculum (reading, arithmetic). (This chapter focuses on the impact of standardized *achievement* tests only.)

As one proceeds up the educational ladder into secondary schools, where instruction is organized around subject matter areas rather than around specific skills, commercially available test batteries become less specific and less related to what is taught. High school test batteries closely resemble elementary school batteries in that they are more oriented to the basic skills of numeracy and literacy than to what is taught in specific subject fields like mathmematics, physics, history, and English literature. As a result such test scores are less relevant to the work of the high school teacher.[3] However, as we shall see, some of the recent reform reports call for the development of exams for each of the secondary school curricula areas. This has profound implications for curriculum and instruction at that level, an issue we shall explore later in the chapter.

SCORE REFERENT

The main distinction here is between norm-referenced tests, on which performance is assessed by reference to the performance of other students, and criterion-referenced tests, on which performance is assessed by reference to the mastery of specific content domains. It should be noted that norm-referenced information can also be structured to provide criterion-referenced interpretations and vice versa. While criterion-referenced tests are increasingly hailed as superior to norm-referenced ones in terms of information provided to teachers, norm-referenced information is valuable for comparative purposes. Further, the specificity of criterion-referenced information from commercially available tests, relative to what is actually taught at the local level, can often be dubious.

INTERNAL VS. EXTERNAL TESTING PROGRAMS

An important distinction relates to the source of, and/or control over, the testing program. Is it an *internal* or *external* testing program? An internal testing program is one which is carried out within a school at the initiative and under the control of the school superintendent, principal, or teacher. This category includes the traditional norm-referenced standardized achievement testing programs used by school systems since the 1920s, as well as the newer commercially available criterion-referenced achievement tests. Internal testing programs are not limited to the use of off-the-shelf commercial tests; in larger systems they can be built by school system personnel or customized for the system by a contractor. Internal testing programs also include traditional teacher-made tests which we will not treat in this chapter.

External testing programs are those controlled and/or mandated by an external authority, such as a state department of education, the state legislature or a private agency such as the College Entrance Examination Board (CEEB). While it can be a semivoluntary test like the SAT, more commonly it is a test which the state mandates if students, teachers, or school districts are to fulfill certain requirements. State minimum competency exams linked to graduation decisions, the English 'O' and 'A' Levels, the Irish Leaving Certificate Examinations, and the old New York State Regents Examinations are all examples of the latter. External testing programs can use norm- or criterion-referenced tests, off-the-shelf commercially available instruments, tests built by the agency, or those delegated to a contractor.

External tests have long been a part of European educational systems. Until the advent of minimum competency testing, most educational testing in the United States had been internal in origin and control. External testing programs were relatively rare, the New York Regents Examinations and the CEEB examinations being notable exceptions. However, as we shall see, external testing is being mandated increasingly by state boards or legislatures as part of their efforts at educational reform.

HIGH-STAKES VS. LOW-STAKES TESTING PROGRAMS

High-stakes tests are those whose results are seen—rightly or wrongly—by students, teachers, administrators, parents, or the general public, as being used to make important decisions that immediately and directly affect them.[4] High-stakes student tests can be norm- or criterion-referenced, internal or external in origin. Examples include tests directly linked to such important decisions as: (a) graduation, promotion, or placement of students; (b) the evaluation or rewarding of teachers or administrators; (c) the allocation of resources to schools or school districts; and (d) school or school system certification. In all of these examples, the perception of people that test results are linked to a high-stakes decision is in fact accurate. Policymakers have mandated that the results be used *automatically* to make such decisions.

However, there are other uses of test results that do not always immediately and directly affect students but nonetheless are generally perceived by people as involving high stakes. For example, SAT results are of secondary importance in admission decisions for those colleges trying to fill vacant seats in the face of adverse demographics. Nonetheless, individuals and school systems act on the perception that these college admissions tests are of crucial and singular importance. Thus, we find that high schools are increasingly offering courses to prepare students to take these tests, and commercial coaching schools are doing a land-office business.

The Kentucky Essential Skills Test (KEST) is an example of a testing program which unintentionally evolved into a high-stakes situation. The KEST is a well-designed, state-mandated testing program covering grades K-12. It has no important rewards or sanctions linked directly and automatically to test performance. However, the state's newspapers rank the districts on the basis of the yearly KEST results. A recent evaluation found that this ranking was seen by many Kentucky educators as pernicious, misleading, detrimental to morale, and fostering an unhealthy competition between districts and schools within districts. Further, and more important, many educators felt that the ranking of districts caused the test to drive the curriculum and teaching in decidedly unhealthy ways.[5] The important point is that it was the media, not any direct mandate of the state legislature, that endowed KEST with such considerable significance.

In contrast to a high-stakes test, a low-stakes test is one which is perceived as not having important rewards or sanctions tied directly to test performance. An example would be traditional school district standardized and norm-referenced testing programs where results are reported to teachers, but there is no immediate, automatic decision linked to performance. In such programs teachers are free to ignore any results which they feel are discrepant. Further, the results are not perceived by them as being used to evaluate their teaching. This does not mean that results from such programs do not affect teachers' perception of students, nor that student placement decisions are not sometimes related to test performance. The important distinction is that teachers, students, and parents do not perceive test performance as a *direct* or *automatic* vehicle of reward or sanction.

The Impact of Tests: General Principles

Perhaps the most convenient way to summarize the considerable literature on the power of testing to influence the curriculum, teaching, and learning, is to list the major conclusions in the form of rules or principles.

Principle 1. *The power of tests and examinations to affect individuals, institutions, curriculum, or instruction is a perceptual phenomenon: if students, teachers, or administrators believe that the results of an examination are important, it matters very little whether this is really true or false—the effect is produced by what individuals perceive to be the case.*

Bloom coined this first principle.[6] Its importance lies in the fact that when people perceive a phenomenon to be true, their actions are guided by the importance perceived to be associated with it. The greater the stakes perceived to be linked to test results, the greater the impact on instruction and learning.

Further, Principle 1 encapsulates the symbolic power of tests in the minds of policymakers and the general public. The numerical scores from high-stakes tests have an objective, scientific, almost magical persuasiveness about them that the general public and policymakers are quick to accept. Test results become a synecdoche for standards. Policymakers are well aware of the high symbolic value tests and test results can have in creating an image of progress or reform. By mandating a test, policymakers are seen to be addressing critical reform issues forcefully, in a way the public understands. Thus, a high-stakes testing program is all too often a symbolic solution to real educational problems. It offers the appearance of a solution, and is believed by policymakers and the public to be a true solution. As test scores rise over time, policymakers point to the wisdom of their action and the general public's confidence in the schools is restored. However, the real possibility that the testing program may not be a cure for the underlying problem, and the reality of the power of such programs to distort the educational process must eventually be faced.

Principle 2. *The more any quantitative social indicator is used for social decision making, the more likely it will be to distort and corrupt the social processes it is intended to monitor.*

This principle comes directly from Campbell's work on social indicators.[7] It also reiterates the power paradox discussed above. Its effects are not limited to testing per se; they are much more general in scope, extending to any social indicator that is used to describe, make decisions about, or influence an important social process. Principle 2 is a social version of Heisenberg's uncertainty principle: you cannot measure either an electron's position or velocity without distorting one or the other. Any measurement of the status of an educational institution, no matter how well designed and well intentioned, inevitably changes its status.

This principle reminds us that while testing is historically seen as a relatively objective and impartial means of correcting abuses in the system, the negative effects eventually outweigh the early benefits. When test results are used for important social decisions, the changes in the system brought about by such a use tend to be both substantial and corrupting. How this comes to pass is described in the five remaining principles.

Principle 3. *If important decisions are presumed to be related to test results, then teachers will teach to the test.*

This accommodation to the power of a high-stakes test can be a double-edged sword. High-stakes tests can focus instruction, giving students and teachers specific goals to attain. If the test is measuring basic skills, preparing students for the skills measured by the test could, proponents argue, serve as a powerful lever to improve basic skills.[8] Unfortunately, the only evidence to support this position is that the scores on tests of basic skills rise, not that the skill necessarily improves. People fail to distinguish between the skill or trait itself and a secondary, fallible indicator or sign of them.

If the test is specific to a more specialized curriculum area where higher-level cognitive outcomes are the goal (for example, college preparatory physics), then the examination will eventually narrow instruction and learning, focusing only on those things measured by the tests.[9] Indeed, this narrowing of the curriculum has been one of the enduring complaints leveled at external certification examinations used for the important functions of certifying the successful completion of elementary or secondary education, and admission to third-level education or to certain jobs.

A review of the effects of such exams on the curriculum over many years and in several countries indicates that, faced with a choice between objectives which are explicit in the curriculum or course outline and a different set of objectives that are implicit in the certifying examination, students and teachers generally choose to focus on the latter. In 1938, Spaulding reported that teachers in New York disregarded the objectives in local curriculum guides in favor of those tested in the Regents examinations.[10] Morris found the rigidity of the exams was the principal reason that the chemistry curriculum in Australia remained almost unchanged from 1891 to 1959. He concluded that the proportion of instructional time spent on various aspects of the syllabus was "seldom higher than the predictive likelihood of its occurrence on the examination paper."[11] Similar observations about the influence of the exams on the curriculum have been made in India,[12] Japan,[13] Ireland,[14] and in England.[15] Turner sums up the English experience: "One only has to look at the timetable of the typical comprehensive school to see that the curriculum consists almost entirely of subjects which can be taken in public examinations."[16]

George Orwell illustrated this principle well when, recalling his own school days, he observed:

Subjects which lacked examination value, such as geography, were almost completely neglected, mathematics was also neglected if you were a "classical," science was not taught in any form . . . and even the books you were encouraged to read in your spare time were chosen with one eye on the English paper.[17]

Orwell's reminiscence is by no means unique. The testimony of many writers powerfully confirms the reality of cramming for external certification exams. Fiction, biography, poetry, drama, even the lowly detective novel, contain a large corpus of information directly from authors who have been through an external examination system and have been eminently successful in later life. The theme of cramming in English and Irish literature is pervasive, reaching even to the images evoked by the language. These images include: the student driven over the hurdles in a steeple chase; a goose stuffed for slaughter; a soldier engaged in cold-blooded warfare. The examination is a grinding machine and success is a form of divine election, with Oxbridge as the heavenly Jerusalem. The exam is often the common enemy and any strategy used by teachers or students to cope with it is justified. The stakes are too high to worry about the niceties of a well-rounded education. A related theme that also emerges is the frank admission of the sheer irrelevance of what was first memorized, then regurgitated on the exam, and quickly forgotten.[18]

Why does this happen? First, there is tremendous social pressure on teachers to see that their students acquit themselves well on the certifying examinations. Second, the results of the examination are so important to students, teachers, and parents that their own self-interest dictates that instructional time focus on test preparation. Bloom once recounted to me an experience that vividly illustrates the kind of pressure teachers in India can experience. He visited the classroom of a former student. To show his professor that he was keeping abreast of new developments the teacher departed from his prepared lecture notes. Almost immediately his students drowned him out with the chant: NOE! NOE! NOE! They forcefully reminded him that the material was *Not On the Exams*, and hence irrelevant.

Writing in 1888 about tests used at that time in the midwest for grade-to-grade promotion, the superintendent of the Cincinnati public schools described the twin pressures exerted on teachers by society and their own self-interests:

In the very nature of things, the coming examination with such consequences must largely determine the character of prior teaching and study. Few teachers can resist such an influence, and in spite of it teach according to their better knowledge and judgment. They cannot feel free, if they would. They shut their eyes to the needs of the pupils and put their strength into what will "count" in examinations.[19]

It is not necessary to use nineteenth-century educators, literary figures, or anecdotes from far away India to describe the effects of Principle 3. On a more contemporary note, Gregory Anrig, the former commissioner of education in Massachusetts, after taking office as the new president of the Educational Testing Service, described the dilemma of teachers with regard to Principle 3:

I don't know of any good teacher who wants to narrow what he or she does in order to ensure success on a specific test. No test is worth teaching to. But if you place too many conditions on the testing program, if you place too much importance on it, you could end up with teaching to the test. If you connect the test scores with such decisions as pupil promotion, teacher evaluation, or the distribution of financial aid, you will accomplish the kinds of pressures that narrow the public school curriculum. I'm not supportive of that.[20]

But, as I have mentioned already, there is a positive aspect associated with Principle 3. A high-stakes test can lever new curricular material. New curricula in physics, chemistry, and mathematics made an immediate impact in Irish schools when in the early 1960s they were prescribed and examined for the Leaving Certificate Examination.[21] Primary teachers in Belgium accepted curricular reforms only when, in 1936, the external exams given at the end of primary school were modified to incorporate the ideas of the new curriculum.[22] In New York State, curriculum specialists from the State Department of Education had little success in moving the emphasis in modern language teaching from grammar and translation to conversation and reading skills, until the corresponding changes had been incorporated in the content of the Regents examination.[23] Revisions of the College Entrance Examination Board (CEEB) mathematics achievement tests to include modern mathematics played an important part in the radical revision of mathematics curricula in the 1960s.[24]

However, a paradox still remains. Despite the ability of the examination to introduce new material, the weight of examination precedent soon takes over and the way in which the new material eventually comes to be taught and learned is determined by the examination. Generally, if one looks at passing rates, the percentage drops sharply with the introduction of new exam material; then, each year for the next several, the passing curve rises until it eventually reaches and stabilizes at the original level. The question that educators must ask themselves is whether the positive aspects associated with Principle 3 outweigh the disadvantages that also flow from it. The answer is a value judgment and depends on one's view of education, the learner, teaching, curriculum development, and testing. My view is that in the long term, the narrowing of instruction and learning associated with this principle far outweighs any advantages.

Principle 4. *In every setting where a high-stakes test operates, a tradition of past exams develops, which eventually de facto defines the curriculum.*

Given Principle 3, the question remains: "How do teachers cope with the pressure of the examination?" The answer is relatively simple. Teachers see the kind of intellectual activity required by previous test questions and prepare the students to meet these demands. Some have argued strongly that if the skills are well chosen, and if the tests truly measure them, then coaching is perfectly acceptable.[25] This argument sounds reasonable, and in the short term, it may even work.[26] However, it ignores a fundamental fact of life: When the teacher's professional worth is estimated in terms of exam success, teachers will corrupt the skills measured by reducing them to the level of strategies in which the examinee is drilled. Further, the expectations and deep-seated primary agenda of students and their parents for exam success will put further pressure on teachers to corrupt the educational process. The view that we can coach for the skills apart from the tradition of test questions, embodies a staggeringly optimistic view of human nature that ignores the powerful pull of self-interest. It simply does not consider the long-term effects of the examination sanctions.

Principle 4 is beautifully illustrated in George Orwell's recollection of his history studies for the scholarship exam: "Did you know for example, that the initial letters of 'a black negress was my aunt; here's her house behind the barn' were also the initial letters of battles in the Wars of the Roses?"[27] Figure 1 offers an Irish example of the same phenomenon. A retired school inspector provided me with samples of student essays taken from the Primary Leaving Certificate examination of 1946-48.[28] Figure 1 shows how variations of the set theme are handed from one generation of examinees to the next through the memorization of stock responses that can be adapted to almost any prompt. Thus, a high score on the exam may not have indicated well-developed writing skills at all, but instead, simply the ability to use memorized material with whatever the theme for that year. The test-taking strategies mastered by students to meet the tradition of past tests vitiate the validity of the inferences about the students' ability to write.

A bicycle ride (1946)

I awakened early, jumped out of bed and had a quick breakfast. My friend, Mary Quant, was coming to our house at nine o'clock as we were going for a long bicycle ride together.

It was a lovely morning. White fleecy clouds floated in the clear blue sky and the sun was shining. As we cycled over Castlemore bridge we could hear the babble of the clear stream beneath us. Away to our right we could see the brilliant flowers in Mrs. Casey's garden. Early summer roses grew all over the pergola which stood in the middle of the garden.

A day in the bog (1947)

I awakened early and jumped out of bed. I wanted to be ready at nine o'clock when my friend, Sadie, was coming to our house. Daddy said he would take us with him to the bog if the day was good.

It was a lovely morning. The sun was shining and white fleecy clouds floated in the clear blue sky. As we were going over Castlemore bridge in the horse and cart we could hear the babble of the clear stream beneath us. Away to our right we could see the brilliant flowers in Mrs. Casey's garden. Early summer roses grew all over the pergola which stood in the middle of the green.

A bus tour (1948)

I awakened early and sprang out of bed. I wanted to be ready in good time for our bus tour from the school. My friend, Nora Greene, was going to call for me at half-past eight as the tour was starting at nine.

It was a lovely morning. The sun was shining and white fleecy clouds floated in the clear blue sky. As we drove over Castlemore bridge we could hear the babble of the clear stream beneath us. From the bus window we could see Mrs. Casey's garden. Early summer roses grew all over the pergola which stood in the middle of the garden.

Figure 1. Examples of compositions from the Irish Primary Certificate Examinations, 1946-1948.

An interesting result of Principle 4 is that if the examination is perceived as important enough, a commercial industry develops to prepare students for it. In the United States this phenomenon can be seen in the rise of commercial firms in virtually every major city, selling coaching services to students in preparation for the College Entrance Examination Boards (CEEB). Haney noted that one sign of the growing importance of commercial coaching schools in the United

States is that the phrase "test taking skills" first appeared as a separate indexing category in volume 33 of the *Education Index*, covering the period from July 1982 to July 1983. Many of the articles referenced under this new category dealt with improving admissions test scores through coaching provided either by commercial firms or computer tutorial soft-ware.[29] In Japan it is common for parents to enroll their children in special extra-study schools known as *juku*.[30] Beginning in the nineteenth century a whole industry of private coaching schools called "crammers" developed in Europe to prepare students for a fee for the tradition of important examinations. In the 1950s tutorial programs geared to the British 11+ examination were common, more so among parents of higher educational levels than among those of lower levels.[31] The important point about these coaching schools is not whether they are successful in preparing students for the exam; it is instead that the public perceives them as helpful and is willing to pay for their services.

Wilfred Sheed's description of one such crammer offers an amusing insight into the power of past examinations to affect preparation for a forthcoming exam. A student was sent to the Jenkins Tutorial Establishment in London which

offered . . . successful examination results as it might a forged passport . . . [bypassing] education altogether. Their only texts were examination papers— all the relevant ones set in the last fifty years, with odds of repetition calculated and noted as in the *Racing Form*. . . . Within six months, I was able to pass London matriculation without knowing any of the subjects involved; and by applying Jenkins' method later, to pass every exam that ever came my way afterwards. Hence I remain a profoundly uneducated man.[32]

The danger associated with Principle 4 is precisely the fact that while pupils may become proficient at passing tests by mastering the tradition of past exams, they may, as Sheed puts it, remain profoundly uneducated.

Principle 5. *Teachers pay particular attention to the form of the questions on a high-stakes test (for example, short answer, essay, multiple-choice) and adjust their instruction accordingly.*

The problem here is that the form of the test question can narrow instruction, study, and learning to the detriment of other skills. Rentz recounts a negative effect associated with Principle 5 which occurred as a result of the Georgia Regents Testing Program, a program designed to assess minimum competencies in reading and writing on the part of college students in that state. The head of an English department lamented:

Because we now are devoting our best efforts to getting the largest number of students past the essay exam . . ., we are teaching to the exam, with an entire course, English III, given over to developing one type of essay writing, the writing of a five-paragraph argumentative essay written under a time limit on a topic about which the author may or may not have knowledge, ideas, or personal opinions. Teaching this one useful writing skill has the beneficial effect of bringing large numbers of weak students to a minimal level of literacy, but at the same time, it devastates the content of the composition program that should be offering the better students challenges to produce writing of high quality. Because the Regents Test is primarily designed to establish a minimal level of literacy, our teaching to this test, which its importance forces us to do, tends to make the minimal acceptable competency the goal of our institution, a circumstance that guarantees mediocrity.[33]

Principle 5 has profound implications for the curriculum specialists. Given our free enterprise system, publishers have begun to look at state-mandated minimum competency tests, or basic skills tests, in order to design materials to better train pupils to take them. Children are apt, therefore, to find themselves spending more and more time filling out dittoed answer sheets or work books. Deborah Meier, a successful principal of a public school in Manhattan, testified at the 1981 NIE-sponsored hearings on Minimum Competency Testing (MCT) that in New York City reading instruction has come to resemble closely the practice of taking reading tests. In reading class, students, using commercial materials, read dozens of little paragraphs about which they then answer multiple-choice questions. Meier described the materials as evolving to resemble more and more the tests students take in the spring. She went on to point out that when synonyms and antonyms were dropped from the test of word meaning, teachers promptly dropped commercial material that stressed them.[34] A Connecticut superintendent recently told me that when that state adopted a cloze-type reading test his district immediately discarded materials they had used to prepare students for the more traditional multiple-choice state reading test in favor of drill material incorporating the cloze format. Someone must begin to challenge a practice whereby the method of measuring reading determines the materials and type of practice used to develop the skill. Along these same lines it is also interesting to note that in 1983 sales of ditto paper were way up nationally while sales of lined theme paper were down.[35]

Principle 6. *When test results are the sole or even partial arbiter of future educational or life choices, society tends to treat test results as the major goal of schooling rather than as a useful but fallible indicator of achievement.*

Of all of the effects attributed to tests those embodied in this principle may well be the most damaging. It is best summed up by the following observation from a nineteenth-century British school inspector who saw first-hand the negative effects of linking teacher salaries to pupil examination results:

Whenever the outward standard of reality (examination results) has established itself at the expense of the inward, the ease with which worth (or what passes for such) can be measured is ever tending to become in itself the chief, if not sole, measure of worth. And in proportion as we tend to value the results of education for their measurableness, so we tend to undervalue and at last to ignore those results which are too intrinsically valuable to be measured.[36]

Sixty years later, Ralph Tyler echoed the same message, warning readers that society conspires to treat marks in certifying examinations as the major end of secondary schooling, rather than as a useful but not infallible indicator of student achievement.[37]

We see the importance society places on test scores to the exclusion of other indicators in such things as: the media attention to declines in SAT scores; reports that our schools score lower than those of other countries on tests of mathematics and science; the Education Department's Wall Chart that ranks states by their performance on the SAT or ACT; newspapers ranking school districts and/or schools within districts by their performance on standardized tests; the use of test results by real estate agents in selling homes; and the money spent by parents on coaching schools for the SATs. The list could go on and on.

Principle 7. *A high-stakes test transfers control over the curriculum to the agency which sets or controls the exam.*

The agency responsible for a high-stakes test assumes a great deal of power or control over what is taught, how it is taught, what is learned, and how it is learned. This principle is well understood in Europe where a system of external certification examinations, controlled by the central government, or by independent examination boards, operates at the secondary level. And while this shift in power is also understood in this country by policymakers who are mandating graduation and promotion tests, the implications of the shift from the local educational authority (LEA) to the state department of education (SEA) have not received sufficient attention and discussion.

Nor have the ideological differences between the educational values and bureaucratic values inherent in such a shift received sufficient attention. Further, since the tests for most state-level programs are developed and validated for the state department by outside contractors, it is important to realize that the state may be effectively delegating this very real power over education to a commercial company whose interest is primarily financial and only secondarily educational.[38]

The Effects of Internal Testing Programs

In the United States, unlike Europe, our system of education evolved based on local rather than state control. Circumstances of the time, the size of the nation, difficulties in communication and transportation helped to build a uniquely democratic system of education in a network of local units. With the exception of the New York State Regents examinations there generally were no state syllabi or state-mandated examinations. These are much more recent phenomena.

Thus, when commercial testing, based on an individual differences model, emerged after World War I, there was a ready market for tests that could be used for local rather than state purposes. These tests were designed not to certify individuals or make interdistrict comparisons, but to predict and select; to help make intradistrict and interschool comparisons; to diagnose individual learning needs; to group children and to compare local district performance to a national norm. By 1960, most all districts, aided by the National Defense Education Act, purchased a standardized, norm-referenced test along with scoring services from one of the big five test publishers.

Recently, policymakers at the local level have discovered the accountability potential, and the power to influence teacher and student behavior inherent in attaching rewards and sanctions to standardized, multiple-choice, test performance. This section, therefore, deals first with the effects associated with traditional school system testing programs, and then with effects associated with the newer policy-related use of such tests by LEAs.

School-level effects. A consideration of the possible effects at the school level of using standardized tests suggests that one might expect effects on school organization and in a number of school practices. However, there has been relatively little systematic research on the impact on school districts, or on schools within districts, of using standardized tests in traditional ways. The assumption is often made that certain decisions and actions, such as the tracking of pupils and the allocation of slow learners to remedial classes, are taken on the basis of standardized test information. For example, Kirkland considers evidence relating to the effect of ability grouping on student achievement; however, she provides no evidence that the grouping was carried out in the first place on the basis of test information.[39] A variety of decisions relating to school organization and student placement can be and are made in the absence of test information. Evidence concerning the exact role of standardized test information in making such decisions is far from clear.

Sproull and Zubrow, after an intensive small-scale study in Pennsylvania, concluded that test results from traditional school district testing programs were not very important to central office administrators, and that administrators are not major users of test information.[40] Similarly, an experimental study of the effects of introducing traditional standardized testing in the schools of the Republic of Ireland found that school principals, when questioned about various aspects of school organization and practice, indicated that the overall impact of the standardized testing program at the administrative and institutional levels was slight.[41]

Teacher-level effects. The large-scale research that is available on teacher-level effects of traditional standardized testing is based on surveys of teachers. Surveys by Goslin[42] and by Beck and Stetz,[43] although a decade apart, present quite similar pictures of teacher perceptions about the usefulness of standardized testing for pupil-centered purposes; teachers tended to perceive such testing as useful for assessing individual and group status, for reporting to parents, and for planning instruction. However, Beck and Stetz also found that teachers were less positive about the use of tests in the context of school or teacher accountability. These latter negative attitudes about test use came at a time when the accountability movement was just beginning to gather momentum, but before the impact of state legislation linking test results to major sanctions (for example, pupil graduation or promotion, school or district accreditation, merit pay) could be felt.

In the 1980s two additional studies shed light on teacher attitudes and perceptions about standardized testing. Leslie Salmon-Cox[44] found that standardized test information was not used much by teachers, did not shape the curriculum, and did not lead to increased within-class grouping. Kellaghan, Madaus, and Airasian found that the opinions of Irish teachers remarkably resembled those of the teachers surveyed by Goslin, by Beck and Stetz, and by Salmon-Cox.[45]

How does one explain the rather consistent finding that standardized tests, while viewed favorably by teachers, were not of great relevance in their work? Salmon-Cox claims that the lack of relevance was due to the narrow range of outcomes the tests measured, that is, only certain aspects of the teachers' cognitive goals for pupils and almost none of their affective goals. Another possible explanation for the gap between teachers' attitudes toward tests and their reported use of them may be a function of the isolation experienced by teachers in their work. Perhaps tests are highly regarded because they basically confirm teachers' own judgments. In a profession in which there is relatively little professional interaction among practitioners, or between practitioners and other professionals, this confirmation may be of considerable significance for the teacher. The Irish data lend some support to this latter explanation and suggest an additional one. To the extent that test results are perceived as providing accurate information about pupils—though not as accurate as teachers' own perceptions—it is likely that the availability of test results will not be seen as having great relevance, and consequently will not exert great influence.[46]

For teachers, traditional standardized test scores can only be what Husserl has termed "occasional expressions."[47] They constitute data which cannot be interpreted by the teacher without recourse to additional information about the student—his or her home background, personal characteristics, or the circumstances under which the test was taken.[48] Further, the test data are always interpreted in light of the teacher's "hidden knowledge" of the pupil: knowledge gained from countless and constant daily evaluations made by the teacher in his or her everyday work.[49] Quite often, the test information simply confirms this "hidden knowledge."

It may well be that when the test results carry with them important consequences for the pupil, teacher, or school, as is the case with many externally imposed testing programs, then the perception of their relevance might be quite different. In a high-stakes testing program teachers cannot ignore results or treat them as occasional experiences, or interpret them in light of their hidden knowledge. The results leave no room for teacher input into the decision. Thus, teacher perceptions of test relevance might be quite different in such situations. We simply do not know.

Kellaghan, Madaus, and Airasian found that teachers in fact do make more use of test results than they are consciously aware of. Teachers' perceptions of pupils are affected by test information, perhaps to a greater extent than they realize. Furthermore, test information is somehow mediated to students and may affect their scholastic performance. This does not happen in the case of all students, or even most students, but it happens to a greater extent than one would predict from a consideration of teachers' reported uses of test information.[50] While these findings indicate that test information does play a role in influencing teachers' expectancies regarding pupils, perhaps even more significantly they underscore the influence of teachers' expectancies on pupils' scholastic performance in a more general way. Whether or not traditional standardized test information is available, teachers form expectancies for pupils which can affect how they perform scholastically.

Whether the influence of tests in altering teachers' perceptions of pupils is beneficial or not is difficult to assess. For some pupils, standardized test information can provide the teacher with a discrepant view of the pupil which leads the teacher to revise his or her expectations. Certainly, we know that teachers' ratings of pupils are more often raised than lowered when they have access to test information.[51] If higher ratings lead to higher expectations and ultimately to superior scholastic performance, then standardized test information would appear to be beneficial more often than it is not.

Student-level effects. It seems reasonable to assume that standardized test score information has its most serious impact on the student. Thus, it is not surprising to find that most research on the effects of standardized testing has been concerned with possible effects on pupils.

Bloom has argued that if the standardized test information is understood and utilized properly by students and teachers, it can do much to enhance a student's learning as well as his or her self-concept.[52] On the other hand, it is not inconceivable that learning the results from a test might adversely affect an individual's self-concept, level of aspiration, or educational plans. However, empirical evidence relating to the impact of providing students with test information in noncognitive areas is surprisingly scant. Part of the reason that research in this area is so sparse is the complexity of investigating the issue. Important distinctions have to be made between the pupil's level of education (test results often are not directly communicated to young pupils but are to secondary students); the kind or amount of information provided (norm- or criterion-referenced information, achievement or ability information); and the type of testing program involved (external test with important sanctions associated with the results or traditional school-based testing programs). The measurement of the students' self-concept is also no easy task, since it is not a unitary trait.

In considering findings on the effects of traditional standardized test information on pupils, a number of investigators have reiterated a point made by Flowers that traditional test information is of itself insufficient to overcome the effects of other variables such as differences in the communities, in the composition of school populations, in school assignments, in teacher types, and in other considerations.[53] As we discussed, the impact of traditional standardized test information on teachers is merely a part, and probably a relatively small part, of the pressure exerted on them by the educational environment. Even if expectancy processes operate in the classroom, standardized test information is only one factor in the network that creates such expectancies, and it is in such a context that any possible role it may have to play in affecting students has to be considered.[54]

INTERNAL HIGH-STAKES TESTING PROGRAMS

The research findings to date on the effects of traditional standardized test information, despite what many critics have said, indicate that the role is not a very major one. These findings cited above speak *only* to the effects of information from traditional school district testing programs. They were carried out before the advent of state-mandated testing programs aimed at reforming education, and before recent efforts by superintendents to use test information for accountability, to drive instruction, or to monitor student achievement continuously.

The most common use of high-stakes tests by LEAs is for purposes of student promotion from grade to grade, often referred to as "gates" testing, and for teacher accountability and in merit pay schemes. To date there have been few systematic evaluations of these uses of test information by LEAs. However, there is increasing anecdotal testimony that the seven principles enunciated above apply to such programs. We have already discussed the Meier testimony on the impact on instruction and curriculum material of gates testing in New York City. In 1974, when some New York City teachers perceived that the standardized tests used in grades two to nine might be used to evaluate them, someone leaked copies. An investigation determined that in a few schools the actual booklets had been used for coaching purposes. As a result the entire testing program had to be reconstructed with heavy emphasis on test security.[55]

In 1983-84 a National Board of Inquiry, formed by the National Coalition of Advocates for Students (NCAS) and chaired by Harold Howe II, assessed barriers to excellence in American education. One of their conclusions based on extensive testimony of teachers and administrators was that these newer uses of test information by LEAs were fast becoming a barrier to excellence, and were being used as exclusionary devices impacting heavily on low-income, minority, and handicapped children.[56] More recently, NCAS has found mounting evidence that some teachers are finding ingenious ways of removing low-scoring students from the test pool because of fear that they will lose their jobs if they do not keep test scores up.[57] Teachers quickly adopt strategies to deal with this type of accountability. There is historical precedent for this last finding. For example, a time-series analysis of promotion rates during the period when the Irish Primary Certificate exam was in effect showed an overall decrease. The data indicate that pupils who were not likely to pass the examination were prevented from failing by not being allowed to sit the exam. The teacher quickly realized that if a weak student was retained twice during the primary grades, then he or she would have attained the school leaving age at or before exam time and would leave school without sitting it. Thus, by weeding out weak students through retention in grade, schools achieved relatively high pass rates for pupils who sat the exam.

There is a need to evaluate systematically LEA sponsored high-stakes testing programs, to measure the positive and negative aspects of the program in order to arrive at a cost-benefit analysis of their effects. For example, will the various "gates" programs which use test results for grade-to-grade promotion improve student learning, or will they eventually increase the dropout rate? However, the difficulty with proposing such evaluations is that the policymakers who implement programs have a vested interest in them. They see their use of tests as a mechanism of power by which they can reform the system. Consequently, there is an understandable reluctance on their part to spend money to question the wisdom of their mandate.

One other growing use of test information by LEAs is in programs of continuous monitoring of student achievement (CAM).

CONTINUOUS ACHIEVEMENT MONITORING

The effectiveness of CAM programs, as well as that of measurement-driven instruction, has to date been assessed primarily by looking for improvement in pupil performance on the tests developed for the program itself, as well as on traditional commercially available standardized norm- or criterion-referenced tests. However, the impact on the administrative practices of district and school level administrators, and the impact on school organization, scheduling, or other areas of the curriculum not included in such programs, have not yet been systematically evaluated.

LeMahieu's evaluation of a CAM program in the Pittsburgh Public Schools is a rare exception and sheds some light on how these measurement-driven instructional programs work. His results indicated that the program had generally positive effects on students' achievement as measured by test scores.[58] The CAM program clearly focused the attention of students and teachers on the skills to be measured, and this largely accounted for the improvement in achievement.

However, LeMahieu also found this focusing phenomenon raises the following issues related to the seven principles: (a) the routinization of instruction by some teachers who may adopt the objectives of the monitoring program as the sole content of instruction in that domain; (b) a loss of residual learning outside of the CAM content; (c) competition for an extremely important and limited resource—instructional time—may increase as additional areas of the curriculum are added to the CAM program. In fact, Pittsburgh teachers reported that they took the time for supplemental instruction in mathematics (the area covered by CAM) away from other subjects. LeMahieu suggests that these difficulties can be overcome by careful planning and wise management but that these dangers are real and ever present.

Support for LeMahieu's first concern about the routinization of instruction comes in testimony to the NCAS Board of Inquiry regarding the Chicago Mastery Learning Reading (CMLR) program. A sequence of 273 separate reading "subskills" had to be mastered, one at a time, and then tested before the student could move on. Grade-to-grade promotion was based largely on success in the program. A teacher described how her teaching was affected:

Because CMLR is mandatory and accountability is emphasized with charts and reports about how many students have passed 80 percent of their tests, and because in many schools basal readers and other books are in short supply, or even nonexistent, CMLR becomes the central part of the reading instruction, and children never get a chance to read real books. CMLR crowds out real reading.[59]

The teacher's testimony speaks forcefully to the validity of the seven principles.

The Effects of External Testing Programs

During the last five years, efforts to reform education, particularly at the state level, have increasingly employed tests and test results in various ways. And this use of external tests in the policy sphere is a growing trend. For example, a fifty-state survey of reform measures conducted by *Education Week* found that: twenty-nine states required competency tests for students, and ten other states had such a requirement under consideration; fifteen states required an exit test for graduation, four additional states had such a measure under consideration; eight states employed a promotional "gates" test, while three others were considering such a mandate; finally, thirty-seven states had some sort of state assessment program, and six additional states had such a program under consideration.[60] This growing use of tests in the policy sphere by agencies external to the LEAs cannot help but affect what is taught, how it is taught, what is learned, and how it is learned.

The discussion of effects is organized around two principal policy uses. The first is the use of test information to *inform* policymakers about the current state of education. The second is the use of tests as *administrative devices* in the implementation of policy. In the former case, test results are used exclusively to describe the present state of education or some aspect of it, or in lobbying efforts for new programs or for reform proposals. The effects of this informational, descriptive use of test results on the educational process are indirect. This is in sharp contrast to the administrative use of test results whereby results automatically trigger a direct reward or sanction being applied to an individual or to an institution.

THE USE OF TEST RESULTS TO INFORM POLICY

The 1867 Act establishing the Department of Education recognized the need for gathering descriptive information about "the condition and progress of education in the several states and territories." Of course, at that time testing as we now know it did not exist. From the 1920s to the 1960s, standardized tests had little or nothing to do with state or federal policy. It was not until the early 1960s with the establishment of the National Assessment of Educational Progress (NAEP), that the Department began to gather test data systematically as part of its original mandate. Further, state departments of education have only recently begun to collect test data systematically to describe the status of education at the state level.

There were several reasons for this recent shift at the state level. First, the concept of equality of educational opportunity evolved from a concern about equality of inputs, resources, and access to programs into a preoccupation with achieving equality of outcomes. As a result, test scores began to be used as a primary indicator of educational outcomes. Second, advocates for minority groups began to point to the large discrepancies between the test scores of middle-class students, and their constituents began to lobby successfully for compensatory funds for programs to reduce these disparities. Third, the large expenditures in the 1950s and 1960s for curriculum development and compensatory programs led policymakers to ask for student test data as an indicator of the effectiveness of these programs. Fourth, as noted above, NAEP was designed as a basis for public discussion about, and a broader understanding of, educational progress and problems.

More recently, the numerous educational reform reports have used test results, including SAT and NAEP data for two purposes: first, to alert the country to what they conclude to be the mediocre state of American education, and second, to lobby for improvement programs to redress these weaknesses. Clearly, test data form an important basis for the current negative descriptions of the status of American education; this in turn has helped policymakers to pass reform legislation that might otherwise not have been instituted. While much of the reform legislation is clearly welcomed and needed, the question remains as to the validity of the inferences about the status of our schools made from available test data. Is the academic performance of our students as poor as it is painted in the various reports? While there are weak spots, particularly at the secondary level with higher-order skills, one could look at the same data and conclude that our schools are doing a quite creditable job and declines and weak spots may be due in large part to nonschool factors.

An illuminating example of how these indicators are actually used to inform such reports is provided by the Twentieth Century Fund Report. It opens with the following gloomy assertion: "The nation's public schools are in trouble. By almost every measure the performance of our schools falls far short of expectations."[61] However, in a commissioned background paper, published as an appendix to the Report itself, Peterson examines all of the available indicators, including test scores, and concludes that "nothing in these data permits the conclusion that educational institutions have deteriorated badly."[62] It would seem that the Task Force did not take cognizance of its own commissioned paper.

Stedman and Smith in their excellent review of these reform proposals point out that they are quintessential political documents. Testing evidence was used selectively to buttress arguments and ignore evidence that might lessen the impact of the message. They examined critically the way test score indicators were interpreted and concluded not only that it was sloppy, but also that we have little in the way of valid, longitudinal national indicators of the academic performance of students. NAEP is the single exception to the latter indictment.[63] The reform reports are excellent illustrations of the pitfalls associated with using test data in the policy arena where careful analyses, contradictory inferences, and caveats about the limitations of the data are at best not understood, or at worst not welcome.

THE USE OF EXTERNAL TESTS AS ADMINISTRATIVE MECHANISMS IN POLICY

During the 1960s state boards and legislatures began to use external tests as a mechanism of power. They began to attach rewards or sanctions to student performance on mandated tests. The test results in effect became a triggering device to make things happen automatically to individuals, schools, or districts. Tests quickly became a principal weapon in the arsenal of policymakers interested in school reform. It was felt that the fear of diploma denial because of a low score on a state test would motivate a target population of lazy or recalcitrant students. Further, the test was viewed as a strong and useful weapon in the armament of the school when they had to tell parents that their child was not ready for promotion or graduation. The weapon metaphor used by advocates to describe this use of tests is very revealing.

Impact on administrative practices and school organization. There has been little research evidence on the impact of using external test results as an administrative mechanism on school organization or administrative practices at the local level. However, certain aspects of these mandated testing programs directly affect pupil placement and therefore should, it seems, affect school organizational practices and the allocation of resources. For example, some minimum competency testing programs mandate that districts must provide students falling below the cut-score with remediation; whether this is done as part of the regular class or on a "pull-out" basis, it involves decisions about instructional organization and the allocation of resources. Other state-level programs require that once a predetermined number of pupils fall below the cut-score the district, or a school within the district, must submit an improvement plan to the state education agency. The development of such a plan requires a series of actions on the part of school administrators. In short, linking important rewards or sanctions to performance on an externally mandated test *should* begin to affect what district and school administrators do regarding resource allocation and their organizational and curricular decisions.

In conjunction with its testing program some states have allocated money for programs to remediate anticipated failures. However, to date, the nature and effectiveness of these efforts have not been adequately evaluated. There is some evidence that remediation becomes equated with test preparation. For example, in Florida a State Task Force on Educational Assessment studying that state's Functional Literacy Test reported that "in all cases observed, spot remediation was being practiced. That is, students were being coached on the specific skills represented by questions they missed on the 1977 test."[64] In testimony to the Florida State Board of Education, a history teacher reported that students were absent from history class for two periods and on return were declared remediated. He concluded that "what really counts here is successful passing of the functional literacy test."[65] New Jersey teachers testifying at the NIE-sponsored 1981 Clarification Hearings on Minimum Competency Testing, reported a similar phenomenon. More recently, the NCAS Board of Inquiry found that, despite the fact that the tests were justified on the basis of ensuring remedial help, there was "no guarantee that such help will be forthcoming; nor do schools take precautions to protect students who do not meet test standards from being stigmatized as 'failures'."[66] The power of the exam and the type of questions posed seem in many instances to dictate the type of remediation offered students.

Impact on teachers. There has been an absence of systematic data concerning the impact of external state testing programs on teachers. What data there are indicate that the tests are narrowing instruction as the first seven principles become operative. For example, the NCAS Board of Inquiry reported that many teachers and parents saw tests as the real curriculum, affecting the daily practice of teaching. They reported that the tests narrowed the curriculum and fostered teaching to the test.[67] In Florida, the State Task Force concluded that "time for remediation [on the basic skills measured by the test] is obtained by having students drop one or more of their regular subjects to spend less time in them." Further it was found that accompanying remediation was a tendency "to reduce investment in elective areas, such as art and music, but key academic programs were affected as well."[68] In New Jersey, the Department of Education admitted that teachers teach to that state's basic skills test, and even provided districts with copies of previous tests that some teachers used for extensive drill work weeks or even months before the exam.[69]

Impact on students. While there are no hard data available, there was considerable anecdotal evidence presented at NIE-sponsored hearings on minimum competency testing that many students who failed a graduation test the first time dropped out of school and never took the test again. These students came to be referred to as "ghosts." Whether or not their decision to drop out is directly or indirectly related to failing the graduation test is unknown. However, as we noted above, NCAS found that high-stakes tests, whatever their origin, were being used as exclusionary devices, and were impacting most adversely on the poor, minority, and handicapped students. There is a great need to study seriously the extent to which state-level high-stakes tests may be influencing the dropout situation. Again there are serious political problems in attempting such a study because of the vested interests of some policymakers in the success of the program.

Richman, Brown, and Clark have examined how personality dimensions of high school students change after the students learned of their success or failure on a state minimum competency test (MCT) linked to the receipt of their high school diploma. Students who were at high risk to fail the MCT, and subsequently did fail, showed

marked increases in neuroticism and apprehension with a corresponding decrease in general self-esteem, responsibility, assertiveness,
warmheartedness, and leadership potential. This is the only study we
know of that examined the direct effects on noncognitive traits of
providing external test information to students.[70]

Popham, Cruse, Rankin, Sandifer, and Williams report that
student test scores have risen dramatically in Texas, Detroit, South
Carolina, and Maryland.[71] In all of these locations, measurement was
perceived as a catalyst to improve instruction. In addition, a number of
people have pointed to a sharp decrease in the numbers of students
failing minimum competency graduation tests as evidence of the
program's success.[72] This phenomenon of pointing to increases in
passing rates is not unusual. For example, in 1881 Sir Patrick Keenan
justified a system of paying teachers on the basis of student
examination results in Ireland by reporting that over the ten-year
period the percentage passing in reading had increased from 70.5
percent to 91.4 percent; in writing from 55.7 percent to 93.8 percent;
and in arithmetic from 54.4 percent to 74.8 percent.[73] However,
alternative explanations for these gains have never been sufficiently
explored. They may be due solely to teaching to the test, which was
certainly the case in the payment by results example. They may not
generalize to other measures of the same construct and in fact may
change the original construct the test was designed to measure.[74] A
recent Congressional Budget Office (CBO) study sheds some light on
such claims. It concluded that the end of the achievement score decline
began about 1968-69, before the advent of external state testing
programs. Further, the data suggest that declines in basic skills might
generally have been less severe than those associated with higher-
order skills.[75]

In short, once again there is a need for carefully designed studies of
the impact of high-stakes state-level achievement tests on schools,
teachers, and students. We would predict that effects associated with
the seven principles would eventually begin to assert themselves.

Testing and the Reform Reports

Several of the recent national educational reform reports have
called for a system of national, but not federal, examinations at major
transition points administered by an agency external to the local
school district. Some have dubbed these exams maximum competency
tests to distinguish them from present minimum competency

certification tests. Consider, for example, this recommendation in *A Nation at Risk*:

Standardized tests of achievement (not to be confused with aptitude tests) should be administered at major transition points from one level of schooling to another and particularly from high school to college or work. The purposes of these tests would be to: (a) certify the student's credentials; (b) identify the need for remedial intervention; and (c) identify the opportunity for advanced or accelerated work. The tests should be administered as part of a nationwide (but not Federal) system of State and local standardized tests.[76]

This proposition, and a similar one in the Carnegie Commission Report,[77] are in essence very similar to the English examination system leading to the General Certificate of Education (GCE), Ordinary (O) level and Advanced (A) level. English students, depending on their career plans, take a number of individual exams in various content areas such as physics, chemistry, mathematics, English Literature, and French. These exams are quite different from basic skills competency tests used in some of our states for certification, which are skill oriented, not subject matter or program specific. There are five troubling issues associated with proposals to transplant an analogous system here. To date these issues have not received sufficient attention.

First, there is the tension that runs through these reports between the perceived desirability of maintaining a decentralized system of education controlled by individual communities on the one hand, and the call for a national external examination program used for certification on the other. The administrative mechanism used to insure that standards are met (an external test) in effect greatly diminishes cherished local control over what is taught as well as over how it is taught and learned. European secondary schools, while more independent than their American counterparts in some ways, have no control over the curriculum. When you buy into an external certification test, you accept ipso facto the straightjacket of constraints on your syllabus and instruction. This particular dilemma did not receive attention in any reports.

Second, assuming that we are willing to diminish further local control by mandating a new type of national external testing program, we have no independent boards that could exercise such a role. In England, on the other hand, there are eight respected examinations boards ranging from the prestigious Oxford and Cambridge School Examinations Board and the University of London Board to lesser known regional boards such as the Welsh Joint Education Committee, all under the coordinating aegis of the National Council for Examinations. Our present solution at the state level would probably be to issue a request for proposals and contract to construct and score the tests. But this is a state-by-state solution; it would not result in the nationwide examination system called for in some of the reports. The Carnegie study of American high schools recommended that the College Entrance Examination Board (CEEB) build what they labeled a new Student Achievement and Advisement Test.[78] It seems unlikely that the fifty states would agree on common syllabi, or approve of the transfer of such enormous power over the curriculum to any outside body.

However, even if it were possible to set up acceptable, independent boards and turn over to them the management of a national certification examination system, they would most likely be conservative, narrow, and rigidly stereotyped. H. G. Wells remarked of such boards, "They must never do the unexpected because that might be unfair."[79] In Tom Sharpe's *Vintage Stuff*, the fictional headmaster, Dr. Hardbolt, humorously explains this inherent conservatism of examination boards thus:

Now where most teachers go wrong is in failing to apply the methods used in animal training to their pupils. If a seal can be taught to balance a ball on his nose, a boy can be taught to pass exams. "But the questions are surely different every year," said Mr. Clyde-Browne. Dr. Hardbolt shook his head. "They can't be. If they were, no one could possibly teach the answers. Those are the rules of the game."[80]

This conservatism was also true of our own homegrown version of external certification exams—the New York State Regents. In 1938, Spaulding reported that exam questions were rejected on the ground that:

"They will not be expecting that," or "They have never had a question like that." The result is that the examinations, instead of leading the way toward better teaching, have often tended merely to perpetuate the kind of teaching to which a majority of teachers had become accustomed.[81]

Spaulding's observation about perpetuating a certain cozy, predictable, conservative style of teaching brings us to the third issue about which we need much more discussion, that is, the long-term negative effects of teaching for the examination flowing out of the seven principles. Inevitably, both the behavior and content of exams become institutionalized. There is a passage from Lewis Carroll which describes beautifully the corrupting process of an established examination tradition.

[The] pupils' got it all by heart; and, when Examination time came, they wrote it down; and the Examiner said Beautiful! (What depth!). They became teachers in their turn, and they said all these things over again; and their pupils wrote it down; and the Examiner accepted it; and nobody had the ghost of an idea what it all meant.[82]

The fourth issue related to proposals for the establishment of maximum competency testing is the tendency for such a system to become elitist. There is bound to be university bias to such GCE-type exams which equate scholastic and academic skills with merit. What about the needs of the nonacademic student? Perhaps we will end up with a double system of external exams like England. There, in addition to the GCE, there is also a Certificate of Secondary Education (CSE) which is based on curricula that are more general and practical. What are the implications of a dichotomized diploma which depends on the type of exams taken? Will such a system slam the doors to higher education for those taking the less prestigious nonacademic exams? It happens in Europe.

The danger in imposing a similar external exam system here is that it may, in fact, close doors to the poor and to minorities. We have been quite successful in this country in steadily raising the final attainment level of students. A very high proportion of our students get their high school diploma. Green warns us that if we now replace indices of attainment, that is, the last level or grade reached, with those of achievement, that is, test scores, we can expect that this will work in opposition to further marginal gains in attainment.[83]

If achievement levels are tightened or raised through external certification exams, and these exams expel failures from the system, then we need to consider this cost in personal and national terms. The Board of Inquiry of NCAS found that tests were already becoming an exclusionary device, affecting the poor, minorities, and the handicapped. Further, as mentioned above, no one has examined whether minimum competency tests—never mind maximum competency tests—have affected the dropout rate. Green also reminds us that having the high school diploma is no big deal today, but not having it is a disaster. We need considerably more discussion and thought concerning the potential of a system of certification tests to create such a disaster for certain vulnerable populations.

Finally, in all the reports there is a tension between the recommendations to upgrade the professional status of teachers and those related to certification testing. Certification testing essentially takes promotion or graduation decisions out of teachers' hands. It seems that the public and policymakers have come to mistrust teachers' judgments and want to replace them with external examinations. They point to the number of students they see passed on from one grade to the next solely on the basis of seat time, as evidence that teachers can not or will not make the tough calls. The simple solution seems to be to hand over critical decisions to a surrogate teacher—a multiple-choice test.

Teachers could use external test results to inform their decisions, but they are diminished as professionals if they, in the final analysis, do not make such decisions. While European secondary teachers may be content to delegate this function to an anonymous external agency, American teachers have traditionally accepted the role of final arbiter as part of their professional responsibilities. As a North Carolina teacher testifying at the NIE Clarification Hearing put it:

Allowing an [external minimum competency test] to make the decision for us, I think, is a copout. Instead as educators we need to accept full responsibility for these difficult decisions. We must look at teacher observations, a child's academic, physical, social, and emotional growth, a child's performance on classroom tests and criterion-referenced tests to fairly evaluate any child.[84]

Those interested in curriculum development, instruction, teaching, and testing need to think through the implications inherent in these proposals for a new type of certification test. Do we want a national curriculum in secondary school subjects that would follow from a national test? There is need for considerably more public debate around these issues than has taken place to date. Ultimately, the decision will be based on the prevailing philosophy of education of those in power and how they view the external tests as a mechanism of power. Historically, the dangers of embarking on this road are clear.

Implications for Curriculum Development and Instruction

Can curriculum recapture its rightful role in defining the goals for our schools? What counterstrategies are available to minimize the potentially corrupting influences of high-stakes tests on the curriculum, teaching, and learning? Given the present political mood of the country—educational reform is currently good politics—there are no easy answers. Policymakers will not readily abandon the use of high-stakes tests to drive instruction and learning.

Consequently, people from various educational disciplines must begin to frame and justify attractive counterstrategies to the use of high-stakes tests. Further, any counterstrategies must include the use of test information. That is, if a counterstrategy is to be taken seriously, it must acknowledge the fact that standardized testing has a legitimate role to play in curriculum and instruction. The late French philosopher-historian Michel Foucault, during a visit to America, made the following observation: "Its cost, importance, the care that one takes in administering it, the justification that one tries to give for it seem to indicate that it possesses positive functions."[85] He was describing Attica prison, not examinations, but the statement easily encompasses the place of examinations in education. The point is that an institution or mechanism of discipline and control cannot be reduced to its negative functions. And, while I have chosen to concentrate on what I regard as the long-term negative consequences of using high-stakes tests as a mechanism of power to drive instruction and learning, formal testing programs can provide valuable descriptive information about achievement.

To begin with, I feel that those concerned with curriculum and instruction need to lobby for a lowering of the stakes associated with test performance per se. Currently test results in most high-stakes situations *automatically* trigger an action without regard for other, possibly contradictory information that might contraindicate the mandated course of action. It is this automatic disposition that gives those who control the test their power over the actions of others. Those concerned with curriculum, teaching, and learning must make the case that test information be *one* piece of information used alongside other indicators, when a person(s), rather than a test score, authorizes a critical decision about pupils, teachers, programs, schools, or school systems.

There is also a need to make the case against the overreliance on the administratively convenient multiple-choice format as the principal indicator of educational outcomes. Frederiksen correctly points out that the economies associated with the multiple-choice format have "nearly driven out other testing procedures that might be used in school evaluation."[86] Further he reminds us of the fact known at least since the Tyler-Wood controversy of the early 1930s, multiple-choice tests tend not to measure more complex abilities.

One counterstrategy offering an alternative that might lessen some of the negative effects associated with present high-stakes testing can be found in the *Paideia Proposal*. Paideia recognizes the need for testing, but of a kind essentially different from that recommended in other reform reports. First, testing is squarely in the hands of the LEAs; in fact, tests would be designed and administered by teachers. Second, Paideia calls for examinations which do not merely involve the regurgitation of textbook or course material, the ever present danger associated with the external exams proposed in other reports. Paideia envisions examinations in the fuller sense of the term: direct, supply-type indicators of student outcomes quite different from the usual multiple-choice, selection format.[87]

Sizer suggests that a good way to operationalize a Paideia curriculum is to have teachers work out examinations—in the fuller sense of the term—which would be used at "key checkpoints." Such an exercise focuses curricular and instructional issues for teachers, and sharpens their priorities.[88] His discussion and the testing philosophy it embodies closely resemble Ralph Tyler's work in the Eight Year Study and later, when he was University Examiner at the University of Chicago.[89] Essentially, in both instances Tyler worked with classroom teachers to help them crystallize their course objectives; teachers had to make explicit the evidence they would accept that their objectives had been realized. The examination flowed out of this interaction. Direct measures were always used until such time as there was evidence that indirect techniques yielded essentially the same results; direct measures were the criterion for the validation of any indirect measure of an objective.

A problem with implementing a Paideia-type testing program is that it lacks the administrative simplicity and low cost of the other reform proposals. To work, it also needs measurement people skilled in the Tyler approach to cooperate closely with teachers—a resource in short supply in many LEAs, particularly in small to medium size and poorer districts. Alternatively we would need teachers much better trained in Tyler's approach to student evaluation than is presently the case. Further, the experience of the University Examiners Office shows that this approach is expensive. There, the exam became available in the bookstore after each administration, which was both costly and sometimes demoralizing for the

Examiner's staff, which had to begin to build a new exam from scratch. Nonetheless, Paideia advocates could read Tyler with profit, for what they are advocating is certainly nothing new.

Despite problems, Paideia offers a possible way to restore the balance between curriculum, teaching, learning, and testing. But, Paideia is not the only nor necessarily the best solution to restoring the balance between testing, curriculum, and instruction. What is needed at this juncture in American education is more discussion of creative counterstrategies that have curriculum and instruction driving testing rather than testing driving curriculum and instruction— counterstrategies in which testing is the servant not the master of curriculum, instruction, and learning.

FOOTNOTES

1. Walter Haney, "College Admissions Testing and High School Curriculum: Uncertain Connection and Future Directions," in *Measures in the College Admissions Process*, ed. Renee Gernand (New York: College Board, in press).

2. For a full discussion of the ways in which tests can be differentiated, see Thomas Kelleghan, George F. Madaus, and Peter W. Airasian, *The Effects of Standardized Testing* (Boston: Kluwer-Nijhoff Publishing, 1982).

3. For a full discussion of the sensitivity of commercially available tests to detect the effectiveness of instruction, see George F. Madaus, Peter W. Airasian, and Thomas Kelleghan, *School Effectiveness: A Reassessment of the Evidence* (New York: McGraw-Hill, 1980).

4. I first heard the term "high-stakes test" used by W. James Popham at a conference sponsored by the Connecticut Department of Education. I was struck by its appropriateness and adopted the term.

5. Center for the Study of Testing, Evaluation, and Educational Policy, "An Evaluation of the Kentucky Essential Skills Tests in Mathematics and Reading," (Chestnut Hill, MA: Boston College, 1986). Paper submitted to the Kentucky Department of Education.

6. Benjamin S. Bloom, "Some Theoretical Issues Relating to Educational Evaluation," in *Educational Evaluation: New Roles, New Means*, ed. Ralph W. Tyler, Sixty-eighth Yearbook of the National Society for the Study of Education, Part 2 (Chicago: University of Chicago Press, 1969).

7. Donald T. Campbell, "Assessing the Impact of Planned Social Change," in *Social Research and Public Policies: The Dartmouth/OECD Conference* (Hanover, NH: Public Affairs Center, Dartmouth College, 1975).

8. W. James Popham, "The Case for Minimum Competency Testing," *Phi Delta Kappan* 63 (October 1981): 89-92; W. James Popham, Keith L. Cruse, Stuart C. Rankin, Paul D. Sandifer, and Paul L. Williams, "Measurement-Driven Instruction: It's on the Road," *Phi Delta Kappan* 66 (May 1985): 628-635.

9. George F. Madaus, "Public Policy and the Testing Profession—You've Never Had It So Good?" *Educational Measurement* 4 (Winter 1985): 5-11.

10. Francis T. Spaulding, *High School and Life: The Regents' Inquiry into the Character and Cost of Public Education in the State of New York* (New York: McGraw-Hill, 1938).

118   THE   INFLUENCE   OF   TESTING

11. G.C. Morris, "Educational Objectives of Higher Secondary School Science" (Doct. diss., University of Sydney, Australia, circa 1969).

12. S.N. Mukerji, *History of Education in India: Modern Period* (Baroda: Acharya Book Depot, 1966); J.T. Srinivasan, "Annual Terminal Examinations in the Jesuit High Schools of Madras, India" (Doct. diss., Boston College, 1971) and A.K. Gayen et al., *Measurement of Achievement in Mathematics: A Statistical Study of Effectiveness of Board and University Examinations in India*, Report I (New Delhi: Ministry of Education, 1961).

13. William K. Cummings, *Education and Equality in Japan* (Princeton, NJ: Princeton University Press, 1980).

14. George F. Madaus and John Macnamara, *Public Examinations: A Study of the Irish Leaving Certificate* (Dublin: Educational Research Centre, St. Patrick's College, 1970).

15. Patricia Broadfoot, ed., *Selection, Certification, and Control: Social Issues in Educational Assessment* (New York: Falmer Press, 1984). See also: J.D. Koerner, *Reform in Education: England and the United States* (New York: Delacorte Press, 1968); E.G.A. Holmes, *What Is and What Might Be: A Study of Education in General and Elementary in Particular* (London: Constable Press, 1911); Robert Bell and Nigel Grant, *A Mythology of British Education* (Frogmore, St. Albans, Herts, England: Panther Books, 1974); Peter Gordon and Dennis Lawton, *Curriculum Change in the 19th and 20th Centuries* (New York: Holmes and Meier, 1978); Norman Morris, "An Historian's View of Examinations," in *Examination and English Education*, ed. S. Wiseman (Manchester: Manchester University Press, 1961).

16. Glenn Turner, "Assessment in the Comprehensive School: What Criteria Count?" in *Selection, Certification, and Control*, ed. Broadfoot, p. 69.

17. George Orwell, "Such, Such Were the Joys," in *The Collected Essays, Journalism, and Letters of George Orwell, In Front of Your Nose, 1945-1950*, ed. S. Orwell and I. Angus (New York: Harcourt Brace Jovanovich, 1968), p. 336.

18. Martin Rafferty, "Examinations in Literature: Perceptions from Nontechnical Writers of England and Ireland from 1850 to 1984" (Doct. diss., Boston College, 1985).

19. Emerson E. White, "Examinations and Promotions," *Education* 8 (1888): 518.

20. Robert J. Braun, "Education Firm Chief Warns of Stress on Skills Tests," *Newark Star Ledger*, 11 October 1981, p. 80.

21. Madaus and Macnamara, *Public Examinations*.

22. F. Hotyat, "Evaluation in Education," in UNESCO, *Report on an International Meeting of Experts Held at the UNESCO Institute for Education* (Hamburg: UNESCO, 1958).

23. Ralph W. Tyler, "The Impact of External Testing Programs," in *The Impact and Improvement of School Testing Programs*, ed. Warren G. Findley, Sixty-second Yearbook of the National Society for the Study of Education, Part 2 (Chicago: University of Chicago Press, 1963), pp. 193-210.

24. Commission on Mathematics, *Program for College Preparatory Mathematics, U.S.A.* (New York: College Entrance Examination Board, 1959).

25. Popham, "The Case for Minimum Competency Testing"; Popham et al., "Measurement-Driven Instruction"; Jason Millman, "Protesting the Detesting of PRO Testing," *NCME Measurement in Education* 12 (Fall 1981): 1-6.

26. The following exchange between the Bishop of London and Matthew Arnold during the latter's testimony to the Royal Commission on Education against payment by results captures the view that if the skills are well chosen and measured correctly then measurement-driven instruction is proper and beneficial. Keep in mind that the

discussion assumes a supply-type rather than selection-type answer on the part of the student.

Bishop of London (BL): "Do you think there is any difference between doing a sum in an examination and doing it on the counter of a shop?"

Matthew Arnold (MA): "I think there is a difference between preparing them to do rightly the sort of sums that are set in an examination and preparing them to use their heads on matters of calculation."

BL: "Certainly, there is a very great difference. But that merely means that the sums are wrongly set, as it were, that the sums set at the examinations are not of the right character?"

MA: "Yes, I think so; that is what I mean."
Royal Commision on Education, *Minutes of Evidence*, Fifteenth Day, 7 April 1886, pp. 208-209.

27. Orwell, "Such, Such Were the Joys," p. 337.

28. For a full description of the Irish Primary Certificate, see George F. Madaus and Vincent Greaney, "The Irish Experience in Competency Testing: Implications for American Education," *American Journal of Education* 93 (February 1985): 268-294.

29. Haney, "College Admissions Testing."

30. Cummings, *Education and Equality in Japan.*

31. P.E. Vernon, ed., *Secondary School Selection: A British Psychological Society Inquiry* (London: Methuen, 1957).

32. Wilfred Sheed, *Transatlantic Blues* (New York: E.P. Dutton, 1982), p. 117.

33. L.B. Corse, as quoted in Robert Rentz, "Testing and the College Degree," in *Measurement and Educational Policy*, ed. William B. Schrader (San Francisco: Jossey-Bass, 1979), p. 76.

34. National Institute of Education, *Transcripts of the Minimum Competency Testing Clarification Hearings*, Washington, DC, July 8, 9, 10, 1981 (prepared by Alderson Reporting Co., Washington, DC, 1981).

35. David Grady, "The New #2 Pencil," *Computer Update* 6 (May/June 1983): pp. 65-67.

36. Holmes, *What Is and What Might Be*, p. 128.

37. Tyler, "The Impact of External Testing Programs."

38. Madaus, "Public Policy and the Testing Profession."

39. Marjorie C. Kirkland, "The Effects of Tests on Students and Schools," *Review of Educational Research* 41 (October 1971): 303-350.

40. Lee Sproull and David Zubrow, "Standardized Testing from the Administrative Perspective," *Phi Delta Kappan* 62 (May 1981): 628-630.

41. Kelleghan, Madaus, and Airasian, *The Effects of Standardized Testing.*

42. D.A. Goslin, *Teachers and Testing* (New York: Russell Sage Foundation, 1967).

43. M.D. Beck and Frank P. Stetz, "Teachers' Opinions of Standardized Test Use and Usefulness" (Paper presented at the Annual Meeting of the American Educational Research Association, San Francisco, April 1979).

44. Leslie Salmon-Cox, "Teachers and Standardized Achievement Tests: What's Really Happening?" *Phi Delta Kappan* 62 (May 1981): 631-633.

45. Kelleghan, Madaus, and Airasian, *The Effects of Standardized Testing.*

46. Ibid.

47. E. Husserl, *Formal and Transcendental Logic*, trans. Dorian Cairns (The Hague: Martinus Nijhoff, 1969).

48. K.C.W. Leiter, "Teachers' Use of Background Knowledge to Interpret Test Scores," *Sociology of Education* 49 (1976): 59-65.

49. Philip W. Jackson, *Life in Classrooms* (New York: Holt, Rinehart and Winston, 1968).

50. Kelleghan, Madaus, and Airasian, *The Effects of Standardized Testing.*

51. Ibid.

52. Bloom, "Some Theoretical Issues."

53. C.E. Flowers, "Effects of an Arbitrary Accelerated Group Placement on the Tested Academic Achievement of Educationally Disadvantaged Students" (Doct. diss., Teachers College, Columbia University. 1966).

54. Kelleghan, Madaus, and Airasian, *The Effects of Standardized Testing.*

55. Anthony J. Polemini, "Security in a Citywide Testing Program," *NCME Measurement in Education* 6 (Summer 1975): 1-5.

56. National Coalition of Advocates for Students, *Barriers to Excellence* (Boston: National Coalition of Advocates for Students, 1985).

57. Joan McCarty First and Jose Cardenas, "A Minority View on Testing," *Educational Measurement: Issues and Practice* 5 (Spring 1986): 6-11.

58. P.G. LeMahieu, "The Effects on Achievement and Instructional Content of a Program of Student Monitoring through Frequent Testing," *Educational Evalutation and Policy Analysis* 6 (Summer 1984): 175-187.

59. National Coalition of Advocates for Students, *Barriers to Excellence*, pp. 48-49.

60. *Education Week*, 6 February 1985.

61. Task Force on Federal Elementary and Secondary Education Policy, *Making the Grade* (New York: Twentieth Century Fund, 1983).

62. Ibid., p. 59.

63. L.C. Stedman and M.S. Smith, "Recent Reform Proposals for American Education," *Contemporary Education Review* 2 (1983): 85-104.

64. Task Force on Educational Assessment Programs, "Competency Testing in Florida: Report to the Florida Cabinet," Part I (Tallahassee, FL: Florida State Department of Education, 1979), p. 10.

65. State of Florida, "Recorded Minutes of the Cabinet Meeting, August 15, 1987" (Tallahassee, FL: Florida State Department of Education, 1979), p. 67.

66. National Coalition of Advocates for Students, *Barriers to Excellence.*

67. Ibid.

68. Task Force on Educational Assessment Programs, "Competency Testing in Florida," p. 11.

69. Robert Braun, " 'Politicizing' Skills Test Scores Carries Great Risk for Students," *Newark Star Ledger*, 12 October 1981, p. 15.

70. C.L. Richman, K.P. Brown, and M. Clark, *Personality Changes as a Function of Minimum Competency Test Success/Failure*, NIMH Grant PHS 1R01 Mh 36491, n.d. Request for reprints may be made through C.L. Richman, Wake Forest University.

71. Popham et al., "Measurement-Driven Instruction."

72. Ralph D. Turlington, "Good News from Florida: Our Minimum Competency Program Is Working," *Phi Delta Kappan* 60 (May 1979): 649-651.

73. P.J. Keenan, *Address on Education to National Association for the Promotion of Social Science* (Dublin: Queen's Printing Office, 1881).

74. Robert Linn, George F. Madaus, and Joseph J. Pedulla, "Minimum Competency Testing: Cautions on the State of the Art," *American Journal of Education* 91 (November 1982): 1-35.

75. Congressional Budget Office of the Congress of the United States, *Trends in Educational Achievement*, April 1986, pp. 59-115.

76. National Commission on Excellence in Education, *A Nation at Risk: The Imperative for Educational Reform* (Washington, DC: U.S. Government Printing Office, 1983), p. 28.

77. E.L. Boyer, *High School: A Report on Secondary Education in America* (New York: Harper and Row, 1983).

78. Ibid.

79. H.G. Wells, *An Experiment in Biography* (New York: Macmillan, 1934), p. 280.

80. Thomas Sharpe, *Vintage Stuff* (London: Penguin Press, 1982), p. 47.

81. Spaulding, *High School and Life*, p. 198.

82. Lewis Carroll, *The Penguin Complete Lewis Carroll* (London: Penguin Press, 1939), p. 563.

83. Thomas F. Green, *Predicting the Behavior of the Educational System* (Syracuse, NY: Syracuse University Press, 1980).

84. National Institute of Education, *Transcripts of the Minimum Competency Testing Clarification Hearings*, p. 300.

85. Michel Foucault, in an interview with John Simon, "Michel Foucault on Attica," *Telos* 19 (1974): 156, cited by James Bernauer, S.J., "Foucault's Political Analysis," *International Philosophical Quarterly* 12 (March 1982): 89.

86. Norman Frederiksen, "The Real Test Bias," *American Psychologist* 39 (March 1984): 193-202.

87. Mortimer J. Adler, *The Paideia Proposal: An Educational Manifesto* (New York: Macmillan, 1982).

88. T.R. Sizer, Appendix III in *Paideia Problems and Possibilities: Consideration of Questions Raised by the Paideia Proposal by M.J. Adler* (New York: Macmillan, 1983).

89. For a description of the Eight Year Study, see Eugene Smith and Ralph W. Tyler, *Appraising and Recording Student Progress* (New York: Harper, 1942). For a description of the University of Chicago Examiner's Office, see Benjamin Bloom, *All Our Children Learning: A Primer for Parents, Teachers, and Other Educators* (New York: McGraw-Hill, 1981), pp. 245-266.

CHAPTER VI

The Textbook Controversies

DANIEL TANNER

"The significant position of textbooks in the program of American education is so generally recognized that the Society seems to be fully justified in sponsoring a yearbook on the theme 'The Textbook.' It is the textbook that in thousands of classrooms determines the content of instruction and as well as the teaching procedures."[1]

These were the opening words of the Thirtieth Yearbook, Part II, of the National Society for the Study of Education, published in 1931. More than half a century later, the textbook was still being described as "the predominant classroom resource," accounting for up to 80 percent of the subject matter in the course of study.[2]

Throughout the twentieth century textbooks have been variously criticized by progressive educators for determining the curriculum, whereas radical romanticists have favored the virtual elimination of textbooks and the preplanned curriculum,[3] while those on the far right have sought to censor textbooks so as to eliminate the treatment of unsettling ideas and issues. Then there are the futurists who became so enamored with the new electronic media during the 1960s and early 1970s that they predicted that print will play only a secondary role in the classroom of the future.[4] In a publication commemorating the centennial year of the U.S. Office of Education, a scenario of schooling was presented as a vision of the future (the year of 1997) in which textbooks and other books, and even teachers, would be replaced by the computer.[5] (Ironically, the futurists who predict the virtual demise of conventional print media for teaching and learning invariably use the book to convey their message to the education profession and the general public.)

Why is the textbook, along with other books in the classroom and school library, so dominant and durable? In an age of microelectronic-media technology, why is it that the textbook and other conventional print media continue to serve as the predominant classroom resource? Is the dominance of the textbook and other conventional print media largely attributable to the resistance of the school to change? Or are there unique attributes and functions indigenous to these conventional print media which distinguish them from other media as a principal teaching-learning resource? These are some of the questions, along with related issues, to be addressed in this chapter.

Dominance and Durability of the Textbook

In *The Textbook Problem*, published in 1927, Ellwood P. Cubberley noted that because of the greater standardization of the curriculum in European schools, teachers there did not have access to the great variety of textbooks available in the United States; and with the greater standardization and uniformity of instruction and instructional tools in Europe, there was less reliance on the textbook. "In no country are there more teachers engaged in the work of textbook-making, and nowhere are textbooks in preparation subjected to such a severe trying-out process before publication. In no country, moreover, are the textbooks in use revised more frequently to keep them abreast of the progress of knowledge and the best educational thought," wrote Cubberley. He went on to point out that "nowhere does the experienced and capable teacher have so many supplementary texts to put into the hands of her pupils as do the teachers in the United States."[6] Nevertheless, a survey by William C. Bagley, reported in the Thirtieth Yearbook of the National Society for the Study of Education, found that modern educational theory in the preparation of teachers was bringing about less reliance on the " 'straight' recitation from the single textbook," and that this was "affecting elementary school practice in a fairly profound fashion, and it is apparently not without its influence upon the secondary school." Bagley also found that this transformation was in greater evidence among teachers who had participated to a greater extent in programs of teacher education. Moreover, the beginning teacher was more likely to depend upon formal textbook methods than teachers with several years of experience.[7]

More than half a century later, Goodlad reported in his study of schooling that there was evidence of the use of a wide range of textbooks and materials in classrooms, although heavy emphasis was being given to workbooks and worksheets in a mode not always distinguishable from testing. Goodlad also found that textbooks dominated the instruction in the sciences and mathematics, although workbooks and worksheets were commonplace in the latter subject.[8]

In the Thirtieth Yearbook of the NSSE (1931), Nelson B. Henry reported that books used in public elementary and secondary schools amounted to only 1.6 percent of the total school expenditures. Henry concluded that "textbooks are surprisingly inexpensive, especially when their importance in the education of the children of this country is considered."[9] A half century later, in the widely heralded report, *A Nation at Risk: The Imperative for Educational Reform*, issued by the National Commission on Excellence in Education, under the auspices of the U.S. Department of Education, the following finding was highlighted:

Expenditures for textbooks and other instructional materials have declined by 50 percent over the past 17 years. While some recommend a level of spending on texts of between 5 and 10 percent of the operating costs of schools, the budgets for basal texts and related materials have been dropping during the past decade and a half to only 0.7 percent today.[10]

Nevertheless, the textbook continues to serve as the predominant classroom resource in determining the content of instruction as well as the teaching procedures, and one must reach the same conclusion today as did Henry: "textbooks are surprisingly inexpensive." Yet to this day, in seeking to reduce the school budget, school boards and administrators tend to look first at reducing expenditures for textbooks and collateral curricular materials as students are made to work with shopworn books for yet another year.

The decline in expenditures for textbooks and other instructional materials by 50 percent over the past seventeen years, as noted in the report of the National Commission on Excellence in Education, appears to have been the result of the back-to-basics retrenchment of the 1970s and early 1980s. With most of the states embarking on minimum-competency testing, and with school districts seeking to hold the line on school budgets, teachers were focusing instruction on facts and skills in teaching-to-the-test while resorting to inexpensive workbooks, and photocopied materials.

The report of the National Commission on Excellence in Education (1983) failed to attribute the decline in expenditures for textbooks and other instructional materials to the factors cited above, or to any other factors. Interestingly, in the section of its report on "Recommendations: Standards and Expectations," the Commission offered eight recommendations, of which five were focused on textbooks and related instructional materials. These recommendations called for the upgrading of textbooks and materials so as to assure (a) more rigorous content by enlisting "university scientists, scholars, and members of professional societies, in collaboration with master teachers . . . as they did in the post-Sputnik era"; (b) the systematic evaluation of textbooks through field trials and other means; and (c) the funding of textbook development in "thin-market" fields (for the disadvantaged, disabled, and gifted learner).[11] No mention was made as to why the unprecedented national curriculum reforms during the crisis of the cold war and post-Sputnik I era had failed to achieve what had been promised, nor how the misguided efforts of the past might be rectified.

Nevertheless, it was clear that the call to upgrade textbooks was a response to what was increasingly being perceived as the "dumbing down" of textbooks as a result of the back-to-basics retrenchment and of the objections that had been raised by various special-interest groups to the treatment of controversial ideas, problems, and issues in textbooks. Before returning to the problem of the "dumbing down" and censorship of textbooks and collateral curricular materials, a brief examination of the unprecedented national efforts to upgrade school textbooks and other instructional materials in the wake of the cold war and Sputnik I is in order.

Nationalizing Influences on the Textbook

"The National Science Foundation, which has recognized expertise in leading curriculum development, should again take the leadership role in promoting curriculum evaluation and development for mathematics, science, and technology."[12] So stated a report issued in 1983 for the National Science Board of the National Science Foundation. In making this recommendation, the report was referring to the national curriculum reform projects financed under the auspices of the National Science Foundation during the effort to mobilize our schools in the sciences and mathematics to meet the alleged crisis of the cold war and post-Sputnik I era.

The rationale undergirding this national curriculum reform effort in the wake of Sputnik I was explicated by Jerome Bruner in a report of a conference in 1959 called by the National Academy of Sciences.

In the opening paragraph of the report, Bruner linked the need for a national effort for curriculum reform with "what is almost certain to be a long-range crisis in national security."[13]

The final chapter of the report was devoted to the place of the newer instructional media in these national curriculum projects. In examining the potentials of programmed instructional materials and teaching machines, Bruner held that it was unlikely that such devices will dehumanize learning any more than books dehumanize learning. "A program for a teaching machine is as personal as a book," contended Bruner.[14] During the early stages of the leading national curriculum projects, it was indicated by some project leaders that explorations were being made into the possibility of developing programmed instructional materials. But none of these projects actually developed such materials. Clearly, with these projects claiming to embrace the inquiry-discovery mode, the convergent mode of programmed instruction was inimical to the presumably emergent inquiry-discovery approach.

Although the leading national curriculum reform projects of that era proceeded to develop multimedia approaches in their curriculum packages, the mainstay, nevertheless, was the textbook. Hence, in the preface to the early editions of the text *Physics* by the Physical Science Study Committee, James R. Killian, Jr., president of the Massachusetts Institute of Technology, described the textbook as "the heart of the PSSC course."[15] Soon, the magnitude of textbook sales was to become the criterion for gauging enrollments and determining the success of these projects; however, it was eventually revealed that the enrollments in the new science courses were being inflated by the project administrators by over 100 percent.[16] At the same time, the authors and publishers of competing texts were claiming that their textbooks were indeed embracing the main elements and currents of the "new" physics, biology, chemistry, mathematics, and so on. In effect, the national curriculum projects exerted a pervasive nationalizing influence on the textbook industry. But as it became apparent that the national curriculum reform projects were failing to measure up to the extravagant claims made for them, alternate approaches began to appear. However, the crisis of the cold war and space race was to become overshadowed by the crisis of student protest and disruption in the wake of the prolonged war in Vietnam, with the result that the role of the National Science Foundation in curriculum reform in elementary and secondary education went into a virtual eclipse.

The Textbook and Codified Knowledge

Why did the textbook serve as the dominant vehicle for the national curriculum reform projects led by university scholar-specialists during the late 1950s and the decade of the 1960s? In *The Structure of Scientific Revolutions*, Thomas Kuhn makes the case for textbooks as indispensable devices in science education in which they serve to "expound the body of accepted theory, illustrate many or all of its successful applications, and compare these applications with exemplary observations and experiments."[17] Kuhn holds that in the social sciences, history, and other fields, where the paradigms are relatively weak as compared with the sciences, textbooks are more likely to be accompanied by parallel readings than in the sciences because in these fields, the student "has constantly before him a number of competing and incommensurable solutions to . . . problems, solutions that he must ultimately evaluate for himself."[18]

With university scholar-specialists leading the national curriculum reforms during the 1950s and 1960s, discipline-centered knowledge became the focus of curriculum redevelopment, and the social scientists endeavored to imitate their colleagues in the natural sciences in seeking to demonstrate the "structure" of their disciplines. And with disciplinary knowledge being the focus of curriculum reform, it was inevitable that the textbook would serve as the principal vehicle for embodying the codified knowledge said to represent each discipline. Hence the school curriculum was to be comprised of separate disciplines or domains of codified knowledge.

By the late 1960s, it had become increasingly apparent that the discipline-centered basis for curriculum reform had neglected the nature of the learner and the need for interdisciplinary curricular structure to serve the function of general education in a free society. In other words, to meet the function of general education, the design of the school curriculum must take into account the nature of the learner and must reveal knowledge applications in the life of the learner and in the wider social life. In contradistinction, the national curriculum reforms had been focused on specialized, abstract, and puristic disciplinary knowledge representing the theoretical knowledge edifices of the university scholar-specialist.[19]

In seeking to study the problems connected with federal involvement in school curriculum development, especially in connection with the rise and fall of the national curriculum projects of the 1950s and 1960s, the National Institute of Education formed a Curriculum Development Task Force in 1975. In the introductory chapter of a book containing the papers commissioned for the Task Force, the chairman of the Task Force attributed the collapse of the federally supported curriculum projects largely to the forces of censorship, capped by a congressional attack on one of these projects in 1975.[20] Although the new biology textbooks had been attacked in some quarters by antievolutionists, the fact remains that most of the projects were not targets of censorship and were already in a state of decline by the late 1960s for reasons cited earlier.

Despite Kuhn's view that there is relatively little disputation in the natural sciences where the disciplinary paradigms are strongest, in contrast to other fields, school textbooks in biology, ecology, and general science have been subjected to enormous pressures of censorship and "dumbing down" to an extent no less portentous than in the social studies, history, and literature. One only has to cite the continued controversy over evolutionary theory in school science textbooks and the pressures by religious fundamentalists demanding that equal treatment be given in science textbooks to the doctrine of creationism as a viable alternative "theory." Or one can cite the opposition raised in some quarters to the study of human reproduction in biology textbooks.

Clearly, although the paradigms in the natural sciences are stronger than in other disciplines, the natural sciences are no less immune from disputation when the subject matter interfaces with philosophical ideas, personal and social views, and social applications. The censorship of ideas has reverberations throughout the school curriculum and cannot be confined to a given discipline or subject as long as that discipline or subject has relevance to the life of the learner and the wider social life. No discipline or subject matter is an island in the curriculum although, in the departmental knowledge edifices of the university, the disciplines or subject fields are often treated as independent, self-serving entities.

Textbook Censorship

At the opening of this chapter, the question was posed as to why the textbooks and collateral print media continue to serve as the predominant classroom resource during an age of microelectronic technology. A number of factors have been explored in this chapter, explaining the certain unique properties and functions of the textbook and conventional print media. Some of these properties become evident when addressing the following question: Why is it that efforts to censor ideas in the school curriculum tend to be centered on textbooks and other books used in the classroom and school library, and not on computer programs, programmed textbooks, or workbooks?

Apparently, beyond the more rudimentary levels of treatment of subject matter, and with the exception of technical subject matter and the subject of school mathematics, textbooks, along with other books used in the classroom and found in the school library, are of enormous potential use in exposing the learner to powerful ideas and unsettling issues that cannot be broached in any comparable way through the computer program, programmed textbook, or workbook. Whereas the computer program and other programmed instructional materials are geared predominantly to *established-convergent* learning situations, in which all action-relevant aspects of the system are specifiable and predictable, textbooks and library books can serve as pedagogical vehicles not only for *established* learning, but for *emergent* learning situations through which the student can explore problems and issues in open-ended ways.[21]

A PERSISTENT HISTORICAL PROBLEM

It is indeed baffling that the contributors to the Thirtieth Yearbook of the National Society for the Study of Education, *The Textbook in American Education*, examined so many ramifications of the textbook without addressing the problem of censorship. Not only had history and social studies textbooks undergone attack in the name of Americanism during the 1920s, but it was over the use of the textbook *Civic Biology*, authored by George Hunter, that John T. Scopes, a Tennessee high school teacher, was brought to trial in 1925 for having violated a state statute prohibiting the teaching of evolution. The case, which was called "the world's most famous court trial,"[22] came about when Scopes had commented to some friends that any teacher using the state-approved biology textbook could not help but violate the Tennessee statute against the teaching of evolution. With William Jennings Bryan on the side of the state and Clarence Darrow representing the defense, the case attracted great national and international notoriety, and eventually was dramatized in the theatre and as a motion picture. Scopes was convicted and fined $100. On appeal the state Supreme Court ruled the law constitutional, but reversed the lower court's decision on a technicality, thereby obviating the possibility of an appeal to the U.S. Supreme Court to test the constitutionality of the Tennessee law. The Tennessee law in question was eventually replaced by a statute prohibiting the use of any textbook containing subject matter on evolution without the qualifying statement that evolution is a theory and not a scientific fact.

In *Anti-intellectualism in American Life*, the late Richard Hofstadter concluded, "Today the evolution controversy seems as remote as the Homeric era to intellectuals in the East, and it is not uncommon to take a condescending view of both sides."[23] Hofstadter not only failed to recognize the growing national influence of Christian fundamentalism, but also that textbooks are used nationally and that any timidity or self-censorship by textbook authors and publishers has ramifications in schools in every sector of the nation. As discussed later, the problem of censoring and the "dumbing down" of schoolbooks so as to avoid controversial ideas was to reach a critical state in the mid-1980s.

Only three years following the publication of Hofstadter's book, and some forty years after the Scopes decision, a biology textbook used by a high school teacher in Little Rock was found in violation of an Arkansas statute against the teaching of evolution. Although the lower court decision was upheld by the state Supreme Court, the decision was reversed by the U.S. Supreme Court, which ruled the statute an establishment of religion in violation of the First Amendment.[24] The evolution-creationism textbook controversy has continued to this day, and in 1986 reached the U.S. Supreme Court once again.[25]

Aside from the very large number of court cases involving school textbooks as related directly to the curriculum, there is the continuing problem of censorship of textbooks and collateral reading materials. Before examining the contemporary situation, mention should be made of two notorious series of censorship incidents that occurred during the years toward the end of the Great Depression, and extended into the early cold-war period following World War II. By far the leading social studies textbook series for the junior and senior high schools during the decade of the 1930s and extending into the first years of the 1940s was *Man and His Changing Society* by Harold Rugg at Teachers College, Columbia University. The frame of reference for this textbook series was the evolution of modern American democracy with a focus on the pervasive problems and issues confronting our contemporary society. By the late 1930s, Rugg's textbooks came under full attack by the National Association of Manufacturers, the Advertising Federation of America, the Hearst press, the American Legion, and other ultra-right-wing groups and individuals seeking to portray the Rugg textbooks as subversive of American ideals and institutions.[26] Although the American Historical Association's Commission on the Social Studies had come under similar attack during this same period by ultrarightists, the Rugg textbooks became the main target and, eventually, the casualty of the onslaught. Articles in *Time, Saturday Evening Post, Forbes, Nation's Business*, and other magazines were attacking progressive education and, more specifically, the Rugg textbooks. To no avail, noted authors, educators, and textbook publishers protested the removal of the Rugg textbooks from the schools and described the situation as a "state of panic" in which "prejudice and hatred are displacing reason and tolerance essential for the functioning of democratic institutions."[27] During the early 1940s the Rugg textbooks were undergoing full eclipse as school boards were urgently ordering their removal from the schools.

Considering the great notoriety of the Rugg textbook controversy and the stifling effect on the school curriculum and on the school textbook industry as a result of the censorship of the Rugg textbooks, it is puzzling that Hofstadter made no mention of this episode in his Pulitzer-prize winning work, *Anti-intellectualism in American Life*. Nor did Hofstadter mention the notorious episode of censoring the *Building America* series of social studies books which followed the Rugg episode. Curiously, Hofstadter chose to portray progressive education largely as an antiintellectual movement, as he failed to recognize the continuing and courageous battle on the part of leading progressive educators against the censorship of schoolbooks and in defense of academic freedom.[28]

Soon after the Rugg episode, during the cold-war years immediately following World War II, the *Building America* series of supplementary social studies texts came under the fire of the superpatriots and special-interest groups.[29] Created during the Great Depression by the Society for Curriculum Study (which later merged with the NEA Department of Supervision and Directors of Instruction, leading to the creation of the Association for Supervision and Curriculum Development), *Building America* was conceived to provide for the thoughtful examination of contemporary socioeconomic problems in the social studies curriculum in junior and senior high schools. The first editorial board of *Building America* (1934) included such figures as Paul R. Hanna, who created the series and served as chairman, Edgar Dale, Harold Hand, Jesse Newlon, Hollis L. Caswell, and James E. Mendenhall—young individuals who were to go on to make lasting contributions to American education. All of them contributed their own money to get the project under way. The first issue, "Housing" (1935), led to a grant from the General Education Board of the Rockefeller Foundation to cover the expenses of the project during its first year. Additional grants were made by the Foundation during the early years of publication. In 1940 the *Building America* series was being published by the Americana Corporation. By 1945, sales of the monthly paperback texts had reached more than a million copies per issue. The monthly texts were also published in hardbound annual editions. Over a period of thirteen years of publication (1935-1948), the widely acclaimed *Building America* series included ninety-one texts bearing such titles as "Food," "Power," "Health," "Youth Faces the World," "Our Constitution," "Social Security," "We Consumers," "Education," "War or Peace?," "Crime," "Civil Liberties," "Women," "Advertising," "Italian Americans," "Our Water Resources," and "Our Land Resources"— all focused on topical issues.

But 1945 was the year when attacks on the *Building America* series were to begin in earnest by the conservative press and ultra-right-wing groups seeking to portray the texts as un-American. The locus of these attacks was mainly in California where the texts and the editorial board of *Building America* were targeted for scrutiny by the State Joint Legislative Fact-Finding Committee on Un-American Activities. Authors of the *Building America* texts and members of the editorial board were accused of being affiliated with communist-front organizations. When the charges were disproved, these individuals were attacked as having been "fooled" by communist-front organizations. As chairman of the editorial board, Paul R. Hanna, professor of education at Stanford University, took much of the brunt of the attacks. Pressures were being exerted to confine the curriculum to the fundamentals and to eliminate social studies and controversial ideas in favor of American history focused on factual subject matter and patriotic treatment.[30]

Although the *Building America* series had been approved by the California Board of Education upon the unanimously favorable recommendations of the California Curriculum Commission, the notoriety of the case led to a sharp decline in the sales of the texts and the withdrawal of Americana as publisher. The last issue in the *Building America* series appeared at the end of 1948 as school boards were having the texts removed from the schools.

The "Dumbing Down" of Schoolbooks

One only has to review the current issues of the American Library Association's *Newsletter on Intellectual Freedom* to realize that the censorship of schoolbooks is not only a continuing problem, but a heightened problem for American education. Virtually every issue of the *Newsletter* contains reports of incidents of the censorship of school library books or textbooks, along with related court decisions. Obviously, only a small fraction of the incidents of schoolbook censorship is reported, as most school administrators, teachers, and school librarians seek to avoid making a public issue over a local censorship incident. Then there is the common problem of self-censorship in which teachers avoid the use of collateral reading materials that might contain unsettling ideas.

WATERING DOWN THE CURRICULUM
TO AVOID CONTROVERSY

It is not only teachers who engage in self-censorship. Textbook authors and publishers also yield to real or imagined pressures as to what is acceptable or unacceptable to various constituencies. A notable example is the Human Sciences Program of the Biological Sciences Curriculum Study (BSCS), designed for students between ten and fourteen years of age. Although the BSCS leadership had been outspoken in defending academic freedom, the director of BSCS, William V. Mayer, acknowledged that a modular approach was taken in the Human Sciences Program so as to allow for the substitution (or elimination) of modules on topics that may be objectionable, such as the module on human reproduction and population. Mayer wrote:

We have, in the absence of data to the contrary, refrained from full explication of certain social matters that are still contentious within the population in order that students may not be disadvantaged by community refusals to use BSCS materials. We can and have rejected community pressures we regard as unfounded or motivated outside the scientific sphere, such as creationism in lieu of or parallel to evolution. But we cannot fight all battles in all communities simultaneously and effectively. . . . Our Board has given us directions in this regard.[31]

In the process of marketing the Human Sciences Program, BSCS proceeded to feature the modular organization of the materials and subject matter as "flexibility in packaging," allowing teachers and administrators to "modify the program to meet local needs by deleting activities either not germane or considered inappropriate for the local population." This was billed by BSCS as providing for "curriculum flexibility," rather than as serving to compromise the curriculum.[32]

The "watering down" of the curriculum is the inevitable consequence of externally imposed or self-imposed censorship, violations of the academic freedom of teachers, and curricular reductionism whereby the curriculum is confined mainly to basic skills and factual subject matter devoid of controversial ideas, problems, and issues. Essentialists typically take the position that academic freedom is the province of higher education, not elementary and secondary education. According to Raymond English, "academic freedom in its true sense has no place in precollege education" on the ground that "the schools and the teachers in them are servants of the community and of the families that make up the community."[33] Not only does such a view ignore the fact that education is a state function, but it relegates the majority of the rising generation who do not go on to college to the status of second-class citizens. Such a narrow view also assumes that the "community" is necessarily manifested in the form of the lowest common denominator of public enlightenment. It fails to recognize that "community" can also mean "cosmopolitan" in exemplifying the highest, widest, and wisest ideals and practices for public education. At the turn of the century, Dewey advised parents and educators that, "What the best and wisest parent wants for his own child, that must the community want for all of its children. Any other ideal is narrow and unlovely; acted upon, it destroys our democracy."[34]

Enlightened, well-educated parents want an enriched idea-oriented curriculum for their own children. When schools provide such a curriculum for the more advantaged children and youth while delimiting the disadvantaged to an error-oriented curriculum through the use of mechanical exercises in workbooks, ditto sheets, and programmed instructional materials, such differentiation mitigates against equality of educational opportunity.[35] There is a commonly held notion that higher-ability students prefer curricular materials and methods that are less directive and more discovery oriented, whereas lower-achieving students respond better to more directive and structured materials and methods. In reviewing the research on learning from media, Clark reports that the opposite seems to be the case:

Higher-ability students seem to like methods and media that they perceive as more structured and directive because they think they will have to invest less effort to achieve success. However, these more structured methods prevent the higher ability students from employing their own considerable skills and yield less effort than the less directive methods and media. Lower-ability students seem to like less structured and more discovery-oriented methods and media.[36]

Those who hold the position that the school curriculum should properly be limited to subject matter concentrated on facts and fundamental skills have exerted a powerful influence on textbooks. Surprisingly, this position is shared by many in higher academe who see the school mainly as a "tooling up" for college. Hence Daniel Bell, a leading advocate of general education in college, proceeded to delimit the function of the secondary school as appropriately "concentrating on facts and skills," whereas he portrayed the college years, through general education, as "a broad intellectual adventure" and as an experience in "the testing of oneself and one's values."[37]

Not only does this view raise ominous consequences for a free society when the majority of youth who do not go on to higher education are denied the opportunity to engage in a "broad intellectual adventure" and the testing of their values in school, but it assumes that the engagement of intellectual curiosity and the formation and testing of values are inappropriate during the developing years of adolescence. To deny such experience is to deny adolescence as a critical period of human development and to place the adolescent in "no-man's-land." For most adolescents, the high school years are the last opportunity they will have to investigate controversial issues systematically in the formal educational setting.

In growing recognition that the forces for censoring schoolbooks and delimiting the school curriculum to established-convergent learning through facts and fundamental skills have great reverberations for higher education, the American Association of University Professors established in 1985 a Commission on Academic Freedom and Pre-College Education. The Commission's first report was focused on the problem of challenges to elementary and secondary school textbooks, library books, and other curricular materials. "The interest of higher education in threats to freedom in the schools is beyond doubt," declared the report as it went on to recommend ways through which universities can work with schools in combating censorship pressures.[38]

By the mid-1980s it was becoming increasingly apparent that the avoidance of controversial ideas in the curriculum, and more specifically in textbooks, was resulting in a watered down curriculum. This was particularly disturbing to many educators in view of the mounting evidence revealing widespread deficiencies in higher-order thinking abilities on the part of students after years of back-to-basics retrenchment.[39]

Bettelheim and Zelan criticized reading texts for focusing on dull, repetitive drills, rote learning, and the failure to engage children in dealing with interesting ideas.[40] In this connection, there is a need to assess the extent to which the widespread use of readability formulas in the preparation of textbooks has resulted in the watering down of subject matter. Paradoxically, such formulas often serve to make the textbook less stimulating as interesting ideas are avoided in favor of more simplistic prose and mechanistic treatment.

A study commissioned by the Advisory Panel on the SAT Test Score Decline, sponsored by the College Board and the Educational Testing Service, found that the cognitive levels of textbooks in social studies, literature, grammar and composition had undergone a decline in level of cognitive maturity over a thirty-five-year period, and that the less challenging textbooks were associated with lower SAT scores by students using such texts. However, the researchers found that sixth-grade basal readers had become increasingly difficult since the late 1960s.[41]

In an address to school administrators in 1984, U.S. Secretary of Education Terrel H. Bell accused the publishers of "dumbing down" their textbooks, but Bell failed to acknowledge that the "dumbing down" of textbooks is the inevitable result of curricular reductionism through "back-to-basics" and censorship pressures.[42]

A STATE RESPONDS

In an ironic turn of events some forty years following the attacks on the *Building America* series in California, the California Board of Education in the fall of 1985, upon recommendation of the State Curriculum Development and Supplemental Materials Commission, unanimously rejected every science textbook submitted for use in seventh- and eighth-grade classes on the ground that the textbooks were "watered down" to avoid controversy. The Board and State Superintendent Bill Honig criticized the publishers for producing textbooks that avoid or fail to address adequately such controversial topics as evolution, human reproduction, and environmental problems. Within several months, the publishers produced revised editions of their textbooks. One publisher, who did not even list the topic of evolution in the textbook index, soon produced a revised edition with an entire chapter on evolution. Honig also announced that textbooks for all other subject areas would come under the same scrutiny as the science textbooks.[43]

Within a year following the action taken on the science textbooks, the California Board of Education voted to uphold the recommendation of the State Curriculum Development and Supplemental Materials Commission in rejecting every mathematics textbook for use in grades K-8. The Commission failed the textbooks for stressing "apparent mastery" of mechanical skills without engaging students in the understanding of concepts and in applying their mathematical knowledge, skills, and experience in problem-solving situations that are new or perplexing to them.[44] As in the case of its earlier report on science, the Commission based its recommendations on the evaluations of a panel of experts composed of university professors in the discipline and in education, curriculum directors and specialists from various school districts, and teachers. In conducting the evaluations, a framework of criteria was used, drawn from the research literature in mathematics and science education.[45]

The remarkable speed with which publishers proceeded to respond to these criticisms and recommendations by issuing revised textbooks can be appreciated when it is realized that if California were a nation, it would rank sixth among the nations of the world in the size of its economy.[46] "We now know that as a state representing 12 percent of the textbook market, we can stand up and be counted," stated Superintendent Honig. He went on to note that "publishers are willing to make changes based on quality criteria, if we ask them, and educators across the country have applauded our efforts."[47] However, as discussed earlier, publishers also respond to the narrow-minded influences of special-interest pressure groups when such influences are dominant.

The power of state adoption in the textbook marketplace as discussed in the recent incidents in California is, of course, a two-edged sword in that the practice of state adoption by a few "super states" can serve to shape the content of textbooks (and the curriculum) nationwide. Consequently, it is essential that the textbook selection committee be comprised of leading professional educators who have the expertise upon which the State Board of Education can rely. It is also essential that state-approved lists be sufficiently comprehensive so as to meet local needs. In these respects, the contemporary structure for textbook adoption in California, where the State Board of Education relies on the professional expertise of the Curriculum Development and Supplemental Materials Commission, and where the approved lists are comprehensive, serves to mitigate against the kinds of episodes that occurred in California and elsewhere during the 1940s in connection with the Rugg textbooks and the *Building America* series. Whereas the recent actions in California were based upon the best available professional knowledge, the actions of the 1940s were narrowly political, censorial, and contrary to the best available professional knowledge. Unfortunately, the historical record reveals that educators have been all too willing to abrogate their professional responsibilities as they readily yield to the dominant tide of the times, no matter how ill conceived and narrowly directed. The mark of a profession is that decisions are based upon the best available evidence, not on political opportunism or expediency.

Censorship and political interference and distortion of the curriculum can best be prevented at the local level when textbook evaluation and selection are based upon the best available professional knowledge. This requires a structural arrangement whereby textbook selection and evaluation are made by the professional staff of the school and school district in the form of a standing curriculum committee. The superintendent of schools must exercise considerable leadership acumen in educating the local board of education on their need to draw upon the expertise of the professional staff. There have been instances where school administrators have been censured by local boards of education for having censored textbooks and other curricular materials. Censorship is less apt to occur when the school board serves to represent the wider public interest, and not narrow individual or special interests. Obviously, this also applies to state boards of education.

Research on the Textbook

Content analysis has served as a useful device in gauging the extent of inclusion or exclusion of topics, ideas, and issues in textbooks and other curricular materials. Unfortunately, however, it has also been used for narrow political purposes to eliminate controversial ideas or to inject the biases of special-interest groups into the curriculum. For example, in its attacks on Rugg's textbooks during the early 1940s, the National Association of Manufacturers (NAM) engaged Ralph Robey, a professor of banking and economics at Columbia, to prepare "objective" abstracts of the material in the textbooks so as to ascertain the author's attitude toward our governmental and economic institutions. Despite the establishment of a committee of the American Historical Association to investigate the approach taken by Robey and the NAM in using the textbook abstracts, Robey and the NAM were successful in creating notoriety in connection with the Rugg textbooks and in using the abstracts to build their case against Rugg.[48]

In 1986, U.S. Secretary of Education William J. Bennett cited studies financed by the U.S. Department of Education to buttress his contention that school textbooks fail to give appropriate recognition to the contributions of religion to American culture. Bennett was quoted as citing these studies as evidence of "the assault of secularism on religion."[49] One of the studies was conducted by Paul C. Vitz, a psychology professor at New York University, who made a content analysis of the social studies textbooks for grades 1-6 from ten publishers. Vitz held that these textbooks "are representative of the nation as a whole." Among Vitz's reported findings were the following: "Serious Christian or Jewish religious motivation is featured nowhere. . . . Patriotism is close to nonexistent in the sample. Likewise, any appreciation of business success is seriously underrepresented. Traditional roles for both men and women receive virtually no support, while role-reversal feminist stories are common."[50]

Secretary Bennett was criticized by U.S. Senator Lowell P. Weicker, chairman of the Senate Education Appropriations Subcommittee, for subsequently approving Vitz for another grant for the content analysis of textbooks despite the low rating given to Vitz's research proposal in peer review. He also criticized Bennett for seeking to use the offices of the Department of Education for bringing his ideologies into school textbooks, when the law governing the department's organization prohibits it from exercising "direction, supervision, or control" over school textbooks.[51]

School textbooks and school library books have been subjected to the pressures of ideologies from the left as well as the right extremes of the political spectrum. Vocal minorities have influenced the treatment of material in textbooks ranging from basal readers to high school history and literature. Books have been removed from the curriculum and from school libraries because of pressures from vocal minorities as well as from right-wing groups.

Considering the great significance of the textbook in the curriculum, and the great disputations attaching to the content and uses of the textbook, it is surprising how little research has been conducted on how textbooks influence teaching and learning. "Textbooks command attention because they not only provide the basic source of school instruction but also transmit culture, reflect values, and serve as springboards for the intellectual development of individuals and the nation," commented Eloise Warming. She went on to note that "little, if any, research has been done on the effectiveness of learning from conventional textbooks."[52]

In the third edition of the *Handbook of Research on Teaching*, only one index entry is made for school textbooks, and the single entry is for the natural sciences. In this connection, the authors note that textbooks "receive far less attention in science education than many other instructional variables."[53]

In the first edition of the *Handbook of Research on Teaching*, Lumsdaine sought to explain the paucity of research on the textbook in these words:

The usual textbook does not control the behavior of the learner in a way which makes it highly predictable as a vehicle of instruction or amenable to experimental research. It does not in itself generate a describable and predictable process of learner behavior, and this may be the reason why there has been little experimental research on the textbook.[54]

Was Lumsdaine explaining the problem by explaining it away, or was he alluding to the special attributes of the textbook? Unlike convergent teaching-learning materials such as workbooks or programmed instructional materials, textbooks can be designed so as to provide for a great range and variety of emergent ideas and uses, or they can be limited mainly to established-convergent knowledge in the form of facts and skills. So limited, textbooks are no longer textbooks as Kuhn describes them. Instead, they become workbooks. Rather than being used to open up areas of inquiry to the learner, they become closed-ended.

Over many decades it has been recognized that effective teachers use textbooks in more emergent ways than less effective teachers and make use of a wide range of collateral reading materials and activities to supplement and enrich the textbook. Nevertheless, the potential for experimental research on the different uses of the textbook by teachers, and on student attitudes toward a subject as the result of having used alternative kinds of textbooks, remains an untapped mine.

Conclusions

Schools in a free society are distinguished from those in a totalitarian society through a commitment to using the best available evidence in examining ideas, problems, and issues in the curriculum. As emphasized throughout this chapter, the enormous disputation evoked by the textbook since the time of its inception is testimony to its unique power as a medium for teaching and learning.

The better school textbooks exemplify organized knowledge in provocative and emergent ways, rather than in established-convergent or closed-ended ways. Nevertheless, effective teachers have long recognized that the textbook should not determine the curriculum. A rich variety of penetrating resource materials and activities must be provided to relate the curriculum to the life of the learner and to the wider social life. Obviously, when textbooks and other curricular materials are used for emergent learning rather than merely for established-convergent learning, teachers and school administrators run the risk that special-interest groups and individuals in the local community will seek to restrict or eliminate the use of such books or materials.

The following conclusions and recommendations are offered in connection with the problems and issues raised in this chapter:

1. The selection of textbooks and other curricular materials should be based upon the best available professional evidence, rather than narrow political or special interests. Hence such selection should be the responsibility of the professional staff of the school and school

district. The superintendent of schools has the responsibility for "educating" his board on these matters. The same should apply at the state level where state approval of school textbooks is practiced.

2. The educational interests of the learner are ill served when the learner is denied the opportunity to investigate controversial ideas, problems, and issues of common concern in a free society. The professional staff of the school and the local school board should be knowledgeable about and committed to the policy statements on academic freedom as developed by the leading professional associations, such as the American Association of School Librarians, Association of Supervision and Curriculum Development, National Council for the Social Studies, National Council of Teachers of English, National Science Teachers Association.

3. A standing curriculum committee composed of faculty, supervisors, head school librarian, and the curriculum director should be responsible for handling complaints lodged against the use of any textbooks, school library books, or other curricular materials, and to protect individual teachers from censorship attacks. The complaints of individuals or special-interest groups should never be the basis for removing or restricting books or other curricular materials. The school administration and school board should rely on the recommendations of the curriculum committee.

4. The school curriculum committee should be able to call upon the expertise of university or college faculty whenever it is felt that assistance is needed in evaluating textbooks and other curricular materials for adoption, and in assisting the school in countering censorship pressures. University and college faculties should be available to assist their school colleagues in these matters.

5. The recent "back-to-basics" retrenchment of the curriculum has resulted in the watering down of textbooks and the excessive use of workbooks and mechanical exercises on ditto sheets. Emphasis has been given to error-oriented teaching at the expense of idea-oriented teaching. There is a growing recognition that such practices have resulted in the decline in higher-order thinking abilities. Textbooks and other curricular materials should be evaluated as to the extent to which they stimulate students to engage in emergent learning and not merely established-convergent learning.

6. A selling point of many publishers is that their school textbooks follow a strict control through readability formulas. The readability of texts is enhanced by interesting ideas. Texts should be

built on the richness of idea development or concept development rather than being regulated by "word count."

7. The proportion of the school budget allocated for textbooks and other curricular materials is negligible, especially considering that textbooks and collateral materials are so central to the content of instruction and instructional procedures. Consequently, budgetary allocations for textbooks, school library books, and other curricular materials can be increased markedly without effecting an appreciable increase in the total school budget.

8. The copyright date should not be the chief criterion for ascertaining whether a textbook should be replaced by an "up-to-date" book. A new copyright date does not signal that the book is necessarily updated in content and superior in quality. Textbooks need to be evaluated by the professional staff and by responsible scholars to ascertain the extent to which they meet qualitative criteria as determined by the best available evidence in the professional literature.

9. No textbook, no matter how excellent it may be, should serve as the sole source of the course of study or should determine the modes of instruction. Students need to learn to work with a wide range of resource materials, and teachers must draw upon a rich variety of resource materials to meet the comprehensive needs of their students. Curriculum guides and lesson plans should not be derived principally from textbooks. Unfortunately, this is the case in far too many schools where "curriculum development" is largely a matter of textbook adoption.

10. A principal criterion in the evaluation of a textbook, and other curricular material, is the extent to which it interfaces with other studies in the total school curriculum. Textbooks and other curricular materials should not be adopted and used as though the subjects in the school curriculum are isolated and independent knowledge compartments. At the secondary school level, the departments should not work in isolation in adopting textbooks and other curricular materials.

11. Aside from the illegality of the all too common practice of reproducing copyrighted material without the consent of publishers, is the matter of denying students the opportunity of using the source material in its original, unexpurgated form. This is indeed poor economy in view of the minute fraction of the school budget devoted to schoolbooks and other curricular materials. Such practices also

make it uneconomical for publishers to keep valuable materials in print.

12. Students should not only be allowed, but encouraged, to take their schoolbooks home.

13. Books and materials in the school media center should not be restricted. In far too many schools, controversial works of fiction and nonfiction are "closeted away" from students.

14. Homework assignments should extend beyond the textbook and beyond other conventional classroom materials by engaging students in the systematic use of reference resources in the school media center, the community library, and other educative community agencies. Homework assignments should stimulate student engagement in emergent learning.

15. Greater attention needs to be given in programs of preservice and in-service teacher education to the selection and uses of the textbook and other curricular materials, particularly in connection with the scope and sequence of the total school curriculum.

In too many instances, school boards, administrators, and teachers have allowed individuals and special-interest groups to determine what is and what is not appropriate in the school curriculum. Under such circumstances, school administrators and their faculties are abrogating their professional responsibility for ensuring that special interests are not served at the expense of the wider public interest.

The function of general education in a free society is to foster the development of a common universe of discourse, understanding, and competence for an enlightened citizenry. This cannot be accomplished when the curriculum is reduced to basic education or focused on specialized technical knowledge to the exclusion of pervading ideas, problems, and issues affecting the life of the learner and the life of society. Textbook adoption has proceeded as though each textbook defines a particular subject matter independent of all other subject matters in the curriculum. Indeed, too many textbooks are written in this vein. The consequence is that the vital interdependence of knowledge is neglected along with the crucial function of general education.

Censorship efforts tend to be centered on conventional textbooks and school library books, and not on computer programs, programmed texts, or workbooks. This is testimony to the power of the textbook and other schoolbooks as principal sources of ideas for emergent learning. The textbook also serves as the key vehicle for initiating the learner to various sources of codified knowledge. No other instrument has been able to challenge the textbook for its dominance and durability as a medium for systematized learning.

FOOTNOTES

1. J. B. Edmonson, "Introduction," in *The Textbook in American Education*, ed. Guy M. Whipple, Thirtieth Yearbook of the National Society for the Study of Education, Part II (Bloomington, Ill.: Public School Publishing Company, 1931), p. 1.

2. Eloise O. Warming, "Textbooks," in *Encyclopedia of Educational Research*, 5th ed. (New York: Free Press and Macmillan, 1982), pp. 1934, 1936.

3. Herbert R. Kohl, *The Open Classroom* (New York: Random House, 1969), pp. 14, 41.

4. Neil Postman and Charles Weingartner, *The School Book* (New York: Delacorte, 1973), pp. 88-89.

5. U.S. Office of Education, *OE 100: Highlighting the Progress of American Education* (Washington, D.C.: U.S. Government Printing Office, 1967).

6. Ellwood P. Cubberley, *The Textbook Problem* (Boston: Houghton Mifflin, 1927), p. 4.

7. William C. Bagley, "The Textbook and Methods of Teaching," in *The Textbook in American Education*, ed. Whipple, pp. 24-25.

8. John I. Goodlad, *A Place Called School* (New York: McGraw-Hill, 1984), pp. 205, 207, 209, 211, 215.

9. Nelson B. Henry, "The Cost of Textbooks," in *The Textbook in American Education*, ed. Whipple, pp. 223, 233.

10. National Commission on Excellence in Education, *A Nation at Risk: The Imperative for Educational Reform* (Washington, D.C.: U.S. Department of Education, April 1983), p. 21.

11. Ibid., p. 28.

12. National Science Board, *Educating Americans for the 21st Century* (Washington, D.C.: National Science Foundation, 1983), p. 46.

13. Jerome S. Bruner, *The Process of Education* (Cambridge, Mass.: Harvard University Press, 1960), p. 1.

14. Ibid., p. 84.

15. James R. Killian, Jr., "Preface to the First Edition," in Physical Sciences Study Committee, *Physics*, 2nd ed. (Boston: D.C. Heath, 1965), p. vi.

16. Wayne W. Welch, "The Impact of National Curriculum Projects: The Need for Accurate Assessment," *School Science and Mathematics* 68 (March 1968): 225-234.

17. Thomas S. Kuhn, *The Structure of Scientific Revolutions*, 2d ed. (Chicago: University of Chicago Press, 1970), p. 10.

18. Ibid., p. 165.

19. See Daniel Tanner and Laurel N. Tanner, *Curriculum Development: Theory Into Practice*, 2d ed. (New York: Macmillan, 1980), chaps. 11, 12; Alvin M. Weinberg, *Reflections on Big Science* (Cambridge, Mass.: M.I.T. Press, 1967).

20. Jon Schaffarzick, "Federal Curriculum Reform: A Crucible for Value Conflict," in *Value Conflicts and Curriculum Issues*, ed. Jon Schaffarzick and Gary Sykes (Berkeley, CA: McCutchan Publishing Corp., 1979).

21. Daniel Tanner and Laurel N. Tanner, *Supervision in Education: Problems and Practices* (New York: Macmillan, 1987), pp. 124-127; Robert Boguslaw, *The New Utopians: A Study of Systems Design and Social Change* (Englewood Cliffs, N.J.: Prentice-Hall, 1965), pp. 7-9, 21.

22. *The World's Most Famous Court Trial, Complete Stenographic Report* (Cincinnati: National Book, 1925).

23. Richard Hofstadter, *Anti-intellectualism in American Life* (New York: Alfred A. Knopf, 1970), p. 129.

24. *Everson v. Arkansas*, 393 U.S. 97 (1968).

25. *Edwards v. Aguillard*, No. 85-1513 (1987).

26. Donald W. Robinson, "Patriotism and Economic Control: The Censure of Harold Rugg" (Doct. diss., Rutgers University, 1983).

27. "Publishers Protest Removal of Rugg Textbooks," *Publishers Weekly*, 22 June 1940, p. 2345.

28. Hofstadter, *Anti-intellectualism in American Life*, pp. 305, 323-390.

29. Robert E. Newman, Jr., "History of a Civic Education Project Implementing the Social-Problems Technique of Instruction" (Doct. diss., Stanford University, 1960).

30. California Senate Committee on Education, "Proceedings in the Matter of Investigation in Regard to Textbooks and Educational Practices in the Public Schools" (April 17, 1947).

31. William V. Mayer, "The BSCS Past," *BSCS Journal* 1 (November 1978): 9.

32. "The Human Sciences Program," *BSCS Journal* 3 (April 1980): 1-2, 4.

33. Raymond English, "The Politics of Textbook Adoption," *Phi Delta Kappan* 62 (December 1980): 278.

34. John Dewey, *The School and Society* (Chicago: University of Chicago Press, 1899), p. 7.

35. Goodlad, *A Place Called School*, p. 298.

36. Richard E. Clark, "Reconsidering Research on Learning from Media," *Review of Educational Research* 53 (Winter 1983): 455.

37. Daniel Bell, *The Reforming of General Education* (New York: Columbia University Press, 1966), p. 181.

38. Committee on Academic Freedom and Pre-College Education, American Association of University Professors, "Liberty and Learning in the Schools: Higher Education's Concerns," *Academe* 72 (September-October 1986): 31a.

39. Arthur N. Applebee, Judith A. Langer, and Ina V. S. Mullis, *The Writing Report Card: Writing Achievement in American Schools* (Princeton, N.J.: National Assessment of Educational Progress, 1986), p. 11.

40. Bruno Bettelheim and Karen Zelan, *On Learning to Read: The Child's Fascination with Meaning* (New York: Alfred A. Knopf, 1982).

41. Jeanne S. Chall, Sue S. Conard, and Susan Harris, *An Analysis of Textbooks in Relation to Declining SAT Scores* (New York: College Entrance Examination Board, 1977).

42. Cited in Edward B. Fiske, "Are They "Dumbing Down" the Textbooks?" *Principal* 64 (November 1984): 44.

43. California State Department of Education, *News Release*, 10 December 1985, p. 3.

44. Curriculum Development and Supplemental Materials Commission, State of California, *Report on Mathematics Instructional Materials* (Sacramento: California State Department of Education, 1986).

45. Science Curriculum Framework and Criteria Committee, *Science Framework Addendum* (Sacramento: California State Department of Education, 1984).

46. *New York Times*, 21 September 1986, p. 40.

47. California State Department of Education, *News Release*, 10 December 1985, p. 2.

48. Robinson, "Patriotism and Economic Control: The Censure of Harold Rugg", pp. 384-393.

49. *New York Times*, 3 June 1986, p. C1.

50. Paul C. Vitz, "Religion and Traditional Values in Public School Textbooks," *Public Interest* 84 (Summer 1986): 90.

51. *Chronicle of Higher Education*, 16 April 1986, pp. 13, 24.

52. Warming, "Textbooks," p. 1933.

53. Richard T. White and Richard P. Tisher, "Research on Natural Sciences," in *Handbook of Research on Teaching*, 3d ed., ed. Merlin C. Wittrock (New York: Macmillan, 1986), p. 880.

54. A. A. Lumsdaine, "Instruments and Media of Instruction," in *Handbook of Research on Teaching*, ed. N. L. Gage (Chicago: Rand McNally, 1963), p. 586.

CHAPTER VII

Are We Improving or Undermining Teaching?

KAREN K. ZUMWALT

Lettering

1. SHOULD BE A SIMPLE BLOCK LETTER OF UNIFORM THICKNESS.

2. Words should be lettered horizontally and not vertically or diagonally.

3. All letters within each word should be of the same color and size except where capitals are desired.

4. Spacing of letters and words is done visually, without rules.

5. Curved letters should be closer to other letters, and straight line letters are further apart in order to give the appearance of uniform spacing. Short phrases promote legibility.

6. No serifs (feet) or decorative letters should be used.

7. Include only those words which are needed to convey the message. Letters are to be neatly and firmly attached to the display area.

8. Important words such as titles may be made larger than others.

A 1986 Teachers' Manual on Bulletin Boards

Satire? Unfortunately, there is nothing fictional about these rules. They are part of three pages of instructions on bulletin boards appearing in a 1986 teachers' manual for an urban public school ironically dedicated to developing students' artistic expressions.

While this may be an extreme case, teachers in other schools as well are increasingly burdened by petty rules and regulations that undermine their sense of professionalism and detract from the satisfactions of teaching. Such regimented "administrivia" are symbolic of much more destructive trends that are also aimed at improving schools but which threaten to chase our most promising teachers from many public schools, leaving them staffed by technicians and paraprofessionals. Besides the tendency to overregulate the behavior of teachers in trivial matters, the three other trends undermining good teachers and teaching are: (a) overstandardization of curriculum, (b) measurement-driven instruction, and (c) research-based prescriptions for effective teaching. Such control efforts, while providing a temporary facade of improvement are ultimately doomed because they devalue the teacher—relegating the teacher's role to that of a technician delivering the "curriculum."

Such efforts not only undermine our attempts to attract and to retain quality teachers. They also have a devastating effect on the actual (enacted) curriculum by restricting teachers' discretion in designing curriculum and in responding to the emerging curriculum in the classroom in a manner that best meets the needs of their particular students and context. Efforts to improve our schools guided by a control mentality are based on a restricted view of the teacher's role and an unsophisticated view of curriculum as a package to be delivered to an undifferentiated student group.

In speaking to research audiences, I have found they are often less aware than the public about the subtle but profound changes that have been occurring, often explicitly legitimized by research. Hence I feel the need to share more of the teachers' manual quoted above to illustrate how these trends are playing themselves out in some schools. After giving some examples from the manual, I will discuss insights from two recent studies of teachers in relation to the impact these changes have on teachers and curriculum. An alternate vision of teaching and its relationship to curriculum is suggested by these studies. It is this vision, rather than the one creeping into too many schools, combined with some of the proposed reforms of the teaching profession that hold promise for supporting good teachers and teaching, ensuring a curriculum responsive to the needs of students as well as of society.

Beyond the Bulletin Board

Excessively detailed rules and regulations, as exemplified by the bulletin board instructions above, attempt to control specific details of the teacher's job in the effort to insure uniform quality. This control mentality has spread to the curriculum. Earlier attempts to provide a "teacher proof" curriculum generally failed as teachers, most of the time thoughtfully, adapted the commercially prepared curriculum in response to the needs of the students and the local context. Unfortunately, in too many cases, this has led to more stringent attempts to control in the name of insuring quality, such as:

- mandated systemwide textbook series which must be covered;
- mandated times to teach reading and mathematics systemwide or schoolwide;
- mandated tests, keyed to text coverage, administered as frequently as biweekly to assess student, as well as teacher, progress;
- mandated whole-group, direct instruction;
- mandated mastery learning approaches requiring that a certain percentage of students achieve a certain level of mastery before moving on;
- mandated conceptions of subject matter.

Specific manifestations of this overstandardization of curriculum and measurement-driven instruction can be illustrated by the teachers' manual referred to above.

The school's approach to developing literacy is prefaced with the following statement of philosophy:

Reading is both a tool for learning and a vehicle for recreation. This concept must be central to our philosophy of instruction. Our students will not read well until we encourage them to read for a purpose, that of finding out or that of enjoying themselves. Our reading instruction must also address specific skill development.

In reality, however, the goal for the "literacy skills workplan" reveals a more limited conception of literacy, driven by standardized measurement practices. The goal is "to ensure that our students enter the 'minimal' average range of students achieving on or above grade level in reading (aim: 50 percent on grade level)."

"Administrative guidelines" further control the teacher's discretion on how to meet this measurement-driven curricular goal:

1. Every student will receive a minimum of ninety minutes literacy skills instruction daily.
2. Forty-five minutes of this time will be devoted to instruction on the schoolwide reading program, the KBRP [abbreviation for a major commercial reading series].
   2.1. Each child must have a KBRP cumulative record card which is maintained in the cumulative record folder and updated by the teacher.

2.2. Each child should have a basic reading text (maintained in school) and a corresponding workbook.

2.3. KBRP unit tests must be administered and results indicated on the KBRP record card.

3. KBRP instruction occurs daily between 9:50 and 10:35 A.M.

4. Fifteen minutes of instruction must be devoted daily to test-taking skills instruction applicable to standardized reading tests.

5. The remaining thirty minutes of basic literacy skill instruction may be devoted to any combination of:

5.1. Development of Word Attack Skills: Phonics and Structural Analysis

5.2. Development of Vocabulary

5.3. Development of Comprehension Skills

5.4. Development of Literature Appreciation

Mathematics is detailed in similar fashion with a pacing calendar indicating which units must be covered in each grade each month. The teachers are told that the textbook manual "guides the scope and sequence (what is taught and when it is taught) of mathematics instruction." Tests must be administered as indicated. In many schools using this mathematics system, the tests must be sent to the district office to be scored (and reviewed).

Teachers are essentially seen as implementors of a curriculum carefully sequenced and developed by experts for the mythical average class. The underlying idea is that if one forces the teachers to cover the prescribed curriculum, then the students will score better on standardized achievement tests.

The same assumption underlies some currently popular approaches to the professional development of teachers, which are essentially attempts to remediate perceived deficiencies in teacher behavior to improve test scores. Often research is used as the justification to train teachers in a certain set of behaviors which have been shown to be correlated with achievement test scores. It is assumed that if teachers only did what the research indicated, they would be better teachers, or more accurately, better at producing students who score higher on achievement tests.

An example of the direct application of research aimed at improving teaching is found in the mathematics section of the teachers' manual. Taken from the work of Good and Grouws,[1] the manual describes the "key instructional behaviors in mathematics" which teachers must follow in all their mathematics lessons.

Daily Review   (First eight minutes except Mondays)
   a. Review the concepts and skills associated with the homework
   b. Collect and deal with homework assignments
   c. Ask several mental computation exercises

Development   (About twenty minutes)
   a. Briefly focus on prerequisite skills and concepts
   b. Focus on meaning and promoting student understanding by using explanations, illustrations, and so on
   c. Assess student comprehension
      1. Using process/product questions (active interaction)
      2. Using controlled practice
   d. Repeat and elaborate on the meaning portion as necessary

Seatwork   (About fifteen minutes)
   a. Provide uninterrupted successful practice
   b. Momentum—keep the ball rolling—get everyone involved, then sustain involvement
   c. Alerting—let students know their work will be checked at end of period
   d. Accountability—check the students' work

Homework Assignment
   a. Assign on a regular basis at the end of each mathematics class except Fridays
   b. Should involve about fifteen minutes of work to be done at home
   c. Should include one or two review problems

Special Reviews
   a. Weekly review/maintenance
      1. Conduct during the first twenty minutes each Monday
      2. Focus on skills and concepts covered during the previous week
   b. Monthly review/maintenance
      1. Conduct every fourth Monday
      2. Focus on skills and concepts covered since the last monthly review

Teachers are to follow this "schema" apparently because it is research-based. It makes little difference that the researchers were studying fourth grade mathematics and never put forth the plan as the prescribed way of teaching all kinds of mathematics at all grade levels to all kinds of students. Here research is inappropriately used to control teachers' behavior in the name of improving education (test scores).

Prescriptions based on research are not limited to teachers' manuals or administrative orders. Sometimes they are incorporated into evaluation ratings of teachers resulting from school or district involvement in one of the popular staff development packages based on research. Often to the distress of the itinerant staff developers/ researchers, school administrators expect teachers to exhibit the behaviors proven to be effective. They redesign their rating systems to evaluate teachers' adherence to whatever they have been trained to do.

Essentially what is emerging is a technical conception of teaching. Teachers are trained to exhibit a defined set of skills, knowledge, and attitudes which lead to predetermined learning outcomes (that is, test scores) for students. Teachers and students can easily be evaluated because the outcomes have been clearly and behaviorally described. Increasing the effectiveness and efficiency of teachers becomes the goal of curriculum makers and administrators. Professional autonomy and discretion are minimized in the name of maintaining high standards for all.

Lost in these attempts to improve education is anything but a superficial notion of curriculum. To upgrade the curriculum of the schools, policymakers only need to increase the number of required subjects and mandated tests. Publishers only need to produce better textbooks. Administrators only need to see that the teachers follow the text and aim for the test. Staff developers only need to train teachers in teaching behaviors that research has demonstrated are effective in raising achievement test scores. And teachers only need to utilize faithfully the identified effective teaching behaviors in implementing the curriculum as defined by the text and tests. And the student, to be judged successful, only has to master the knowledge and skills on which he is to be tested. The notion of curriculum has been reduced to being the predetermined knowledge and skills found in commercially prepared texts and tests or the list of courses or subjects the students must take.

Given this state of affairs, perhaps it is not too surprising that a generation of researchers of teaching, most with training in educational psychology, have found such a receptive audience for their instructional view of teaching. To them, the curriculum and, until very recently, the content were extraneous variables that were basically ignored in their search for generic effective teaching behaviors. Those of us in the curriculum field have failed to portray the more complex visions of curriculum that we have come to take for granted. Distinctions such as the planned, intended, explicit, manifest, enacted, implicit, and hidden curriculum are alien concepts. The idea that good teachers should be responsive to the needs of a particular group of individual students in a particular context and should be examining goals and developing appropriate learning experiences is dismissed as both unnecessary and unrealistic. Surely adaptations are acceptable, but teachers need not develop curriculum: that is someone else's job. While viewing teachers as developers of curriculum is dismissed as misguided, the more sophisticated view that the curriculum is that which is constructed through the interaction of teachers and pupils, and has different meanings for different participants, is dismissed as meaningless. What operates is an impoverished view of curriculum which has profound educational consequences—policy is mandated, with all good intentions, but its net effect may be one of undermining rather than improving education.

The direct undermining impact of this technical conception of teaching on curriculum is addressed elsewhere in this volume. I focus here on its impact on teachers and hence indirectly on the curriculum. This conception of teaching ignores the intertwining of curricular and instructional decisions in the process of teaching. Along with low salaries and low status, it is a major disincentive in attracting and retaining the kinds of able teachers we need in our schools. In fact, its popularization encourages the continuation of low salaries and low status because it devalues the unique contribution of teachers in designing and creating appropriate learning environments for their students. It encourages a vision of the teacher as a skilled technician rather than a professional called upon to make decisions and take discretionary action.

The contradictions involved in current efforts to maintain or upgrade the quality of teachers and to improve education by controlling teachers and curriculum are evident in two recent studies in which I have been involved. The first study was part of an Interactive Research and Development in Schooling project (IR&DS), which attempted to discover the factors keeping teachers in New York City positive in spite of all kinds of difficulties facing them in the early 1980s.[2] The second was a study exploring what had happened to some very able prospective teachers who were prepared as curriculum developers rather than mere implementors. As will be seen below, both studies speak to the necessity of recapturing a sense of the interrelationship of teachers and curriculum if improving education is our aim.

Maintaining Positive Attitudes toward Teaching

The IR&DS research team included five teacher center specialists and one staff developer connected with the New York City Teacher Centers Consortium, and myself, a teacher educator.[3] Our charge was to collaborate in the design and conduct of a study in which research and development were interactive rather than being viewed in a linear fashion where teachers are expected to apply research conducted by others.

The substance of the research was up to us. In trying to decide what to study, we each listed the major concerns and problems facing teachers in 1981. One set of problems was on all our lists: low morale, burnout, and stress. The topic was familiar to all of us. The press had made much of teacher burnout and incompetence. We knew that many of the laid-off teachers in New York City chose not to return to the classroom when they were called back. We knew many teachers were demoralized by low salaries, violence, and the low status of teaching. The high-salaried, high-status, previously male professions now open to women seemed particularly attractive. We knew teachers who felt resentful that such options were not open to them when they chose their careers. And we all knew teachers who no longer cared, who spent most of their time complaining, and who had developed a strict nine-to-three job mentality about teaching.

As we reviewed the literature and discussed possible studies, we became increasingly dissatisfied with a focus on low morale, burnout, and stress. We were afraid that another study on what is wrong with teachers and teaching would just contribute to the problem. We knew there were good things happening in schools despite the bleak image painted by the media. We knew and were encouraged by teachers who have maintained positive attitudes about teaching. These committed, involved, challenged teachers, found in all types of schools and working under a variety of conditions, seemed to have a "take charge" attitude that insured their own continued professional development. They seemed to have a sense of control; they apparently believed that what they do has a consequence in providing a better educational environment for children. Our collective experience indicated that these teachers were easily discernible from teachers who believed that most events and situations within the school occur because of influences external to the individual, and that they therefore were helpless and powerless to effect any changes within the school system or in the particular school in which they worked.

We began to speculate as to the reasons for these different orientations amongst teachers. Were they rooted in rather stable personality characteristics or were there other factors contributing to these different orientations? After much struggling, our primary research question became "What are the factors that enable some teachers to maintain positive attitudes about their jobs?" Specifically, we wanted to know what teachers felt positive about; why they felt positive; how they maintained their positive attitudes; what would make them feel more positive; and how these positive attitudes could be shared with and developed in other teachers.

Developing a suitable methodology that encouraged the interaction of data gathering and dissemination processes was a challenge, which is described in detail elsewhere.[4] Briefly, we chose a two-stage interview process where thirty-five teachers viewed as having positive attitudes about teaching were interviewed in depth and then they in turn each interviewed two other teachers in their school who were viewed as having positive attitudes about their jobs. The following four themes that emerged from a content analysis of the interviews helped to explain why this group of 105 teachers felt positive and how they maintained these positive attitudes: (a) the freedom to be creative and innovative; (b) their capacity to influence and impact students; (c) opportunities for feedback, recognition, and support from adults and students; and (d) opportunities to share and work with other adults. The intrinsic rewards that teachers get from working with students have been a common theme in the literature. Less frequently noted are two other aspects of teaching mentioned by these teachers with positive attitudes. In fact, they run counter to descriptions of teaching as an isolated, lonely job and certainly counter to the lack of autonomy described earlier in this chapter. These teachers continue to maintain positive attitudes about teaching because they have found the opportunity to work with other adults as well as children, and because they feel they have freedom to be creative and innovative in the classroom.

The opportunity to work with other adults went beyond the developing of personal friendships and the sense of collegiality found in some schools. These teachers were involved, on a problem-solving level, with other teachers in small and large groups working on school-related problems or projects. The focus of such groups was often on curricular issues within or across grades or subject areas. Sometimes the arrangements were informal; at other times they were facilitated by administrators or teacher-center specialists.

These were teachers who also felt they had the freedom to be creative and innovative and used this opportunity to implement their own conception of good teaching. They were actively involved in curriculum development, experimenting with their own ideas and trying out innovations designed by others. They seemed to have a sense of autonomy, which in some cases was more the result of administrative indifference rather than support. Basically they were trusted to use their professional judgment in diagnosing and meeting individual, group, and grade-level needs and to use their own talents, interests, and ideas in teaching. They were excited about change and newness, which kept them moving and relieved boredom and tedium. Whether it was teaching reading through puppetry rather than textbooks or taking an inner-city class of sixth graders on a week's trip to Toronto, these teachers exuded much energy and creativity in their daily approach to teaching.

Central to their continued positive attitudes was the freedom to make professional decisions. To them it was part of their responsibility as teachers, and it was this sense of responsibility that continued to stimulate them. Denied this freedom, they would be stripped of the essence of teaching and that which was most rewarding to them. As mere functionaries, they would not last long in teaching. The loss would be ours as well as theirs.

Instead of focusing so much attention on controlling teachers because of the incompetence of a few, the IR&DS team concluded that "we should be capitalizing on the commitment, competence, and creativity of the many positive and potentially positive teachers."[5]

Student Teachers Revisited

Having participated in the IR&DS study and being aware of the many school trends running counter to quality teaching, I became increasingly interested in what had happened to my own student teachers who had graduated from Smith College and Teachers College, Columbia University, in the mid-1970s through the early 1980s. They entered teaching when "direct instruction," "time on task," and "effective teaching" were the rage of the day. I suspected that my former students were finding themselves thrust more and more into a technological orientation to their work.

For teachers educated to see teaching as demanding constant judgments about ends and means in a contextually complex setting and to view themselves as curriculum makers rather than mere implementors, this change in professional expectations might add to their self-doubts about entering or staying in the teaching profession. I feared that this technological orientation would likely discourage very able, creative people who see teaching as more than supervising workbook activities, covering the textbook, and preparing students for achievement tests. As a profession, I feared, "we have so trivialized teaching"[6] that not surprisingly we now have a shortage of good teachers.

Conversely, I was concerned that perhaps those of us who view teachers as curriculum makers have provided our preservice and in-service people with unobtainable ideals. Perhaps our visions not only demand unusual commitment, energy, creativity, intelligence, adaptability, and self-generated reflection and growth, but run counter to what is possible given the reality of schooling today. Perhaps we help "burn out" the academically able, creative teachers by instilling unrealistic expectations of what teachers and teaching could be like in America today.

Given such concerns, and with support from the Spencer Foundation,[7] during the academic year 1984-85 I conducted a follow-up study of the approximately 200 student teachers with whom I had worked at Smith College (1973-76) and at Teachers College (1976-82). The programs at the two institutions were similar in their orientation toward teaching and involved academically able students who had chosen a costly as well as rigorous certification program. (The Smith students included undergraduates and graduates; Teachers College included only graduate students.)

The study involved a seventeen-page questionnaire focusing on the teachers' professional experiences since graduation, their present orientation to curriculum and teaching, their judgments of current proposed remedies to improve the quality of teachers and teaching, and their assessment of their own professional future. The data generated from the questionnaire provided a context for phone interviews with a small sample of teachers (n=34) who had received the highest grades in student teaching. Observation and further interviewing of nine teachers who teach in diverse settings were conducted to develop illustrative case studies. The interviews and observations were designed to provide more understanding of what had happened to the most promising of these academically able teachers.

For the illustrative purposes of this chapter, the focus will be on four teachers who hold rather sophisticated views of curriculum and see themselves as constructors of curriculum, but who demonstrate a range of experiences and satisfactions with teaching. They include:

Barbara, who is in her seventh year of teaching and who is by all indications an outstanding success. But she is very dissatisfied with teaching and does not plan to return to teach after next year's maternity leave.

Terry, who is also in her seventh year of teaching and who is also considered a success. But, unlike Barbara, she sees herself teaching until retirement.

Kathy, who is in her fourth year of teaching and who has begun to distance herself from her teacher identity by taking on administrative responsibilities.

Gillian, who is in her third year of teaching, and who sees herself teaching for at least ten years at which time she plans to reassess her goals.

BARBARA

Barbara realizes that she is recognized as "head and shoulders" above the other teachers. She is given much autonomy in the classroom, gets certain privileges and choices others do not get, and is used by other teachers to help them get what they need. She has been given some released time to help other teachers with their writing curriculum. Although this is her first year teaching kindergarten, she has developed an exceptional, thematically based, integrated curriculum for her inner-city five year olds.

But despite the outward signs of success and recognition which others might envy, Barbara feels very dissatisfied with teaching. Part of her dissatisfaction can be explained as "culture shock" in having moved from teaching in private schools to teaching in an urban public school, and from teaching the upper grades to teaching the lower grades. But it is the technological orientation of the school that she finds most troublesome. She remarks, "I don't feel they really understand the way I think about curriculum, child development, and subject matter—how things can and should fit together." "What bothered me about the principal's evaluation," she continues, "was what he didn't see, not what he said. I'm praised for things that are not that important or things that I should be doing." She has been granted much autonomy in her classroom but she does not sense that the administrators really understand what makes her classroom appear good.

Very idealistic and holding high expectations for herself, Barbara has found that "what's hard about being a good teacher is living with compromises." In her view, prepackaged curricula and teaching "formulas" are just not sophisticated enough to respond to the "multiplicity of variables" that characterize a real classroom. She has a good sense of what could and should be done for her students but realizes that certain conditions, such as class size, limited resources, impersonal technological approaches to teaching, all make it particularly hard to meet the educational needs of the youngsters. And she has vivid memories of the contrasting circumstances that had a profound impact on the curriculum experienced by her former students from more privileged backgrounds.

Barbara would like to work in a school environment that is highly professional, one that will provide time for reflection and dialogue regarding the tough and complex issues and problems surrounding teaching and learning. She desires a workplace that will provide opportunities for teachers to develop curriculum and instructional strategies that will meet the special need of their community and unique student clientele. Although Barbara is aware that many teachers are not prepared to work collaboratively to improve the quality of a school's educational program, she believes that there is a rich knowledge base available to make such improvements. She points out that unfortunately teachers are not typically provided with the time, incentives, or the opportunities to participate professionally in the school organization. She senses that schools are moving away from the ideal of establishing a more professional climate in which collaboration and experimentation would be the norm. Rather, she perceives that technological approaches to teaching and standardized testing are becoming more prevalent at the elementary level. She sees this as a threat to the necessary autonomy and deliberative judgment that teachers must exercise in order to best serve the educational needs of children. She fears that standardization will "disastrously limit the kinds of learning that will go on to the detriment of the children."

It makes her uncomfortable to be reminded that she is "so head and shoulders above other teachers" because it adds to her doubt that she made the right career choice. "I feel like I'm in the wrong generation. I could be good at lots of things, make more money, and have people be interested in me. But I chose to be a teacher. I chose Smith. That was OK in another generation. Now people think I should be a lawyer or a banker. People feel it is strange that I'm a teacher." She realizes the problem is not teaching itself, which can be intellectually challenging and a creative outlet if one holds a view of teaching and curriculum like Barbara's. "The problem is me—my own insecurity. I really feel like a second-class citizen. I've bought the public attitude. I wonder if I can do anything else." She says she really "doesn't buy it," but when she sees other teachers performing their jobs in very perfunctory ways, she fears she will become like them. "I wish society didn't matter to me," she says. But others' views are terribly important to her and are undermining this good teacher.

The real tension is between her objective success as an exceptionally competent and creative teacher and her perception of how others value it. She has a sophisticated view of curriculum and teaching and has been given the freedom to carry it out within the parameters of teaching in an inner-city school where resources are especially stretched to meet the multitude of needs of the students. But as long as she feels that administrators and the public do not understand the complex job facing her as an elementary school teacher attempting to develop an appropriate curriculum for her students, she is saddled with the corresponding low status attributed to a technician rather than a professional. "There are lots of misconceptions about what teaching is and who is capable of doing it well." Hence, she feels impelled to leave classroom teaching to find another job where other people's expectations for her match their expectations for the job.

TERRY

For Terry, teaching and developing curriculum are synonymous. She left her first school after only one year because she felt her philosophy was very different from this private school's orientation. They had a different vision of what was appropriate for kinder-gartners. "In my fury," she remarks, "I always had to remind myself that the head was not trained as an educator." She felt constrained there, but not enough to refrain from developing a unit on Africa to replace the one on seasons "because there were so many African children in the class." Not being able to get a job in the public system, she found a position teaching in another private school where her views of curriculum and teaching were the norm. Basal readers and other standard curriculum material were available, but she was not required to use them. Rather she was expected to develop an appropriate curriculum for her students. In such a supportive environment, she experienced much professional growth.

Although she "was inspired" and "got lots of new ideas from other teachers," she felt a need to move on after several years for "social reasons." Now teaching in Europe in a school which is "very textbook oriented," she is viewed as "the weirdo from New York," but "I am accepted and I can do what I want." She has developed a nuclear issues course for the eighth grade which could have been potentially controversial because some parents work at a nearby cruise missile base. But unlike her early years in teaching when she was most interested in presenting her own perspective, she now feels she pays more attention to the views of her students and their interactions in class in developing a more balanced curriculum. She has lobbied for and took high school students on a trip to Moscow and fourth graders on a four-day camping trip. She is especially proud of a large history unit she developed on Japan for her fourth graders. The reward for her efforts has been increased autonomy and larger than usual salary increases. Terry attributes much to her knowledge of curriculum development, which she feels many teachers do not know. She has met many teachers who "prepare fascinating, isolated, exciting events— but nothing hangs together."

For Terry, teaching is "intellectually, emotionally, and artistically stimulating. The eclectic nature of teaching and working in schools is satisfying to my more creative side." She likes the possibility of mobility—of teaching different ages, different subjects, and in different countries, and combining it with a variety of administrative possibilities. In her present position, which she feels is not as satisfying in terms of professional growth as her previous school, she has asked for and been given some administrative responsibilities (for example, chairing the staff committee in charge of helping the school go through the European accreditation process.) She wants to be able to do some administrative work without leaving classroom teaching.

Like Barbara, Terry's vision of teaching involves heavy demands on her as a developer of curriculum appropriate for her students. If either were forced to deliver one-way, textbook- or test-oriented curriculum, teaching would be stripped of its essence for them. But unlike Barbara, Terry has come to terms with the fact that many view teaching as a much simpler, less intellectually challenging job. The low status of teachers used to bother her in the beginning. "Now I don't care. I love what I do and I do it well."

KATHY

To keep from "getting bored and not doing what's safe," Kathy likes to develop curriculum about topics she knows nothing about— like rocks and minerals or economics. Presently, as a resource room teacher for the gifted, she feels particularly challenged to buck the trend of teaching thinking skills in isolation. She also feels concerned about teachers "going crazy with diagnostic and summative tests" at the expense of teaching.

Kathy feels that the approach to developing curriculum she learned in her graduate teacher preparation program has not only helped her in the classroom and in the resource room, but also in "moving" in the public school system. Although she is only in her fourth year of teaching and in her second year in this particular system, she has already become an influential member of the curriculum committee. And in her present job as resource room teacher, part of her job is to act as a consultant to other teachers. She develops workshops, helps teachers to individualize instruction within their own classroom, works out units with them, and does some team teaching. She works on district as well as school committees, and has set up an enrichment after-school program which is open to children not officially labeled as gifted.

She feels particularly fortunate in having taught in districts where she "fits in." "If I had not gone to the districts I went to, I would be disillusioned with teaching. I went to the districts Teachers College is teaching toward—we were going to be in the vanguard." Besides being in a district in which she has the freedom and support to be a constructor rather than just an implementor of others' curriculum, she is in a district which is unique in the professional opportunities given teachers. The district is responsive to teachers' requests for professional development leaves, travel study, conferences, and information-gathering trips, such as the trip Kathy took to visit a model program for kindergarten screening 3,000 miles away.

Despite recognition, success, and an ideal teaching situation, Kathy has begun to distance herself from her teacher identity. She questions how much longer she will be a teacher. Money is clearly a factor now. "I entered teaching for ideological reasons—to make a contribution to society." Being more materialistic now, she thinks she "might have found a way of working for a cause through volunteer work instead of through my professional work." And like Barbara, the low status of teaching is bothering her. "I keep having to defend what I am doing to people not in education. My friends respect it because they know that I'm not doing it because I can't do anything else" and because they know how hard she has to work. She feels like screaming to others, "Yes, I'm intelligent but I went into teaching!"

She has also decided that she wants a "faster, more creatively competitive pace in my work environment." She feels that others are not as committed as she is, so she has to tone down her enthusiasm. Colleagues have credited Kathy's single, childless status for her seemingly boundless energy when it comes to creating curriculum and other projects which she regards as an integral part of her job but others see as extra. She sees it as more a function of personality. She has little patience with grumbling and doing nothing; when she sees a problem she wants to jump in and try to solve it. She wants to resist actively the routinized teaching many teachers fall into, not because of administrative mandate in this district, but because of the tendency of many to lead routinized personal lives.

Kathy's vision of teaching and the work and status associated with it is probably out of line with the extrinsic rewards of even her present job. She is frustrated because "no matter how hard one works, one can't get a higher salary or a promotion." Her experiences in the classroom have confirmed an earlier expectation that she eventually wants to be involved in education in more than a teaching role. The idea that intrigues her most is to open a school for the gifted. Perhaps there is no way someone like Kathy would stay in classroom teaching given her initial predilection and the mismatch between her conception of teaching and its present remuneration, status, and work ethos. However, the idea of a differentiated hierarchy in teaching positions, if appropriately rewarded, is very exciting to her. But the promise may be too far off—Kathy is now considering getting her administrator/supervisor certificate. If she is going to work this hard, she might as well be paid a salary that enables her to live her life as well.

GILLIAN

In her third year of teaching, Gillian is excited about working in a public school environment where teachers are viewed as curriculum makers and are expected to make decisions as they teach. She is grateful for the emphasis on curriculum development in her teacher education program, not only because it prepared her well for her present position, but because it "provides much of the intellectual stimulation" which she finds essential to any kind of work. Besides developing new curriculum from scratch each year because she has taught at different grades, Gillian is writing the mathematics curriculum for the entire school with another teacher.

Since she teaches in a magnet school serving gifted children, parents and administrators "know that it is supposed to be different— innovative. So they do not react negatively when teachers try new things. If you pull it off, you're OK." In fact, the norm at the school is to do things differently. There is lots of competition amongst the teachers to be creatively outstanding.

But teaching in such a school is not without its frustrations. Gillian, who places an emphasis on developing cognitive skills, thinking skills, and creativity, was distressed when she had to administer standardized tests to her second graders. "I spent the whole year teaching the students not to be calculators, but thinkers. Then they get six pages on the test of four-digit addition problems to do in twenty minutes. Parents 'freaked out' when kids scored only 80 percent on computation. The problem is we have no other measure, even a soft one, of the things we do which are our focus—such as conceptual, creative thinking."

Other problems have to do with administrative instability and the resulting low morale in the school. It has affected some teachers in their classrooms, but she tends to ignore it. "If it was really interfering with my teaching, I'd leave." In fact, she realizes that her autonomy comes partly from norms of the school and partly because the administrators "leave me alone and don't really know what's going on." She is disturbed about her frequent grade change, which is "too much because we have to do our own curriculum," and about the class size (twenty-six). "There's no point in advertising a certain kind of education if you can't deliver it because of large numbers."

Despite these problems and facing the prospect of a fourth change of grade next year, Gillian maintains a realistic attitude about the adjustments one needs to make as one copes with reality. She even admits to having gone to workbooks more now: "You have to because you cannot become the whole curriculum." She is careful to distinguish between the selective use of workbooks and their routine use that often results from the frustrations of first-year teachers. Being overwhelmed, "some teachers end up slapping workbook pages on the desk. It becomes a pattern, an easy way—and that's the end of a good teacher."

Gillian attributes her positive attitude about teaching to having made a clear choice to become a professional teacher. Like Barbara and Kathy, she comes from a family of educators. But unlike them, she resisted becoming a teacher "as long as I could. I wanted to choose something for myself." She tried utilizing her Russian major by working for a left-wing travel agency; next she worked as a paralegal. What she was looking for was a "creative active profession which also felt politically comfortable." "When I made the decision to go to graduate school, I knew what I was doing. Teaching had not been first, but I kept coming around to it." Viewing herself as left of center, she became a teacher because "I wanted my work to reflect how I think people should live and not be exploited. Teaching is a basic political act—you are working with the kids who will be taking over."

She feels she may be more realistic than her classmates because she worked before entering teaching and she saw her mother "work for years and years as a teacher." She went into teaching for herself and will leave if it is not working for her. Right now she envisions teaching for at least another ten years at which time she will reevaluate. She is not sure she would have even stayed in this long if she had not been in a school that allowed her to teach the way she wanted. She does not have much patience with bureaucracy. She feels she could handle a regular public school now. "I have my own sense of self. I consider myself a professional, not a full-time baby-sitter. I value myself too much. If I wasn't valued as a professional, I just wouldn't put up with it. I know I don't have to teach. I could do lots of other things, but I don't want to work anywhere where they value you for the suit you wear." She has never felt trapped—and she wants to teach. And no matter what others think, she views herself as a professional: "They can't take that away from me."

Toward a Different Vision of Curriculum and Teaching

Different tensions for different teachers are illustrated in the four portraits, but the key to their excellence, and that of the positive teachers studied in the IR&DS study, is a conception of themselves as active teachers committed to doing their best for their students. They expect autonomy in making curricular and teaching decisions. And they accept the corresponding responsibility to grow continually as professionals. They are critical of the overstandardization of curriculum, measurement-driven instruction, and research-based prescriptions for effective teaching illustrated at the beginning of this chapter. They seem to have found settings that protect them from the more blatant manifestations of these trends. Yet some are very vulnerable to the general low regard the public holds of teachers, with its corresponding simplistic vision of the role of teacher. The present control mentality permeating efforts to improve education not only strips teaching of its essence for them but also reinforces its troublesome low status.

These teachers are good examples of a vision of teaching that runs counter to the current technological orientation described earlier. This orientation, emphasizing a commitment to reflection and growth sees teaching more from the perspective of a craftsman or a clinician. The process of teaching entails applying the basic tools of the trade—one's experience, intuition, and understanding of particular learners, content, pedagogy, and context—in what is essentially a fast-paced, continuous, complex, problem-solving, and decision-making process. Teaching is a process of constantly making choices about means and ends. Choices are not limited to technical ones. Decisions about priorities amongst goals and subjects, room organization, management style, discipline, grouping arrangements, materials, time allotments, teaching strategies, approaches to subject matter, evaluation techniques, homework, and individual students all involve value judgments in choosing among alternatives and balancing priorities. And all such teacher decisions affect the intended as well as the enacted curriculum.

This orientation to teaching is one I have labeled as "deliberative" as opposed to "technological."[8] It was never articulated as such to any of the student teachers with whom I have worked because I had not articulated it for myself. But even unnamed, it permeated my own teaching and the vision of teaching I attempted to instill within my student teachers. In reflecting upon my own early experiences as a teacher, I have come to realize that I owe much to my first class of twenty-five seventh-grade girls in an all black inner-city junior high school in Cleveland twenty years ago.[9]

We were together every morning for a thematically oriented approach to English, social studies, mathematics, and science. Obviously, the goals of this Title I program were not limited to subject matter learnings; self-image and positive attitudes about learning, school, community, and others were of central concern. Although few miracles happened and there are many things I wish I had done differently, for most of my seventh graders it was a good year—active involvement in school, some academic progress, a sense of belonging, good times, pride in their accomplishments, no pregnancies, twenty-eight consecutive days of perfect attendance, and a positive relationship with a white teacher in a year marked by assassinations and racial riots. I do not know how much they gained on achievement tests; fortunately, for all of us that was not then *the* measure of success. They were convinced that they were the best of the six Title I classes—and so was I. I was stunned when I found out the last week of school that I had the bottom section. The power of positive expectations, now confirmed by research, made a lasting impression on me.

But my girls did more than confirm my faith in expectations. They taught me in the most powerful way that there is no one way in teaching. Coming from a privileged educational background myself, I had entered teaching with certain idealistic conceptions of humane, progressive, academically rigorous education. Yet I found that the only way to hang on to my ideals was to be open to alternatives that I had previously rejected—behavior modification, rote learning drills, and I even succumbed once to a very common practice in this junior high school, paddling.

I learned to be more intentionally eclectic as I taught and attempted to develop an appropriate educational environment for my girls. Yet the importance of considering alternative strategies literally hit home the day Robin finally learned to subtract two- and three-digit numbers. I had just begun to experiment with a new strategy to handle mathematics because the individualized self-pacing materials were no longer engaging the students productively. So while I worked with small groups, I had other students working in carefully matched pairs at the blackboard. The "teacher" was to teach the student the computation skill I had identified for each student. They were excitedly working and I was enjoying my uninterrupted time with my small group when out of the corner of my eye, I saw Tillie hit Robin. Since Robin was not complaining, I decided not to intervene. But after several more hits, I felt compelled to rescue Robin. When I asked Tillie why she was hitting Robin, she quickly responded, "That's the only way she's going to learn." And much to my amazement Robin did learn to subtract that day.

While this is not what the researchers had in mind when extolling the values of corrective feedback and it is not a strategy I would want to encourage, it has served as a vivid reminder to me through the years of the value of openness and flexibility, and the importance of an awareness of a range of approaches and the discretionary judgment of the teacher. Being initiated into teaching through Title I programs definitely shaped my view of teaching as deliberative and the necessity for a teacher to be a curriculum maker. There was no commercial seventh-grade curriculum for a group of eleven- to fourteen-year-olds who tested at the second- to fifth-grade level. Nor was there any commercial curriculum that integrated all four subjects thematically. And it was clear that, regardless of the curriculum which I had carefully planned, the actual curriculum was that which emerged as the students and I interacted daily. It was a big challenge—and also very stimulating.

Actually there is nothing really profound in my "discovery." It is self-evident to most teachers who are seriously committed to their role as educator of all children and to being reflective about their own teaching. It is a view that Barbara, Terry, Kathy, Gillian, and the teachers in the IR&DS study take for granted. But it is a profoundly different view than the impoverished view of curriculum and teaching underlying the current efforts by some administrators and policymakers to control the behavior of teachers. And it is a view profoundly different from that many teachers have received in their own preparation programs and continue to receive in staff development programs. For example, the leader of one of the most popular staff development programs today comments, "While highly related, teaching is distinct from determining the curriculum."[10] Not surprisingly, her approach to improving teaching focuses on improving instructional behavior. While focusing on aspects of instructional behavior might be an appropriate starting point to engage teachers in self-analysis and improvement of their teaching, when such a focus becomes the end point as well, a deceptively simple view of teaching is perpetuated.

Whether curriculum and teaching are separate domains has been one of those perennial questions in the field. Semantics and conceptual clarity aside, I think curricular and instructional decisions are intertwined in practice. By assigning curricular decisions elsewhere and relegating teachers to instructional and managerial decisions, one limits the discretionary freedom expected of most professionals and restricts teachers' ability to create effective educational experiences for their students. The current technological orientation with its mandated methods and curriculum strips teachers of their professionalism and undermines the attainment of excellence in the long run.

Toward a Different Vision of Professional Development

The approach to professional development accompanying a deliberative view of teaching is very different from some of the popular training models. Rather than requiring teachers to imitate certain behaviors, professional development opportunities should stimulate teachers to reflect upon their own practice and facilitate their efforts to improve their practice. The emphasis should be on learning from teaching rather than learning how to teach. A self-analytic stance insures continual professional growth. With an emphasis on empowering, the need for external control should be minimized.

The form such professional development takes will necessarily vary. As Lieberman and Miller remind us, "different people need different things at different times. Sometimes what is rewarding at one time turns out to be draining at another; what one person needs experience in may have always been part of a repertoire of another."[11] Barbara, Terry, Kathy, and Gillian would all make different choices about what would help them grow professionally. And the choices should be theirs.

Unfortunately, staff development is often delivered en masse. Even when teacher input is requested, the results are less than satisfying because teachers are not aware of possible alternatives. Helping teachers clarify and articulate their needs and preferences in relation to professional development was a primary purpose of the 1986 Association of Supervision and Curriculum Development Yearbook on *Improving Teaching*.[12] In it, eleven authors, representing a range of views from technical to deliberative and from instructional to curricular, respond to a hypothetical teacher-initiated professional development activity. Each describes his or her approach based on actual observation of at least two teachers. As expected, they describe eleven different perspectives on how teachers might improve their teaching. In using the book with teachers, I have been most impressed that all the authors are chosen as "favorites" by different teachers for very different reasons. I have also been impressed with how little opportunity they have had to analyze different approaches in more than a superficial manner and how excited they get in understanding and being able to articulate their deeply felt beliefs about teaching.

The IR&DS teachers and the four vignettes also remind us of the futility of attracting and retaining able people to teaching and improving teacher education without changing the reward structure, career patterns, working conditions, and the nature of professional autonomy and responsibility expected of teachers.

Fortunately, we are in an exciting period of change—there is a recognition that our trial-by-fire entry into teaching, where the neophyte assumes full responsibility from day one, makes very little sense and encourages a survival style.[13] Several states are considering or have funded induction programs for new teachers. Under these various plans, first-year teachers are given reduced loads as are the experienced teachers who will work with them. Hopefully, this arrangement will provide the time and nonevaluative support needed as first-year teachers experiment, analyze, reflect, and solve problems while they cope with the new demands of teaching. And, hopefully, this introduction will set a different tone for future years and encourage more good teachers to stay with teaching. But while promising, induction programs will not measurably improve education if the beginning teachers are being inducted into a school context that denies their professionalism or one in which they are expected to act as professionals without having either the preparation to do so or an idea of what that vision entails.

Induction-year programs become mere tinkering when not placed in the larger context of changes in the workplace, and structural and conceptual changes in teaching itself. The complexity of the problem is recognized in the recent Holmes Group report, *Tomorrow's Teachers*.[14] Although most of their proposed agenda has to do with reforming teacher education, the Holmes Group realizes that such efforts are futile unless they also simultaneously work

to make schools better places for teachers to work and to learn. This will require less bureaucracy, more professional autonomy, and more leadership for teachers. But schools where teachers can learn from each other, and from other professionals, will be schools where good teachers will want to work. They also will be schools in which students will learn more.[15]

They propose making schools better places for teachers and students to learn by altering the professional roles and responsibilities of teachers. This will require changes in the authority relationships in schools and in the nature and scope of autonomy for professional teachers. The three-tier system of teacher licensing which will distinguish novices (instructors), competent members of the profession (professional teachers), and high-level professional leaders (career professionals) has been the subject of much attention and controversy. If many of the difficult political and conceptual issues get worked out, such a schema would probably be very attractive to people like Barbara, Terry, Kathy, and Gillian. In some sense, all of them have extended their role outside the classroom and are involved in many of the activities that are envisioned for career professional teachers in the Holmes report. But the current lack of formal recognition and rewards for their efforts is definitely critical for the two who are thinking of leaving teaching now and potentially critical for the two who are less troubled by the discrepancy between their efforts and their status and financial rewards.

Receiving less attention, but as important, is the vision of teaching described by the Holmes Group. Noting that the nature and organization of teachers' work has changed little since the middle of the nineteenth century, their report views teachers as holding "creaky old jobs."[16] Compounding the problem is

mounting evidence that many of this country's teachers act as educational functionaries, faithfully but mindlessly following prescriptions about what and how to teach. Conducting classes in routine, undemanding ways, far too many teachers give out directions, busywork, and fact-fact-fact lectures in ways that keep students intellectually passive if not actually deepening their disregard for learning and schooling.[17]

In contrast to the one-way teaching so often seen in our schools, the Holmes Group advocates "interactive teaching as the hallmark of competent professionals." "Central to the vision are competent teachers empowered to make principled judgments and decisions on their students' behalf."[18] They understand that teaching and learning are interactive. Although not using the term "curriculum," the report in essence describes teachers as developers of curriculum rather than as mere implementors and conveys a sense that "curriculum" emerges from the interaction of teaching and learning. Regardless of the terms used, "teaching is conceived as a responsible and complex activity" rather than "highly simple" work that "any modestly educated person with average abilities can do."[19] By calling for changes in the perceived view of teaching, along with higher standards of entry, improved working conditions, and expanded roles and responsibilities for teachers, the report dreams of a day when the "real regard" for teaching will match the "professed regard."[20]

Whether such proposed changes will ever take place or whether they will actually change the status of teaching as well as the reality of teaching is unknown. In the meantime, we have an uphill battle in countering the current efforts to improve education for children by increasing the controls on teacher behavior. Efforts to insure quality through overstandardization of curriculum, overemphasis on test scores as the measures of success, and research-based prescriptions for effective teaching give the illusion of improvement while in the long run undermining quality education. Standards, test scores, and research on teaching are all important elements in the educational process, but they are potentially destructive when they become driving forces in the deliberations of educators. We need to recapture curriculum and teaching—for our many creative, committed professional teachers and for our children.

FOOTNOTES

AUTHOR'S NOTE: An earlier version of this paper was given at an institute on "Vocational Choice and Realities of Teaching," at Teachers College, Columbia University, July 1986.

1. Thomas Good and Douglas A. Grouws, "The Missouri Mathematics Effectiveness Project: An Experimental Study in Fourth-Grade Classrooms," *Journal of Educational Psychology* 71 (1979): 355-362.

2. Gary Griffin, Ann Lieberman, and Joann Jacullo-Noto, *Interactive Research and Development on Schooling. Final Report*, NIE Grant No. G-80-0179 (New York: Teachers College, Columbia University, 1982).

3. The five teacher center specialists were: Clare Cohen, Stewart Lyons, Carole Nussbaum, Anne Sabatini, and Barbara Scaros. Ellen Saxl served as the staff developer.

4. Griffin, Lieberman, and Jacullo-Noto, *Interactive Research and Development on Schooling.*

5. Karen Zumwalt, "Teachers' Positive Attitudes toward Their Work," Report of the New York City Teacher Center Team, Interactive Research and Development in Schools Project (Paper presented at the Annual Meeting of the American Educational Research Association, Montreal, Canada, 1983), p. 5.

6. Norman Colb, speaking at BOCES Conference, White Plains, New York, December 8, 1983.

7. Karen K. Zumwalt, "Academically Able Teachers: The First Ten Years" (Grant Proposal to Spencer Foundation, January 1984). Arthur Hochman and Richard Weiner served as research assistants on this project.

8. Karen K. Zumwalt, "Research on Teaching: Policy Implications for Teacher Education," *Policy Making in Education,* ed. Ann Lieberman and Milbrey W. McLaughlin, Eighty-first Yearbook of the National Society for the Study of Education, Part 1 (Chicago: University of Chicago Press, 1982), pp. 215-248.

9. Karen K. Zumwalt, "Curriculum" (Paper presented at Conference on Effects of Alternative Designs in Compensatory Education, Washington, D.C., June 1986).

10. Madeline Hunter, "Knowing, Teaching, and Supervising," in *Using What We Know about Teaching,* ed. Philip L. Hosford, 1984 Association for Supervision and Curriculum Development Yearbook (Alexandria, VA: Association for Supervision and Curriculum Development, 1984), p. 170.

11. Ann Lieberman and Lynne Miller, *Teachers, Their World, and Their Work: Implications for School Improvement* (Alexandria, VA: Association for Supervision and Curriculum Development, 1984), p. 94.

12. Karen K. Zumwalt, ed., *Improving Teaching,* 1986 Association for Supervision and Curriculum Development Yearbook (Alexandria, VA: Association for Supervision and Curriculum Development, 1986).

13. Karen K. Zumwalt, "Teachers and Mothers: Facing New Beginnings," *Teachers College Record* 86 (Fall 1984): pp. 138-155.

14. The Holmes Group, *Tomorrow's Teachers: A Report of The Holmes Group* (East Lansing, MI: The Holmes Group, 1986).

15. Ibid. p. 4.
16. Ibid. p. 7.
17. Ibid. p. 29.
18. Ibid. p. 28.
19. Ibid. p. 27.
20. Dan Lortie, *Schoolteacher* (Chicago: University of Chicago Press, 1975), p. 10.

CHAPTER VIII

Who Decides? The Basic Policy Issue

RICHARD W. CLARK

The president dispatches helicopters with troops into the highlands of a Central American nation. He joins his wife on television to announce that this invasion is but one battle in his war against drug abuse in this country. Department of education auditors threaten a local school district with the elimination of federal funds because the school district is not providing a special instructional program for a student who has abused drugs. The secretary of education issues a "What Works" booklet, telling of the problems of drug abuse. Congress rushes to pass legislation that threatens to trample the Bill of Rights as it seeks to stop drug abuse. The governor of the state, not to be outdone, announces that instruction aimed at decreasing drug abuse must begin immediately with very young pupils.

Meanwhile, textbook publishers, aware of the growing national interest, complete revisions of their books incorporating the latest problems, such as the use of crack (cocaine). This revision of textbooks also enables them to discount the findings of the college researchers who say that textbook-based drug abuse programs are having little effect on student behavior. The publishers can now indicate that the studies were done on an earlier edition, not on their new and improved package.

The county prosecutor issues a letter to all local school boards challenging them to join him in the fight against drug abuse. He disseminates a program developed in another state featuring the use of police in the classroom as a means of educating all children on the dangers of drug abuse. Parent organizations and members of the social service community join in demanding action from the local school board. The PTA sponsors a traveling "bong" show to expose parents to the horrors of drug abuse.

The board establishes spending priorities for drug abuse and instructs the central administration of the district to take action to solve the problem. The administration looks at the new textbooks that have been made available by the publisher, hears the mandate from its board, and adopts a new program for all students. In the process of implementing the new program, the central office arranges meetings at which administrators from throughout the district listen to high school students with a history of illicit use of drugs bare their souls and tell how they developed their problems.

With this information and the distribution of additional reading materials, including the "What Works" pamphlet from the U.S. secretary of education, the administration proceeds with its implementation plans. Teachers receive the new books from the publishers. Programs are developed for elementary, middle school, and high school students to assure that all children will have the skills necessary to deal with the social situations in which they will find themselves and the knowledge necessary to make wise decisions in those situations. Teachers participate in two workshops and receive the packaged materials designed to help them deal knowledgeably and effectively with the new programs.

The teachers return to their classrooms and use the new materials they have been given—if they find these new materials useful. Or, the teachers may use other materials to develop students' knowledge and skills. Or, the teachers make decisions indicating that they believe, as some researchers have suggested, that spending much time on the subject is of little value in the war against drug abuse.

* * *

The preceding events occurred within a six-month span of time. They help demonstrate the complexity of the basic policy issue: *Who decides what should be included in the program of general education—the curriculum for all students?* The issues discussed in other chapters in this yearbook all converge in the larger question of who decides. It is of critical importance because when curriculum workers feel that all important decisions are made elsewhere, they are not likely to view improvement of curriculum decisions as their responsibility.

Decisions are made with varying levels of specificity, depending on how far from the student the decisions are made. Generally speaking, as in the example above concerning drug abuse, most of those who speak from the national and state level make statements of broad priorities. The specific events of the instructional episode, including the content students are expected to learn, are ultimately decided by the classroom teacher. A case can be made that the student is the ultimate decider in that he or she may willfully tune out or become involved in the intended curriculum, thus determining the "real" curriculum. However, our focus will remain on what is intended for students. Each of these decisions is a significant one and could be studied for its own sake. To some extent, as was obvious in the commentary on the drug abuse curriculum, the decision made at each level interacts with the decisions made at other levels.

What Is to Be Decided? Some Basic Definitions

Before proceeding, several terms need defining. The first is *policy decisions*, the questions of which option schools should select in dealing with issues. Such questions are considered by some to be best dealt with at some distance from the classroom. However, because we are concerned with what happens to students, we will treat the entire range of curriculum decisions as a form of policymaking. In other words, the governor's decision to emphasize drug abuse education for young children and the teacher's decision not to use provided materials are both "policy decisions." Teachers are policymakers, although they are not recognized as such in most of the literature on educational policymaking. This must be a basic consideration in any discussion of who decides—or ought to decide—what the curriculum for all students should be.

Another concept to be understood before we proceed with the discussion is that of *general education*. What are the learnings that all members of a free society should hold in common? The curriculum must provide a common ground of knowledge, attitudes, and behaviors, and this is the task of general education. The concept of general education has existed in some form or other since the Revolution; from the time of our nation's infancy there was concern for developing a curriculum that contributed to the welfare of individuals and the society. Since the development of our state system of public education, the trend has been toward an increasingly close connection between what students learn in school and what they need to know after they leave school. (Recall, for example, how the Latin grammar schools gave way to a more useful form of education—the academy, which was the precursor of the modern high school.) In the twentieth century, enlightened leaders such as John Dewey were concerned that learning relate to the students' present lives as well as their future lives.

Although some interested citizens argue that the school should limit its function to academic goals, and that nonschool agencies should be responsible for the achievement of such objectives as sex education and driver education, schools are increasingly expected to bear the responsibility for teaching about such problems as traffic safety, the dangers of AIDS, and drug abuse. The trend is expansionist. Goodlad suggests that "the history of the emergence of four broad areas in goals for our schools—academic, social/civic, vocational and personal—provides an initial consensus on breadth of commitment."[1] It is this broad concept with which we will deal in this chapter. For there is no doubt that the public believes that the school should meet each of these goals. Public opinion has always supported, indeed demanded, more educational opportunity. The problem is not with the broad goals but with the way such goals are operationalized and with lack of agreement on which goals should be for all students. Outlooks also differ on how the goals should be met. We are concerned here with those policy decisions which determine what the *education will be for all children*, that education we refer to as general education.

The final concept needing definition before we proceed with our discussion is that of *curriculum*. There are arguments for many definitions of curriculum. They will not be repeated here, but it is necessary to say *what* is being decided before one can speak very usefully to the question of who should decide it. We have already mentioned that decisions about curriculum are made with various levels of specificity, ranging from broad statements of purpose of schooling to the description of classroom interactions of teachers and students during a particular moment. Because we believe that ends and means are inextricably interwoven, we define curriculum as the *process* of making the full range of decisions about what and how children should learn and the *results* of these decisions. Returning to our earlier discussion of events related to education on problems of drug abuse, we would say that the decisions by the federal government giving high priority to drug abuse were part of the curriculum decision-making process just as we would say that the contributions by the textbook publishers in updating their texts and the selection of specific instructional strategies by the teachers were part of that process.

These decisions at different levels are significant only to the extent they have an effect on students. It is at the point of the student that the processes and products, the ends and the means of curriculum come together. In a very real sense, it makes little difference what the secretary of education says works, what the governor includes in his program, or what the school board adopts for the district administration to implement, *if* none of these actions affects what happens between the teacher and the student.

At the school, the decisions to be made should include statements of the objectives of instruction, the determination of the organizing scheme for instruction (the structure used for considering what is to be learned *and* the arrangement of staff and students), the instructional strategies to be employed, and the resources to be used in order to accomplish the desired ends.

As mentioned previously, these decisions are made within a context of expectations established by national, state, and school district policymakers. Who the decision makers are and should be, at these levels removed from the school, is of interest because the nature of the school's transactions with them influences the decision making in the schools. Therefore, although we will place primary importance on those who do make decisions at the school, and on those who should make them, consideration also will be given to the broader arena and the responsibility of actors in that broader arena to enable those in the schools to make wise decisions.

In summary, our concern is with the decisions made about the ends and means of instruction for all children, with particular emphasis on those decisions made in the school and the classroom, but with the recognition of the broader context in which those local decisions are made.

Who Are the Decision Makers?

Having considered *what* is being decided, we turn our attention to the question of *who* is making the decision. The first thing to be recognized is that there are many actors making critical decisions concerning curriculum. We will consider ten different categories of such decision makers.

CATEGORIES OF DECISION MAKERS

The public. Among the members of the public who seek to make decisions concerning curriculum are two subgroups: affiliated members of the public and those seeking to influence curriculum as individuals. Affiliated members of the public are found in a wide variety of interest groups. In this era we are familiar with religious groups who have sought to bar consideration of ideas with which they disagree. They have gone so far in a number of areas as to create home schooling programs that assure protection of the students about whom they are concerned from the content of the general education program being provided to other students. In removing such children from the scene, they affect the schooling of those who remain behind as well. Affiliated groups also include businesses that seek school partnerships. In some instances, businesses have found it useful to promote the understanding of one view of economics or of their particular approach to doing business. Still other groups have attempted to assure that the general education program promotes conservation of natural resources, that students floss their teeth, that there are specific programs for combating drug abuse, ending smoking, promoting safe driving, or emphasizing speaking only the English language. Interest groups have also sought to break down the commonality of the educational program by insisting that students with special needs or special abilities be removed from the general education program. Like a number of the participants in the curriculum decision-making process, affiliated members of the public work at many different levels. That is to say, they are active in influencing broad goals as well as in seeking to modify the implementation activities of classroom teachers. Some of these organizations, such as the national Parent-Teacher Association, have a long history of working in close collaboration with schools at the national, state, district, and local levels. Other organizations, such as the National Committee for Citizens in Education (NCCE), have attempted to maintain a greater autonomy so that they can work in the role of the "loyal opposition" in their efforts to influence the school curriculum.

Nonaffiliated members of the public are more likely to concentrate their efforts at the local school level. Whereas individuals need the base of a recognized organization to get the attention of the media and the formal agencies that is necessary to have influence at the state and national level, individuals interacting directly with the principal and teachers at the school may have profound effects on the shape of the curriculum as students experience it. Individuals who seek to have such influence most generally direct it at the school where their own children are enrolled. Popular magazines frequently offer advice to parents on how to shape the schools to the benefit of their own youngster. Sometimes the consequence of an individual's involvement is to lead to a change in the program received by a group of students. For example, an individual parent may have strong convictions about the need for multicultural education. That individual, working with the teacher, may shape curricular experiences in the classroom with which he or she is working so that the general education for that classroom is considerably different from the general education in the classroom next door.

Political leaders. The next group of actors who seek to influence the determination of the curriculum for all students we will label as the "political." This group is best viewed as containing a number of subgroups beginning with the local community but stretching into state, national, and world political organizations. Some of the efforts on the part of the political scene to influence curriculum are a part of the legitimate role of these institutions. For example, when the state board of education adopts graduation requirements, it is carrying out its mission. However, other contributions to curriculum decision making by the political world are much like the efforts of public interest groups. When the president of the United States or the county prosecutor try to persuade schools to adopt particular approaches to drug abuse education, they are attempting to bring to bear the strength of their political offices in areas that are outside their specific political authority. Because many people do not have a clear understanding of our political institutions, it is not unusual for those within and without the school system to fail to differentiate between the persuasive efforts of politicians and their efforts to carry out their specific authority. Moreover, because some members of the political world do not understand the limits of their authority, they add confusion to the issue. During the last quarter century, the judicial branch of our government has taken a number of steps that have directly influenced general education for all students. For example, in deciding that tracking is not an appropriate educational strategy for the Washington, D.C., schools to employ, the courts directed the schools to increase the extent to which there was a common education for all students. Many instances of court action influencing general education have been in relation to equity issues. However, courts have also made policies concerning students' freedom of expression and the distribution of resources to schools, policies which have greatly influenced curriculum.

Textbook publishers. Actors who are frequently credited with making more decisions than they should about the content and form of education for all students are the textbook publishers. The process of statewide adoption of textbooks in such populous states as California and Texas not only has a considerable influence on the general education of the students in those states, but the experiences of students throughout the country are shaped as publishers prepare their texts to the specifications of these lucrative markets. Thus, when

California requires rewriting of textbooks in science and in mathematics, as they have in recent years, to adapt to different approaches in instruction, the individuals in California establishing those standards are influencing instruction in classrooms throughout the nation. This interaction between state governments and textbook publishers demonstrates that few of the efforts to influence decisions by any of the groups we are discussing occur in isolation. Often the consequences of the interactions of the various groups lead to decisions that are different from what either group would have preferred.

The interaction of textbook publishers and the political scene is not limited to state selection of texts. The famous Scopes trial during the first half of the century may, in fact, be eclipsed by the influence on curriculum of more recent decisions in the courts of Tennessee and Alabama, as affiliated groups from the public come before the courts to obtain the right to veto local school district selection of textbooks that are part of the general education program for students. The decision in the Hawkins case in Tennessee in 1986 (on appeal as of this writing), requiring a local school district to accommodate parents' wishes regarding basal reading texts, is one of the most evident and direct examples of the influences of a court decision on the curriculum for all students.

Textbook publishers often are charged with controlling the content of instruction by publishing materials that limit the scope of student inquiry. What is sometimes not as evident is that textbooks also influence significantly the processes by which learning occurs. To a large extent, the objection to existing textbooks by California authorities was that the texts failed to develop conceptual understanding of mathematics. The method of learning was as much a concern of the textbook adoption commission as was the content of the books.

Test publishers. As George Madaus points out in his chapter in this volume, the publishers of standardized tests powerfully influence the content of general education. With the members of the public calling for accountability, and the legislators and state boards of the various states responding to this perceived demand by the public, test scores have been published on a school-by-school and district-by-district basis. The effect of such comparisons has been to determine the level of funding support of schools, to influence decisions by parents on whether to move to a particular school district, and, in more than one instance, to affect the job security of professional educators. Thus, it is not surprising that attention is given to the content of these tests as the general education program is constructed and implemented. A simple example clarifies this point. There is no national mandate saying that eighth graders must study United States history. However, since most standardized tests that seek to measure student performance in the social studies at the eighth-grade level focus on U.S. history (and for that matter most eighth-grade social studies textbooks focus on U.S. history), one finds few school districts willing to deal with some other social studies topic at that grade level. Even though strong arguments might be put forward for the need to emphasize topics drawn from sociology and psychology when seeking to find a curriculum that is most appropriate for students at the eighth-grade level, the pervasiveness of the testing program discourages districts, schools, or teachers from attempting such a change in the curriculum.

The media. Noting the influence of newspaper publication of test scores introduces the next actors we will consider: the media. Newspapers, radio, television—all influence the general education curriculum in a variety of ways. Because conflict is "news," those affiliated public groups that choose to challenge the status quo find a ready ally in the media. Because the media are aware of the strong interest of the local community in its schools, national and locally prepared documentaries are created to influence decision making. That they do so to a significant degree is evident when one considers the discrepancy between the public's view of schools in general and the public's view of schools with which it has direct connections.[2] The media's role in influencing decisions through direct commentary is much like that of the affiliated interest group in the public at large or the politician seeking to use his or her office to influence school decision making.

However, the content of the media, particularly television which absorbs so many hours of every child's day, has another kind of influence on the general education curriculum. Teachers cannot communicate with students except to the extent there is a common body of knowledge between them and the students. Increasingly, the common knowledge must include reference to the world of television, a world that includes much violence and sham, and one in which the student may spend as many hours of the day as he or she spends in class. Teachers who do not understand this world end up with a different general curriculum than those who do. Lawrence A. Cremin has suggested that schools can counter and neutralize the harmful effects of aggression on television by teaching children that there are nonviolent ways available to people for settling conflicts and by demonstrating what they are.[3] Such teaching becomes another addition to the curriculum. Should it be included in the learnings for all children? Who is to decide? College professors?

Higher education personnel. This brings us to the next set of actors on the curriculum decision-making scene: those who are a part of higher education. For purposes of this discussion, we will consider separately those who are a part of the colleges of education and those in other fields. Periodically, individuals and groups within various subject areas seek to influence the general education of students in the common schools. These influences were particularly apparent at the turn of the century as colleges attempted to direct the nature of the programs of the newly evolving public high schools. Their success in doing this is evident in the close similarity one still finds between general graduation requirements and college entrance expectations. More recently, authorities in various disciplines have sought to construct specific curriculums which could then be used in the schools. In a number of subject areas, including English and biology, subject-matter specialists in colleges attempted in the 1960s and 1970s to craft "teacher-proof" materials. Such efforts were intended to overcome the lack of knowledge of teachers in the classroom and the lack of teacher attention to what the professors viewed as appropriate processes for learning. The interesting coalition of the political realm and higher education on several occasions has seen the federal government involved with professors of various disciplines in the preparation of instructional materials and in specific training of teachers in the proper use of these materials. Most noteworthy of these efforts have been various programs of the National Science Foundation and the National Endowment for the Humanities in the sciences and social sciences.

Experts in curriculum in colleges of education have obviously engaged in the training of curriculum development specialists. This training has focused not only on the development of curriculum to be implemented throughout a state or a school district, but on the curriculum decisions made by the individual teacher in the classroom. Professors of education have not limited their efforts to influence general education to this instructional activity. They also have been influential in attempting to set direction in much the same way as affiliated members of the public and politicians have been active. This is a role successfully undertaken, for example, by many of the college-based authors of other chapters in this yearbook. Still other faculty members of colleges of education have worked to produce directly curriculum materials and to assure their proper implementation. For example, faculty in the University of Hawaii, working with colleagues and academic departments, and faculty members in the public schools have developed and marketed a science curriculum called Foundational Approaches in Science Teaching. In order to assure the implementation of that curriculum as intended, the Curriculum Research and Development Group at the University of Hawaii insists that those who acquire its science materials be trained in their proper use. On the other side of the United States, the faculty at the Bank Street College of Education had a tremendous impact on the early development of instruction in computer education with its creation of the "Bank Street Writer." This kind of influence is continuing with its science and technology materials, "Voyage of Mimi," which again consist not only of curriculum content, but of training packages designed to assure proper implementation.

Professional organizations. The organized profession acts as another influencer of decisions concerning the general curriculum. One segment of this group consists of the various organizations that focus on particular subject areas. Here, higher education faculty members exercise their influence. Groups in fields such as English, social studies, mathematics, and speech not only debate what the proper content of general education should be; they also develop and market specific instructional materials designed for the training of teachers and for use by teachers in the classroom. Often these groups, as do the groups from higher education, join with the publishers of textbooks and tests in collaborative efforts that strongly influence students' general education.

Other organizations within the profession are more general in nature and may focus on general goals and on processes for development. Administrative groups, the Association for Supervision and Curriculum Development, and other professional entities may provide guidance on the processes to be used in selecting instructional materials, influence the structure of the instructional setting, or otherwise contribute to the decisions concerning general education. Finally, organized professional groups function as unions shaping the working conditions of professional employees. In doing so, they directly affect the structure of the classroom environment and may have a direct influence on the experiences of students in their general education program in a variety of other ways.

Central administration. School boards and central administrators within school districts also act to determine general education. Within guidelines provided by the state, they establish the specific graduation requirements and, in most states, approve the goals and general learning objectives for courses of study for students. In implementing decisions of the boards, central administrative staffs may seek tightly coupled solutions and therefore specify the content, textbooks, and other materials to be used, the tests needed to measure student performance, the standards expected of students in relation to those tests, and the procedures to be used by the teachers in carrying out their responsibilities. Such approaches to curriculum implementation, as Cuban has observed, produce a number of consequences, some intended and some unintended. Such central curriculum decision making may be made purely from the top down, in some districts may include top-down and bottom-up activity, or in some rare instances may essentially be developed from the bottom up. When the decision-making process is top-down, student test scores tend to improve at the elementary levels, but not at the secondary levels; the paper flow tends to increase; and internal organizational conflict becomes apparent.[4]

Teacher groups. Curriculum decisions are also made at the building level. Groups of teachers working together may determine the content and method of general education programs to be implemented within guidelines provided from other agencies, or in some cases outside such guidelines. A number of those currently interested in school reform identify the school building as the key place for school improvement, and thus, one would assume, as the locus for making many important decisions concerning general education. David Seeley, who is concerned with community-school partnerships, and Carl L. Marburger, who advocates school-based management, tend to stress that central office and other higher authorities can not be trusted. They therefore advocate direct connections between individual members of the public and the teaching staff at the building level in making essential educational decisions.[5]

Individual teachers. The final group of actors we identify is the classroom teachers themselves. Cuban speaks of the interaction between teacher, student, and content as the iron triangle, to which all other instructional and curriculum decisions are ultimately related.[6] Teachers often complain that the other groups which have been identified make all the important decisions concerning the general education curriculum. In truth, there is considerable evidence that teachers make most of the critical decisions. Cusick, Lightfoot, and

Lipsitz are among the authors who describe the absolute authority the teacher has over his or her classroom once the door is closed and instruction begins.[7] These authors describe in their own ways the phenomenon of the teacher negotiating with the students to determine what will happen in the classroom. As they point out very vividly, what occurs once the teacher and the students have reached their understanding may bear little resemblance to what may have been prescribed by the state, the central office, or even the staff of the school building.

Who, then, *does* decide what general education should include? If we seek our answer from those who have the official responsibility for definition of the curriculum in state and local school districts, one is apt to conclude that there is a tightly defined process that acknowledges the role of various state officials, textbook publishers, test constructors, district curriculum specialists, individuals involved in providing staff development, and teachers who may have contributed to the construction of the curriculum. If, on the other hand, one attempts to determine who decides what should be included in general education by observing practice, one is apt to conclude that there is much less clarity in the picture than the official answer would suggest. Since our task is not only to reflect on who does make these decisions, but to attempt to describe who *should* make them, we face an even more difficult problem.

Actually, under present conditions, all of those actors discussed have considerable influence. Many have much more influence than they realize. Teachers tend to claim that they are powerless and that textbook publishers and central office staff members make all the important decisions regarding the materials that they will use and the kinds of interactions they will have with students. However, the daily decisions made by teachers reveal that they are persons in positions of considerable power.

Textbook publishers deny charges that they have a disproportionate influence on the curriculum, claiming that they simply meet a market. They indicate that they cannot afford to take a risk by publishing a "different" textbook because of the high cost involved in creating a book only to discover that there is no market for it.

Test makers deny charges that they have an undue influence on the curriculum, suggesting that professionals do not always know how to make the best use of the instruments they distribute, and that they cannot be blamed for abuses of the media if the media choose to use the test results in an unintended manner.

Various public groups deny that they are taking control of decision making regarding the curriculum from professionals who are trained to make such judgments. These groups stress that they are merely trying to restore the balance between lay people and professionals—a balance that has been distorted by excessive grabs for power by professionals.

What should be evident from looking at these counterclaims is that *if any two of the ten groups have anywhere near the power that others attribute to them, it is clearly not possible for one group to be dominating the decision making.* Neither is it possible to describe the decision-making process in curriculum matters as a purely technical task engaged in by experts who are trained to prepare curriculum. In fact, as we look at the example of assuring that all children are taught about the problems of drug abuse, and as we consider the above review of the different groups that seek to make decisions regarding the general curriculum, we are reminded of Cuban's assertion that "curriculum is a political question, not a technical question."[8] That is, it is evident that curriculum is the process and the product of many human interactions, not the result of some single dominant force.

CONSEQUENCES OF INVOLVEMENT OF DIFFERENT ACTORS

The consequence of the involvement of these different actors is the creation of a general education curriculum that is largely static, if not stagnant. If one looks at the shape of schooling in the past fifty years, one is struck by the fact that most of the change that has occurred has been in peripheral matters. While it is true that new technologies have been introduced, many have fallen by the wayside and few have produced significant differences in the general education for all children. While the school buildings the children attend may have different designs now than a half century ago, the essential interactions between teachers and students remain relatively unaffected. In *A Place Called School*, John Goodlad reported the unchanging classroom scene as one of the major findings of his extensive examination of schooling in the latter part of the twentieth century.[9] While it is possible to look back over the past to observe temporary changes in emphasis as the schools react to the launching of a Russian Sputnik, or to a concern that the schools have become dehumanized, or to a commissioner of education's determination to focus on career education, or to the nationwide panic over drug abuse, few of these have made significant changes in the education obtained by all children. Emphasis continues to be placed on learning the same group of disciplines. The method of learning continues, particularly at the secondary level, to be characterized by passive student behavior and the classroom to be dominated by teacher talk.

It may be that the power of each of the groups seeking to make decisions is so great relative to the power that other groups have, that we have been unable to develop sufficient national consensus on anything which could lead to significant improvement. On the other hand, it is possible that we have focused too much attention on developing techniques and strategies for decision-making groups that are too far removed from the classroom, when what is needed is a way of improving the decision-making processes in the school and classroom.

One difference found between today's schools and those of fifty years ago is the level of education of the professionals who work in the schools and of the parents of the children attending the schools. However, the system of decision making continues to treat both groups as if they were know-nothings who need to be told how to perform in much the same way that an assembly line worker needs to know how to add a part to a manufactured product as it moves down the conveyor belt.

Ernest Boyer related the following field report from his study on the high school:

The visitor need spend only a brief time in the school before becoming aware of an enveloping bureaucracy. It is the iron fist in the paper glove: memoranda is its hallmark. Daily, the school and its administration face a massive volume of generally unimaginative, arguably unnecessary, and often barely literate directives from Central Board headquarters. In addition to that, there is a union contract which frequently seems to have the effect of severely limiting thoughtful planning and support options.[10]

Boyer went on to note that "heavy doses of bureaucracy are stifling creativity in too many schools, and preventing principals and their staffs from exercising their best professional judgment on decisions that properly should be made at the local level."[11]

DECISION MAKING AT THE BUILDING LEVEL

In attacking the stifling effects of bureaucracy, Boyer joins with other proponents of school reform who suggest that more emphasis needs to be placed on decision making at the building level. However, some still advocate top-down solutions such as increased graduation requirements for all students, increased length of instructional time, and the adoption of specific instructional strategies as standard practices. People who would solve the school's problems in this manner appear to be ignoring the changing professionalism of the teacher and to be failing to take advantage of the increased education level of the parents. They are also ignoring the findings of a number of scholars in other fields regarding the nature of effective modern organization. Hart and Scott, in *Organizational America,* have provided the "weenie syndrome" as one of the most vivid metaphors for the problem. In their discussion they note that "the weenie syndrome involves the assumption by the elite that the mass of people are empty of understanding and that they need to be stuffed with relevant instructions. The world of the modern organization is far too complicated for them, and they therefore must quietly await instructions from a paternalistic elite."[12] In contrast to this traditional approach is the increasing emphasis on participative decision making that takes advantage of the knowledge and skills of the members of the organizations.

Focusing on the individual school as the locus for change, John Goodlad made the following comments:

Principals and teachers concurred in the desire for a rebalancing of power toward greater decentralization and localism. It is fascinating to note that principals put themselves before teachers and teachers put themselves before principals in the preferred authority structure. The preferred order for teachers was themselves first, followed by the principal, the superintendent, and then the board. Principals placed themselves in the top slot, followed by teachers, the superintendent, and the board. The superintendents and board members queried in regard to this issue would place themselves in one or the other of the top two decision-making roles they perceived themselves already holding. All would elevate somewhat the individual and collective role of parents. . . .

The wish for this kind of shift in power comes through clearly for our sample. It implies the significance of the school as the unit for improvement and those associated with the individual school as the persons to effect change. It does not imply, I think, that it would be wise to dismantle completely the educational system, leaving tens of thousands of schools to float free from all external directives and restraints. Some of these undoubtedly would become stars in the constellation of schools, but most, I fear, would fall victim to fad, fashion, orthodoxy, incompetence, and local politics. And there would be gross inequities in the school-to-school quality of the education provided beyond those currently existing. . . .

Again, an either-or approach to this structure—either no system or a highly centralized, bureaucratic one—gets us nowhere. Rather, authority and responsibility must be differentiated and distributed across the system. The central purpose of doing so is to stimulate and support local efforts to provide good programs for the students in each school.[13]

It is not enough to criticize the ineffectiveness of the central bureaucracy, nor to extol the virtues of making use of the teachers and parents at the school level. We need a conceptualization of how these parents and teachers can work together within the context provided by the other actors involved in making curriculum decisions concerning students' general education.

The "Active" School: A Model

The model, which we will call an "active system" of curriculum decision making, focuses on the individual school. However, it does not assume that proper decision making has been achieved, once it has been decided that the school will be the location of the key decisions. In order for an active system to function, three elements must be developed at the school: control, consensus building, and legitimation. The development and implementation of these elements is the responsibility of the building principal. Decision making within the system should be performed by the parents and professionals, and, where appropriate, the students. Figure 1 provides a graphic representation of this model.

The school which has an active decision-making system in place has an effective *control* mechanism operating. Authority, power, and influence interact with the encouragement of dissenting views to achieve the degree of control that is needed. Careful examination is made of the findings of research about student learning. The faculty is knowledgeable in the various disciplines and in the way in which those disciplines are learned. Faculty members and parents who disagree with the prevailing opinion are encouraged to express their views and all examine these dissenting opinions in order to obtain a clear understanding of them. This control mechanism leads to expression of a clear vision of the curriculum in a carefully crafted, written plan.

Interacting with the element of control is that of *consensus-building.* Faculty members, parents, and students are mobilized to participate actively in the developmental processes and the decision making of the school. Not only do they participate eagerly, but their participation is

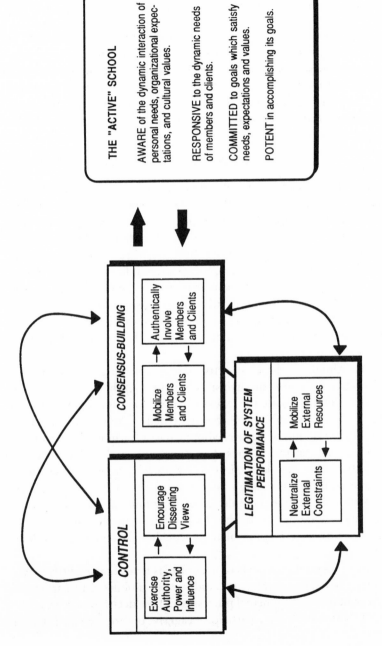

Figure 1. The "Active" School

authentic. In this setting, we do not find parents and faculty members condescendingly asked for "input" so that all-knowing authorities can make the decision. Neither do we find those who are participants in the decision making ignoring the outcome, closing the door, and going on their own way.

The third element is that of *legitimation.* The school neutralizes external constraints and mobilizes external resources in order to carry out the decisions that it has made.

Given the maximization of legitimation, control, and consensus, the active school is aware of the dynamic interaction of personal needs, organizational expectations, and cultural values. It responds to the dynamic needs of the faculty, parents, and, most importantly, the students at the school. It is committed to the goals that will satisfy the needs, expectations, and values of the school, and it is potent in accomplishing these goals. In order to function as an active system, this school draws on the authority of the world outside it without being constrained by that world to the extent that it becomes immobilized.[14]

OVERLAPPING AND INTERDEPENDENT RELATIONSHIPS IN DECISION MAKING

An active school cannot thrive unless it is in an active school district and an active school district requires an active state educational structure. The resources of each level of educational enterprise are insufficient to allow it to exist, even with the most powerful legitimating mechanisms, unless the levels "above" and "below" it are making their contributions to the entire effort.

The active school district maximizes the same elements—control, consensus building, and legitimation—as the active school. *The significant difference is that it concentrates on enabling the school, while the school enables the teacher.* The same relation should exist between the state and the school district. Problems begin to occur when the various levels forget their reason for existence. When state legislators begin to act as if they are members of a school board, or district administrators start playing the role of super principal, conditions are created that make it difficult, if not impossible, for the school to be "active" or the teacher to be successful.

Ideally the three levels interact with each other in an overlapping, interdependent fashion. We use figure 2 in an effort to clarify this relationship. Traditional organizational charts would show the school as subordinate to the district and the district, in turn, responsible to the state and each, therefore, responsible for carrying out mandates handed down to it. As many have observed, while schools are legally linked in this direct fashion, they function with a more loosely coupled relationship. While they may attempt to do so, states that seek to specify curriculum fail to control what happens behind the classroom doors no matter how glossy the guides they create. Central offices of school districts also fail in their efforts to mandate specific teacher behaviors.

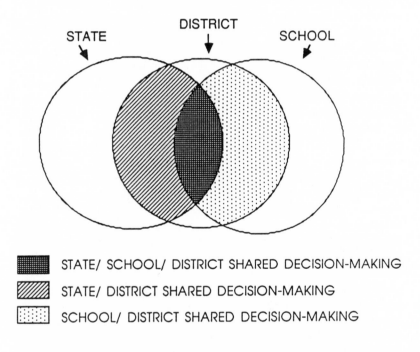

STATE/ SCHOOL/ DISTRICT SHARED DECISION-MAKING

STATE/ DISTRICT SHARED DECISION-MAKING

SCHOOL/ DISTRICT SHARED DECISION-MAKING

Figure 2. Overlapping, interdependent, decision-making relationships

What then is the role of curriculum specialists or other educators who function at the state or district level and who are concerned with the definition of general education for all students? Should there even be such positions? Such positions are, indeed, necessary. However, it is not the role of people in these positions to make the ultimate decisions about what the general education of all students should be.

Rather, it is their role to see that decisions are made by the people who will be most affected by them and that the decisions are of high quality.

Students seldom receive their education in a single school. State and district decision makers, including curriculum specialists, have the obligation to provide the framework within which school-based decisions are made. Such a framework would include a specification of the general content of the common curriculum and of the processes favored for teaching that content. For example, the state specifies general courses of study that it expects of all students, while the district develops statements of general goals for those courses of study and helps schools understand relationships between areas of study. The framework usually consists of a collection of laws, regulations, policies, and guides that district and state specialists need to be sure are understood by people in schools. State and district specialists need to develop this framework through processes that involve parents, students, administrators, and teachers along with a wide variety of subject-matter and curriculum specialists.

People working at the state or district level should not be telling people at the schools what textbooks to use. Rather they should be helping them develop processes that will lead to the adoption of good texts. They should be helping school-based groups ask the hard questions that need to be asked concerning the effects of texts (and other learning materials and strategies) on the learners, the adequacy of the texts in treating the discipline, and the effectiveness of the learning strategies embodied in the materials. (These considerations are addressed in detail by Tanner in chapter 6 of this volume.)

State and district curriculum personnel should not be selling professionals in schools on "teacher-proof" materials but enlisting the professionals in the intelligent description of the structure of the learning activities they want in their school.

Experts outside the school should not be adopting standardized tests for teachers to use to help with instruction but should be helping teachers at a school select assessment strategies and developing school-based professional ability to interpret these instruments. This does not mean that district or statewide assessment may not be necessary. In fact, in order to legitimate the efforts of the state or local district and acquire the funds that the schools will need, assessment of populations larger than a school may well be necessary. This is done to support the school, not the teacher. Recognizing this difference in purpose, the state or district testing effort should focus on a sample of the students, not on all. It should use an instrument designed to give a broad overview of student learning rather than to provide assistance to a teacher working with students.

Curriculum specialists outside the school need to develop models of alternative approaches to learning and of alternative configurations of curriculum so that those working at the school will have a basis for deciding whether to try something new in their own environment. They will need to provide information from research and theoretical studies so that the school-based decision makers have broader perspectives than their daily experiences would otherwise provide.

They need to ask the "hard" questions that stimulate true scholarly inquiry among those at the school and they need to help the school-based decision makers learn to ask such questions themselves. Thus, when staff members at a school return from a workshop, enthusiastic about the latest approach to teaching reading, the outside curriculum specialist needs to remind them to examine the research and theoretical base for the approach. Specialists need to help the school staff separate the "hype" from the valid educational principles involved in the approach.

Martin, Saif, and Thiel recently reported a national survey indicating that school districts prefer a homegrown curriculum. They concluded their article by observing that "the challenge for American curriculum leaders is to maintain and enhance the teacher-ownership model with its requirement for large investments of time, and to resist the temptation to surrender curriculum decisions to outside forces, both at state and local levels."[15]

Interactions among School, District, and State in a Curriculum Project

Further understanding of the interaction of the state, district, and school may be gained by considering recent experiences of a district in developing a high school core curriculum. The initiative for the study in this instance was taken by the high school principals as they responded to a change in grade configuration of their schools, which added ninth graders to previous three-year schools. While the principals and their faculties were dealing with this shift in student population, the principals were interacting with John Goodlad and other professors at the University of Washington who were helping them interpret the meaning of various calls for school reform. Meanwhile, the state board of education, partially in response to these same national calls for reform, had increased the graduation requirements for students. The school district determined that a comprehensive examination should be made of its four high schools. It also determined that this examination should be school-based once general agreement had been reached on the desirable common characteristics of the high school programs.

A high school study committee involving parents, teachers, and district curriculum people spent a year developing general recommendations under the leadership of one of the high school principals. Hearings were conducted with local community groups. Each faculty was intensively involved in developing recommendations and reacting to preliminary drafts of the recommendations. When the work was completed, it included a variety of recommendations regarding the general nature of the high school program. Specifically, it included the following recommendation: "We recommend that a common content core be identified and taught to all students. This content core should include the essential knowledge and understandings of human heritage and culture to ensure that all students may have a quality adult life regardless of their future roles in society."[16] The districtwide committee also recommended creation of subject-oriented task forces that would be charged to coordinate the high school offerings throughout the district, and to define those aspects of the content core that would be required of all high school students in the district.

Following the completion of this study and board approval of its recommendations, task forces representing every required subject met for a year to describe the high school core curriculum in general terms. Areas included were fine arts, communications, English, health, mathematics, occupational education, physical education, reading, science, and social studies. The work of the task force of teachers was periodically reviewed by a steering committee representing each task force and also representing wider district interests such as special education and equity groups. District curriculum specialists also worked with the task forces, which were under the general chairmanship of one high school principal and the district's director of curriculum and instruction.

The central purpose of specifying the core curriculum was to make certain that every student in the district had experiences with what was deemed essential for education. *This definition of experiences was then used as a guide for a thorough review of the high school curriculum by faculty and parents at each high school.* This review, which took an

TABLE 1

Common Learnings Example

Citizenship Skills	Art	Com	Eng	Hlth	Math	OcEd	P.E.	Read	Sci	SoSt
1 Appreciate a multicultural society in the local community and the world	T R A		T R A	T R A	A	T R A	A	A		T R A
2 Appreciate a society that encourages both men and women in educational settings and in career pursuits regardless of gender	T A	T R A		R A	A	T R A	T R A	A	A	T R A
3 Assign values to decision making	T R A		R A	T R A		T A	A	T R A	T R	T R A
4 Develop a global point of view			T R A	T R A		R	R A	R A	T R A	T R A
5 Develop and practice group participation skills	T R A	T R A	R A	T R A	A	T R A	T R A	T R A	R A	R A
6 Develop and practice leadership skills	T R A	T R A	R A	T R A	A	T R A	T R A			R A

TABLE 1 (*Continued*)

Citizenship Skills	Art	Com	Eng	Hlth	Math	OcEd	P.E.	Read	Sci	SoSt
7 Develop and practice skills that insure fair treatment of all groups of people	T R A	T R A	T R A	R A	A	R A	T R A	R A	A	T R A
8 Identify and fulfill social and community responsibilities	T R A	R A		T R A		T R A		A	T R A	R A
9 Identify social problems and suggest viable solutions		T R A		T R A		T R A	A	T R A	T R A	T R A
10 Know and practice the responsibilities of a citizen in a democratic society	A	T R A		T R A		T R A	T A	R A	R A	T R A
11 Learn and practice conflict resolution skills: compromise, debate, and negotiation	A	T R A	A	T R A		T R A	T R A	T R A	R A	R A

T = Taught   R = Reviewed   A = Applied

additional year, provided an opportunity for each school to describe where and how the experiences were to be offered. It was designed to emphasize the importance of coordinating a multidisciplinary approach to instruction and to examine ways that the curriculum could foster equity for the students. In the course of the self-study, each school was to make a self-evaluation in each discipline and develop a process to tie together interdisciplinary threads. Attention was to be given by the people engaged in the self-study to coordinating the programs they were reviewing with those that occurred in the kindergarten through the eighth grade. Curriculum specialists from the district were to be used as a resource. A list of specific activities was to be developed in each discipline to show how the core curriculum was being implemented. Finally, priorities for improving areas that needed attention were to be established and plans prepared for making those improvements.

In the process of stating the core curriculum, the district task force identified a number of areas where common learnings cut across traditional subject-matter boundaries. These common learnings were organized under the headings of Citizenship Skills, Communication Skills, Learning Skills, Personal/Social Skills, and Reasoning Skills. Staff members working within each discipline then indicated whether the common learning was taught, applied, or reviewed as part of the core curriculum for each student within their discipline. Tables were developed, such as table 1 on Citizenship Skills, to indicate how the various common learnings were being dealt with in each of the major discipline areas. As the schools began their self-study, their task was to seek ways of turning these common areas of learning from discrete activities within the various disciplines into true interdisciplinary learning experiences.

As district and state officials worked with the schools to develop a framework and then to assist them in analyzing the content and processes of their programs, they were clearly exercising leadership roles and contributing to the decisions regarding the education that was to be common for all students. However, the emphasis remained on the individual school where the ultimate decisions regarding the shape of the general education program were being made.

Drug Education Reconsidered: An Alternative Scenario

In order to review our suggestions for who should decide what the general education program should be for all students, let us return to the issue of drug education and consider an alternative to the scenario with which we opened the chapter.

The active school might include attention to drug awareness in its general education curriculum, but if it were to do so, the sequence of events in the decision-making processes would be considerably different than that outlined previously. At "active school" the counselor addresses the school advisory council. He expresses his strong concerns about the drug problem at the school. He notes that not only are there students who are abusing drugs on campus and at extracurricular activities, but there are many students returning from drug treatment programs who are suddenly aware that they have gaps of several years in which no learning has taken place while they have been "stoned." The counselor urges the advisory council to develop a plan of instruction about the problems of abuse of alcohol and other drugs.

At first some of the group expresses doubt that the problem really is worse. But after considerable discussion, all agree that whether the problem is worse or not, it is a serious one needing attention. The faculty decides to place a priority on determining what attention should be given to the problems of drug abuse in the school's curriculum. The advisory council creates a planning committee to work on the problem. The principal arranges for an expert in drug abuse from the local university to meet with the faculty, and one of the parents who is a counselor in a local rehabilitation program arranges for the planning committee to visit the rehabilitation program and to talk with some of the students having problems with drug abuse and to talk also with parents of those students. Arrangements are made for representatives of several textbook companies to make presentations regarding the latest offerings of their company. Teachers in nearby schools who are using these materials are invited to appear before the planning committee and discuss the strengths and weaknesses of the materials. The planning committee works to involve the faculty, student body, and parent groups at large in its exploration of this problem in a series of forums featuring members of a school district committee that had been examining various programs for dealing with drug abuse in other school districts throughout the state. Individual teachers are encouraged to test some of the materials that have been written on the subject. Other teachers work with students and parents to create a core team to serve as a support group for students who are returning to the school after treatment. Another group of teachers and parents joins the principal in meeting with the district's public relations officer to get assistance in telling the story of their approach to drug abuse to the local radio, television, and newspaper reporters. This effort leads to a televised appearance of the parents and students on the core team on a local television talk show.

The planning committee identifies an interested foundation and secures a grant that enables teachers and parents to join with experts from the state drug and alcohol abuse program, the local police department, and the local university, in developing a comprehensive plan for assuring that all students receive instruction in the problems of alcohol and other drugs.

Meanwhile, as a result of the public forums, a group of parents has informed the principal that they are concerned that the school is usurping the role of the home and the church in some of the programs that it is considering. The planning committee meets with this group of parents and encourages them to identify their concerns. The materials complained about are reviewed carefully by the planning committee and, in those instances where it is determined that the materials should be used even though the parents had complained, detailed explanations are provided to those raising concerns. Also, those raising concerns are encouraged to identify other materials that could be used to help eliminate some of their concerns.

While the school planners are at work, the state legislature passes legislation directing the state school superintendent's office to support community efforts to reduce drug abuse. The state superintendent initiates a series of seminars, one of which is attended by two teachers and a parent from "active school." These seminars provide information on successful programs developed elsewhere in the nation, and a university professor shares a model of assessment that the state encourages local schools to examine as a means of monitoring implementation progress. Meanwhile the state directs local school districts to initiate data collecting processes to provide the state office with material it will need in seeking special funds to help schools from the next legislative session.

The district curriculum specialist for health education and the district director of curriculum are pleased with the progress being made at "active school." However, they quickly recognize that if the initiative being taken at this school is not supported by what happens as students leave "active school" and move to the next level, the gains being made by the students will be lost. They also recognize that support will have to be obtained from the local school board in order to protect "active school" from complaints that may come from community members who have not been involved by the school in the development of its programs. With these concerns in mind, the two district officials initiate a communitywide panel to draft a board policy providing the general framework for other schools as they work with the same issues facing "active school." District officials also convene meetings involving "active school" and the school attended by students after they leave "active school" in order to discuss articulation questions. This discussion eventually leads to a districtwide seminar on the problems of articulation, which gives the district health specialist an opportunity to share the results of some recent research on the effects of learning styles on how to approach drug education.

A clear, comprehensive curriculum for all students emerges from these activities of the planning committee, the state, and the district. The plan includes provisions for formative evaluation at all stages of implementation so it is not a static plan to be blindly implemented once constructed, but a constantly self-correcting, dynamic expression of the means and ends of student learning.

After three years of planning and implementing activity, the "active school" advisory council examines the findings of the outside consultant, who was retained to help them evaluate their program, and decides that good progress is being made. Using the results obtained in this project, the advisory council approaches the district's board of directors with a request that it be allowed to take a similar active approach to new concerns that parents and faculty members have begun to express with regard to students' reading comprehension. The school has in place elements of *control, consensus building*, and *legitimation*. The faculty, parents, and students are very much aware of the program and, as the results of the evaluation indicate, drug and alcohol abuse has been significantly decreased, and students and parents feel better about themselves and each other.

The counselor reports to the advisory council that he knows the children in "active school" are part of an exemplary program for dealing with problems of drug abuse. Fortunately, they are also part of a school that knows who should decide what the general education should be for all students and how such decisions should be made.

FOOTNOTES

1. John I. Goodlad, "Individuality, Commonality, and Curricular Practice," in *Individual Differences and the Common Curriculum*, ed. Gary D Fenstermacher and John

1. Goodlad, Eighty-second Yearbook of the National Society for the Study of Education, Part I (Chicago: University of Chicago Press, 1983). While he recognizes the "social/civic" as one of the goal areas for education, Goodlad rejects the notion of direct instrumentality for schools. See John Goodlad, "Rethinking What Schools Can Do Best," in Education in School and Nonschool Settings, ed. Mario D. Fantini and Robert L. Sinclair, Eighty-fourth Yearbook of the National Society for the Study of Education, Part I (Chicago: University of Chicago Press, 1985). Whether schools can be used effectively for specific social purposes is a basic question that faces those who would decide on an appropriate response for the schools in dealing with problems such as drug abuse.

2. Alec M. Gallup, "The 18th Annual Gallup Poll of the Public's Attitudes Toward the Public Schools," Phi Delta Kappan 68 (September 1986): 43-59.

3. Lawrence A. Cremin, Public Education (New York: Basic Books, 1976), p. 22.

4. Larry Cuban, in an address to the Washington Association of School Administrators, Yakima, Washington, October 28, 1986.

5. David S. Seeley, Education through Partnership: Mediating Structures and Education (Cambridge, Mass.: Ballinger Publishing Co., 1981) and Carl L. Marburger, One School at a Time: School-Based Management, A Process for Change (Columbia, MD: National Committee for Citizens in Education, 1985).

6. Cuban, address to Washington Association of School Administrators.

7. Philip A. Cusick, The Egalitarian Ideal and the American High School (New York: Longman, 1983); Joan Lipsitz, Successful Schools for Young Adolescents (New Brunswick, NJ: Transaction Books, 1984); Sara Lawrence Lightfoot, The Good High School (New York: Basic Books, 1983).

8. Cuban, address to Washington Association of School Administrators.

9. John I. Goodlad, A Place Called School (New York: McGraw-Hill, 1984).

10. Ernest L. Boyer, High School: A Report on Secondary Education in America (New York: Harper and Row, 1983), p. 225.

11. Ibid, p. 227.

12. William G. Scott and David K. Hart, Organizational America (Boston: Houghton Mifflin, 1979), p. 98.

13. Goodlad, A Place Called School, pp. 273-274.

14. The reader will find that this view of an active system relies heavily on the conceptualization in Amatai Etzioni, The Active Society (New York: Free Press, 1969).

15. David S. Martin, Philip S. Saif, and Linda Thiel, "Curriculum Development: Who Is Involved and How?" Educational Leadership 44 (December 1986/January 1987): 48.

16. Bellevue Public Schools, "High School Core Curriculum" (Unpublished report of the Bellevue (WA) Public Schools, May 1986).

CHAPTER IX

Issues of Access to Knowledge: Grouping and Tracking

A. HARRY PASSOW

Few educational issues have been written about more than the problem of ability grouping or tracking. Despite the widespread use of various forms of ability grouping at all school levels, few educational practices have been more controversial over the years. The literature in support of or in opposition to ability grouping ranges from scholarly reports of research findings to philosophical statements to emotional polemics.

Begun in the 1840s, the graded school organization had spread widely by the 1860s and, by the turn of the century, a number of procedures had been introduced to provide for the range of differences in ability and/or achievement. William T. Harris's plan, initiated in St. Louis in 1867, is often cited as one of the first systematic efforts to group by ability. Bright pupils, chosen on the basis of their achievement as determined by their teachers, were promoted rapidly through the grades. In 1891, the Cambridge (Massachusetts) Plan was introduced whereby pupils were divided into groups, with the brightest groups completing grades four through nine in four years while the slowest groups took as many as seven or eight years. The Santa Barbara (California) Concentric Plan was initiated at the turn of the century with each grade divided into A, B, and C sections. All three sections mastered the same fundamentals for each subject but the A's did more intensive work than the B's, and the B's more than the C's. Unlike many earlier grouping plans in which the learning rate was differentiated, the Santa Barbara Plan provided for differentiation in curriculum also. Dozens of other procedures were introduced as well and, with the advent of group intelligence tests and standardized achievement tests around World War I, ability grouping became a commonplace practice by which schools attempted to cope with student diversity and provide for individual differences.

Two Reports and Access to Knowledge

At the high school level, two reports—the *Report of the Committee on Secondary School Studies* (better known as the Committee of Ten) and the *Cardinal Principles of Secondary Education*—had a significant impact on secondary school curriculum and organization.[1] The twenty-five years between the two reports (1893-1918) were times of major change in American society and in its schools. The waves of immigration brought about an explosion of population and of schooling. The new immigrants represented a population that was very diverse linguistically, culturally, and socioeconomically. The character of the cities changed as poor immigrants settled in, trying to find work in the expanding industrial economy and to make new homes in this new world. In the high schools, student enrollment multiplied geometrically, doubling every decade. The public schools were pressed to rethink their functions and purposes as well as their programs.

Appointed by the National Education Association to study the demands for more uniformity in college admissions, the Committee of Ten flatly asserted that the preparation of graduates for college was not the principal purpose of the public high school but that its main function was "to prepare for the duties of life that small portion of all children in the country . . . who show themselves able to profit by an education prolonged to the eighteenth year, and whose parents are able to support them while they remain so long at school."[2] But, while declaring that the secondary school must be designed primarily for the great majority of students whose education was to end with high school, the report argued that preparation for college was really the best preparation for life. Moreover, the Committee declared that "every subject which is taught at all in a secondary school should be taught in the same way and to the same extent to every pupil so long as he pursues it, no matter what the probable destination of the pupil may be, or at what point his education is to cease."[3] Bodies of experts in nine subject areas detailed the curricula, spelling out in detail what was to be taught, when instruction was to begin, how often it was to occur and for how long. The Committee recommended "equality of subjects" with modern academic subjects as acceptable for college admission as the classical subjects. The Committee suggested four alternative programs—classical, Latin-scientific, modern languages, and English—with different subject balances but none of the programs was designed for a particular group of students, such as those who were college bound or those who were not. Electives were to be available but the selection of courses was not to be based on whether or not the student was going on to college. Throughout the report there are statements that a subject is "an instrument for training the mind to habits of intellectual consciousness, patience, discrimination, accuracy, and thoroughness—in a word, to habits of clear and sound thinking," that a vast majority of students were capable of acquiring these habits, that this was true for almost all students whether or not they aspired to college, and, therefore, that there was to be no separation of students by curriculum differentiation.[4] Cremin saw the general acceptance of the recommendations as overwhelming with most high schools attempting to implement the report within a decade after it was published. However, as Cremin pointed out, major political, economic, and social changes were taking place which resulted in new demands on the schools and changed the outlook of 1893:

An expanding industrialism, a changing immigration, and a vigorous democracy exerted fundamental new demands on American schools between 1893 and 1918. Equally important in the evolving pedagogy of the era, however, were changes in the conception of the school itself—of its relationship to society and to the individuals who attended it.[5]

Appointed in 1913, the Commission on the Reorganization of Secondary Education issued its report, the *Cardinal Principles of Secondary Education* in 1918. This Commission argued that secondary education "should be determined by the needs of the society to be served, the character of the individuals to be educated, and the knowledge of educational theory and practice available."[6] It detailed changes it saw in society (society required individuals with a higher degree of intelligence and efficiency); in the high school population (in addition to the sharp increase in number of students attending, those students exhibited "widely varying capacities, aptitudes, social heredity, and destinies in life"); and in educational theory and practice (much more was known about individual differences in capacities and aptitudes, the faculty psychology which dominated learning theory needed to be reexamined, and subjects and teaching methods required review). The Commission declared that all education was to be guided by a clear conception of democracy: "Education in a democracy, both within and without school, should develop in each individual the knowledge, interests, ideals, habits, and powers whereby he will find his place and use that place to shape both himself and society toward ever nobler ends."[7] Secondary education needed to fill two functions: one of specialization "whereby individuals may become effective in the various vocations and other fields of human endeavor," and the other of unification, the attainment of "those common ideals, and common modes of thought, feeling, and action that make for cooperation, social cohesion, and social solidarity."[8] The first function, specialization, called for a wide range of subjects, many opportunities for exploration and guidance, adaptation of content and method, flexibility of organization, and differentiated curricula. Unification, on the other hand, called for common studies, especially in English and social studies, and a school organization that provided for social mingling and student participation in common activities.

The Commission asserted that "the comprehensive (sometimes called composite or cosmopolitan) high school, embracing all curriculums in one unified organization, should remain the standard type of secondary school in the United States."[9] Of course, the Commission with all its statements regarding democracy and its support of a comprehensive school organization, ignored completely the de facto and de jure segregation in American schools.

In contrasting the two reports, Cremin observed:

Formerly, when the content and purpose of secondary education had been fairly well defined, equal opportunity meant the right of all who might profit from secondary education as so defined to enjoy its benefits. Now, the "given" of the equation was no longer the school with its content and purposes, but the children with their backgrounds and needs. Equal opportunity now meant simply the right of all who came to be offered something of value, and it was the school's obligation to offer it. The magnitude of this shift cannot be overestimated; it was truly Copernican in character.[10]

The Cardinal Principles of Secondary Education, while focusing on the high school, expressed statements of purpose that applied to "all education in a democracy." With the end of World War I, which was followed by tremendous changes in demography, growing industrialism and urbanization, and social revolutions, the schools found themselves with burgeoning student bodies whose backgrounds, abilities, and aspirations were increasingly diversified. The relative homogeneity of the high school student body at the turn of the century can be seen by the fact that although only 11 percent of high school age youth were then in school, two-thirds of those who graduated went on to college. By the 1920s, a much larger proportion of students came from immigrant, lower socioeconomic, and minority families. The Committee of Ten had proposed a fairly homogeneous curriculum; the Commission on the Reorganization of Secondary Education recommended a curriculum to meet the diverse needs of youth. Differentiated curricula involving grouping and tracking increasingly became one of the more popular means of choice.

Oakes has argued that it was the efficiency movement, the concept of the schools as factories using efficient and scientific methods to turn the raw material ("the children") into finished products ("educated adults"), that affected the nature of schooling beginning at the turn of the century. She observes:

The ethnocentric ideas of Social Darwinism, the push for Americanization to socialize newcomers to their appropriate places in society, and the model of the factory as an efficient way to mass produce an educated citizenry all converged in the concept of the comprehensive high school, complete with differentiated education and with ability grouping and tracking.[11]

However, the Commission on the Reorganization of Secondary Education had proposed the comprehensive high school as a means of social unification to be attained through the mingling of students from all walks of life.

Another important curriculum development during the same period involved what was first introduced as manual training and which later became vocational education. Manual training was first introduced as part of general education for all students, not training for specific trades or occupations. In addition, manual training employed a strategy of "learning by doing" in contrast to the prevalent lecture-recitation approach used in most classes. But, Oakes has observed, "manual education was soon seen as a way to improve the lot or at least properly socialize the new immigrant poor by teaching the dominant values, the virtue of hard work, and discipline."[12] This purpose, together with the views of those advocates who saw vocational education as a means of producing industrial and agricultural workers with necessary technical skills, resulted in the growth of special programs and curriculum. Moreover, as Oakes has noted, "schooling became increasingly seen as a means to contribute to the expansion of the industrial economy," with curricular differentiation, grouping, and tracking becoming ever more commonplace practices.[13]

In her analysis of the growth of curricular differentiation, Oakes concluded:

This curricular differentiation was made possible only by the genuine belief—arising from social Darwinism—that children of various social classes, those from native-born and long-established families and those of recent immigrants, differed greatly in fundamental ways. Children of the affluent were considered by school people to be abstract thinkers, head-minded, and oriented toward literacy. Those of the lower classes and the newly immigrated were considered laggards, ne'er-do-wells, hand-minded, and socially inefficient, ignorant, prejudiced, and highly excitable.[14]

Selden has maintained that the psychologists involved in the development of group intelligence tests were similarly biased.[15] Lewis Terman, for example, reported that about 80 percent of the immigrants tested were feebleminded. Terman viewed this "dullness" as racial "or at least in the family stocks from which they come," and urged that they be segregated in special classes since, although they were unable to master abstractions, they could often be made into efficient workers.[16]

Research and Controversy Regarding Grouping

The practice of grouping in its present meaning reached a peak in the 1920s and 1930s. The practice consisted really of a variety of practices. There was and is, for example, *within-class* grouping wherein teachers, particularly elementary school teachers, grouped students for a particular subject such as reading or mathematics. Most teachers employed three groups although others used fewer or more. There were and are *ability-grouped classes* wherein entire classes at a particular grade level are formed according to ability level. At the elementary level, where the self-contained class is common, students may be assigned to such classes on the basis of ability. At the junior high level, where departmentalization is more common, students may be assigned to a class on the basis of ability and move as a group from teacher to teacher for different subjects. There were and are *pull-out classes* wherein students are grouped on the basis of ability or some other criterion for part of the time. Classes that provide remediation or enrichment on a part-time basis, daily or weekly, are examples of this form of grouping. Mainly at the high school level, but sometimes at earlier levels as well, there has been and is *tracking* wherein students are assigned according to ability or achievement to a particular curriculum track, such as college preparatory, vocational, or general. These students take all or most of their courses within the track to which they are assigned. There have been and are plans which combine special grouping with heterogeneous grouping such as the Joplin Plan and the Dual Progress Plan. The Joplin Plan grouped children on the basis of reading ability. Children from several grade levels but with approximately the same reading ability or achievement were brought together daily during a designated reading period; they were with their grademates for the rest of their program. The Dual Progress Plan brought youngsters together on the basis of ability for instruction in reading and social studies and grouped them heterogeneously for all other subjects. And, there were and are *special schools* wherein students are grouped according to ability, achievement, interest, or some other criteria. There were and are what are called *mixed ability groups* to which students are assigned so as to provide for "planned heterogeneity."

The bases for grouping and the nature of the groups vary considerably. As I have pointed out elsewhere:

Groups may be selected on the basis of ability, interests, aptitude, or motivation. In terms of the total program, groups may meet for a few minutes per day or for the entire school day. They may involve the entire student body or a few students. Schools may form special groups to reduce the range of certain individual differences and facilitate experiences which may be more intensive, or extensive, accelerated, or of a different nature. Groups may be organized to provide greater opportunities for children to stimulate each other through interaction of interests, abilities, and judgments. Special groups may be established to expedite the use of special personnel or resources. Or, groups may be used to facilitate the administration of certain forms of acceleration.[17]

In a survey of grouping practices used mainly in the United States and Europe, Yates reported that the grounds on which "grouping policies are most commonly based [are]: age; sex; religious denomination; race; language; socioeconomic status; special needs or handicaps; ability and attainments. Grouping is also sometimes affected by the manpower requirements of the community."[18] Yates observed that geographical location affected only interschool grouping while the other factors applied both to grouping within and between schools.

A variety of grouping practices emerged in the 1920s and 1930s primarily as a means for "providing for individual differences." On the basis of returns from over 11,000 schools, the 1932 National

Survey of Secondary Education concluded that homogeneous grouping, special classes, and the unit assignment were "core elements in a typically successful program to provide for individual differences."[19] Four years later, Harap reported that ability grouping was still "the most common method of adjusting learning to individual differences."[20]

The main issues regarding ability grouping at that time were discussed in the Thirty-fifth Yearbook, Part 1, of the National Society for the Study of Education titled, *The Grouping of Pupils*. The yearbook was published in response to "the need, for those concerned with practical school organization, of a more authoritative and a clearer statement of the problems connected with pupil classification, and in particular with ability grouping."[21] The authors raised a number of issues, many of which persist to this day. Questions were raised about the use of group intelligence tests as a basis for grouping; the possibility and the desirability of creating homogeneous groups; the social problems of ability grouping; the appropriate emphasis to be placed on individual and group differences; the effects on the social, emotional, and personality adjustment of pupils in groups; the quality and equality of learning; and the extent to which grouping actually facilitates learning, teaching, and administrative organization. In summarizing the "effects of ability grouping determinable from published studies," Cornell concluded:

The results of ability grouping seem to depend less upon the fact of grouping itself than upon the philosophy behind the grouping, the accuracy with which the grouping is made for the purposes intended, the differentiations in content, method, and speed, and the technique of the teacher, as well as upon more general environmental influences. Experimental studies have in general been too piecemeal to afford a true evaluation of results, but when attitudes, methods, and curricula are well adapted to further the adjustment of the school to the child, results, both objective and subjective, seem to be favorable to grouping.[22]

The first serious attempt to study homogeneous grouping with something resembling controlled experimentation occurred in 1916. Numerous other studies followed soon thereafter. One of the earliest critical analyses of research on ability grouping was made by Rock, who included only those studies which he considered "scientific." Rock's conclusions are not unlike numerous other later analyses:

The experimental studies of grouping which have been considered fail to show consistent, statistically or educationally significant differences between the achievement of pupils in homogeneous groups and pupils of equal ability in heterogeneous groups. This failure to realize one of the important advantages claimed for ability grouping is not, however, evidence that homogeneous grouping cannot be attained under proper organization. There was practically unanimous agreement found among teachers involved in the studies that the teaching situation was improved by the homogeneous grouping.[23]

The equivocal results regarding student achievement, the suggestion that such results did not necessarily mean that positive results could not be realized with "proper organization" of groups, and the "unanimous agreement found among teachers" that grouping improved the teaching situation are conclusions that have been regularly drawn from reviews of research on grouping over the years. Rather than resolving the issues raised by ability grouping, attempts at synthesizing and interpreting research seem more likely to reinforce and harden positions already taken. It is difficult to reconcile research studies that have such different designs, such diverse population samples, such different foci. In addition, researchers such as Rock seem puzzled when what seems like simple conventional wisdom is neither confirmed nor supported. To a good many educators and lay persons alike, narrowing the range of ability in a classroom should make it easier for the teacher to arrange more appropriate learning tasks and gear instruction to the "level" of the group so that all students benefit and achievement increases. Because such benefits do not always occur, research findings are ignored, interpreted with caveats, or rationalized. After seven decades, ability grouping continues to be controversial on philosophical, educational, psychological, and moral grounds and, in recent years, on legal grounds as well.

Much of the research assesses the effects of grouping on a single variable—achievement—and often in only one or two subjects such as reading and mathematics. Much of the research on grouping assumes that teachers do modify content and/or methods of instruction to deal with the narrower range of ability levels within the groups formed, although the nature of these modifications is usually not examined. In the case of tracking, curricular differentiation is more clearly established.

When variables other than academic achievement are examined, the findings are more complicated and the conclusions less clear. For example, in a large-scale study by Goldberg, Passow, and Justman involving 3,000 pupils in 86 fifth-grade classes in 45 New York City elementary schools, three general null hypotheses were tested for five major variables. The null hypotheses were:

1. The presence or absence of the extreme ability levels (gifted, slow) has no effect on the changes in performance of the other ability levels.

2. Narrowing the ability range in the classroom has no effect on changes in the performance of the pupils.

3. The relative position of any ability level within the range (that is, whether that ability level is at the top, in the middle, or at the bottom in the particular class) has no effect on changes in the performance of the pupils.[24]

The five variables included: (a) academic achievement at the end of grade six in reading, arithmetic, language, science, social studies, and work-study skills; (b) attitudes toward self; (c) interests and attitudes toward school; (d) assessment of more or less able peers (using stereotyped characters); and (e) teacher ratings. The presence of gifted students had an upgrading effect in science and social studies but in other subjects the effect was neither consistently upgrading nor downgrading. In reading, language, and work-study skills, for example, the presence of gifted students had minimal effects. The presence of slow students had a consistently upgrading effect on the arithmetic achievement of all other pupils. The null hypothesis relating to the effects of ability range on academic achievement was rejected. Generally, achievement increments were greater in the broader than in the narrower ability ranges except for the gifted students for whom average increment in the narrowest range was slightly higher than in the broader range classes. As for the effects of position, no one position was consistently superior to any other for all ability levels in all subject areas. With regard to self-attitudes and academic expectations, the presence of both gifted and slow pupils had statistically significant effects although the results were not consistent. The ability range in the classroom was significantly related to changes in self-attitude and changes in expectations of academic success, but the changes varied with ability level and ability range. Changes in attitudes toward more or less able peers (as depicted by stereotypes) were generally small and were affected only minimally by the grouping pattern, the pupil attitudes remaining fairly stable over the two-year period. As for teacher ratings, there was a consistent positive relationship between ratings and pupils' ability not only regarding intellectual functioning but also personal, social, and work characteristics. The lack of consistent findings for ability levels, ability ranges, presence or absence of gifted or slow students, or class position led Goldberg et al. to conclusions very much like those of Cornell quoted above. They concluded that ability grouping was neither good nor bad; its value was contingent on the way in which it was used:

Where it is used without close examination of the specific learning needs of various pupils and without recognition that it must *follow* the demands of carefully planned variations in curriculum, grouping can be, at best, ineffective, at worst, harmful. It can become harmful when it lulls teachers and parents into believing that because there is grouping, the school is providing differentiated education for pupils of varying degrees of ability, when in reality this is not the case. It may become dangerous when it leads teachers to underestimate the learning capacities of pupils at the lower ability levels. It can also be damaging when it is inflexible and does not provide channels for moving children from lower to higher ability groups and back again either from subject to subject or within any one subject as their performance at various times in their school career dictates.[25]

Goldberg et al. neither praise nor condemn ability grouping but argue that it is "on the differentiation and appropriate selection of content and method of teaching that the emphasis must be placed" so that "grouping procedures can then become effective servants of the curriculum."[26] This support of differentiated curriculum and instructional strategies for pupils of varying ability levels is called into question by some critics who argue that such differentiation leads to unequal access to knowledge and inequities of many kinds.

In recent years, meta-analysis and best-evidence synthesis have been used to make sense out of what has been called "the maze of research on ability grouping."[27] Kulik and Kulik, for example, have reported results from a meta-analysis of findings from fifty-two studies of ability grouping at the secondary school level regarding the effects on academic achievement, student attitudes, and self-concepts. Their conclusions were:

that students gained somewhat more from grouped classes than they did from ungrouped ones. The benefits of grouping tended to be slight in the area of achievement—an average increase of one-tenth standard deviation on achievement examinations, or an increase from the 50th to the 54th percentile for the typical student in a grouped class. The benefits were somewhat greater in the attitudinal area. Students in grouped classes clearly developed more positive attitudes toward the subjects they were studying. Grouping practices, however, did not appear to influence students' attitudes toward themselves and their schools. . . . High-ability students apparently benefited from the stimulation provided by other high-aptitude students and from the special curricula that grouping made possible.[28]

Kulik and Kulik noted that the findings from their meta-analysis tended to differ from those of other reviewers who are critical of ability grouping. They point out that "the effect of grouping is near-zero on the achievement of average and below average students; it is not negative," and "students seemed to like their school subjects more when they studied with peers of similar ability, and some students in grouped classes even developed more positive attitudes about themselves and about school."[29]

Slavin reviewed studies of the achievement effects of five types of ability grouping plans at the elementary school level. He used a best-evidence synthesis technique which combines features of meta-analytic and narrative research reviews and concluded that assigning students to self-contained classes on the basis of general ability or past achievement does not enhance their achievement. Grouping students for reading and mathematics, he concluded, "can be instructionally effective if the level and pace of instruction is adapted to the achievement level of the regrouped class and if students are not regrouped for more than one or two different subjects."[30] Grouping students for reading across grade lines, as is done in the Joplin Plan, increases reading achievement. While the evidence of the effects of nongraded grouping plans is not as consistent as that for the Joplin Plan, Slavin still believes that the findings "support the use of comprehensive nongraded plans." Research on within-class grouping, mainly limited to mathematics, supports the use of this procedure if the number of groups is kept small. Slavin proposed what he called five elements of effective grouping plans:

1. Students should remain in heterogeneous classes at most times, and be regrouped by ability only in subjects (e.g., reading, mathematics) in which reducing heterogeneity is particularly important. Students' primary identification should be with a heterogeneous class.

2. Grouping plans must reduce heterogeneity in the specific skill being taught (e.g., reading, mathematics).

3. Grouping plans must frequently reassess student placements and must be flexible enough to allow for easy reassignments after initial placement.

4. Teachers must actually vary their level and pace of instruction to correspond to students' levels of readiness and learning rates in regrouped classes.

5. In within-class ability grouping, numbers of groups should be kept small to allow for adequate direct instruction from the teacher for each group.[31]

Slavin's "elements of effective grouping plans" suggest that ability grouping can be effective if certain caveats are observed and that these caveats have to do with pedagogical strategies for varying the level and pace of instruction rather than with differentiating curriculum unless level of instruction is meant to include curriculum differentiation.

Tracking and Access to Knowledge

Perhaps the most controversial form of grouping over the years has been that of tracking—the assignment of students to classes, programs, or schools on the basis of ability, achievement, or teacher/counselor judgment. Estimates are that more than three-fourths of all secondary schools use some kind of tracking. A San Francisco Unified School District Curriculum Survey Committee summarized some of the arguments advanced in support of tracking when it recommended that:

beginning with the ninth grade separate, fixed curricula—such as academic, commercial, general, and industrial arts—be established. Students should be held to one of these on the basis partly of achievement, partly of preference and interests, with the possibility of shifting from one curriculum to another according to achievement. Such a system would prevent able students from taking easy courses in order to make high grades with little effort; it would prevent all students from wasting time with dubious or irrelevant electives; and, by reducing programming to a simple routine easily handled by administrative clerks, it would relieve many teachers from counseling and return them to the more important work of teaching.[32]

Oakes points out four assumptions which seem to underlie the practice of grouping: (a) students learn better when they are with other students who are like them academically ("who know about the same things, who learn at the same rate, or who are expected to have similar futures"), so that bright students are not held back and slower students are more easily remediated; (b) slower students develop more positive self-concepts and attitudes about themselves as learners when not in classes with much more able students; (c) the placement processes and decisions are accurate, fair, and appropriate for future learning; and (d) teachers are better able to accommodate individual differences in homogeneous groups that are easier to teach and to manage.[33] As a critic of tracking, Oakes challenges all four assumptions.

Esposito has described the rationale for tracking and grouping as follows:

homogeneous grouping takes individual differences into account by allowing students to advance at their own rate with others of similar ability, and by offering them methods and materials geared to their level; more individual attention from teachers is possible; students are challenged to do their best in their group, or to be promoted to the next level, within a realistic range of competition; and it is easier to teach to and provide materials for a narrower range of ability.[34]

Critics of tracking, such as Schafer and Olexa, argue that: (a) the procedures used for assigning students to a track discriminate against those from lower-income or minority group families intentionally or unintentionally since the tests and teacher judgments are weighted in favor of white middle-class students; (b) "the organizational processes of curriculum assignment are complex, with assumptions made by counselors about the character, adjustment, and alleged potential of incoming students playing an important part in the decision"; (c) the system locks students into educational and occupational career lines prematurely and provides little or no chance for shifting later on; (d) compared to the program offered students in the upper tracks, the education provided lower-track students is of inferior quality resulting from "damaged self-esteem because of the stigma attached to lower tracks, poor peer models, dull subject matter, and ineffective and uninspired teaching"; (e) by imposing economic and racial segregation on the classroom and limiting contact with students with other backgrounds, the school system "fails to prepare students for effective living in an open, multiethnic society"; and (f) tracking actually contributes to the problems schools seek to prevent such as rebelliousness, dropping out, and delinquency by alienating youth, developing negative self-concepts, and lowering their aspirations for the future.[35]

Acknowledging the highly controversial nature of ability grouping in his 1959 study, *The American High School Today*, Conant recommended that in "the required subjects and those elected by students with a wide range of ability [for example, English, American history, ninth-grade algebra, biology, and physical science] the students should be grouped according to ability, subject by subject" into at least three levels—more able, average, and slow readers with the middle group divided into two or three sections.[36] Conant did not want this type of grouping "to be confused with across-the-board grouping [that is, tracking] in which a given student is placed in a particular section in *all* courses."[37]

In his *Paideia Proposal*, Adler describes a multitrack system as "an abominable discrimination" aiming undemocratically at different goals for different groups of children. In a democracy, he argues, there must be the same educational objectives for all, the same course of study for all, and the completion of "this required course of study with a satisfactory standard of accomplishment regardless of native ability, temperamental bent, or conscious preferences."[38] Adler proposes adjusting for individual differences by administering the program "sensitively and flexibly in ways that accord with whatever differences must be taken into account."[39]

Drawing on the same data that Oakes collected for "A Study of Schooling," both Goodlad and Boyer are critical of tracking and ability grouping in their respective reports, *A Place Called School* and *High School*.[40] Boyer observes that: "Curriculum decisions are shaped *most* decisively perhaps by the program or "track" in which a student is enrolled—academic, vocational, or general."[41] The academic track is the most rigorous with the most number of "solid" subjects and its aim is college preparatory. The general track has few academic courses, many more electives, and is more open-ended. Boyer attributes an enrollment jump in the general track from 12 percent in the 1960s to 42.5 percent in the late 1970s to the addition of a variety of "more attractive" courses, to the growth of two-year community colleges, and to the lowering of admissions requirements in four-year colleges. The vocational track for students who will join the work force after graduation includes a core of academic courses plus five or six job-related courses.[42] Resnick and Resnick have observed that with multiple tracks there are different curriculum standards operating simultaneously in high schools: "Although everyone is expected to complete high school and to offer the requisite number of Carnegie units in order to receive a diploma, we have several different tracks or programs that students may follow—each with a different set of requirements." The consequence, they believe, is that "there is no sensible way to address the question of curriculum standards in general."[43]

Goodlad sees tracking practices as creating the myth that there are two kinds of students—those who are "head oriented" and those who are "hand oriented," fast and slow learners, good and poor students, college bound and bound for the workplace. Tracking, he argues, results in a separation between the kinds of curriculum content studied by students in different tracks. Goodlad concludes that:

> This relentless process is justified by resorting, on one hand, to the myth of inevitable and irrevocable human variability and, on the other, to the popular rhetoric of providing for individual differences in learning. A self-fulfilling prophecy appearing to "prove" the prevailing assumptions is created. Practices justified as providing for human individuality appear, rather, to result in giving up on many individuals.[44]

Believing that it is the poor, the minority, and the otherwise disadvantaged students who are blocked from having access to the knowledge they need to advantage them, Goodlad urges that tracking be prohibited since it "serves as an organizational device for hiding awareness of the problem rather than an educative means for correcting it. The decision to track is essentially one of giving up on the problem of human variability in learning. It is a retreat rather than a strategy."[45] The solution Goodlad offers is to abolish all grouping and tracking; to provide "a common core of studies from which students cannot escape through electives, even though the proposed electives purport to be in the same domain of knowledge"; to eliminate all grouping of students on the basis of past performance and random assignment of students to heterogeneous classes; to have better professional preparation of teachers, involving their attitudes, knowledge, and pedagogy—all aimed at offering "the most equity with respect to gaining access to knowledge while still preserving the more advantageous content and teaching practices of the upper tracks."[46]

Fenstermacher, like Goodlad and other critics of grouping and tracking, agrees that individual differences do exist and that some differences are perceived as being so important that they justify differences in what is taught and how, but exactly "what these important individual differences are is not always clear, nor is it in most cases obvious what specific curricular or instructional variations ought to follow from important individual differences."[47] It is the use of curricular and organizational variations, rather than instructional variations, to accommodate to individual differences that denies students equal access to knowledge with such disastrous consequences. Fenstermacher asserts:

No theory of education known to us permits such selective access to knowledge and ideas based upon individual differences in aptitude, ability, or interest. Of course, it is possible that some students may not benefit equally from unrestricted access to knowledge, but this fact does not entitle us to control access in ways that effectively prohibit all students from encountering what Dewey called "the funded capital of civilization."[48]

Can the Issues Be Resolved?

Despite the continued outpouring of criticisms of ability grouping and tracking over the years, it seems clear that these practices persist, have been increasing, and are being used at earlier and earlier grade levels. This is true for many nations, not just the United States. Why this is so has been the object of speculation. The critics assert that schools are agents of cultural reproduction, or that they promulgate a meritocratic system, or that they are locked into inadequate and inappropriate technologies. The proponents assert that grouping is needed to nurture individual potential to the fullest and that there are no better techniques or procedures. Strong arguments can be and are advanced for each of these positions and others as well.

Of the number of issues raised two seem most critical: Can the twin goals of equity and excellence be attained so long as students are grouped and tracked? Is there some appropriate balance to be maintained between curricular uniformity and curricular diversity? Schafer and Olexa put it another way when they asserted that schools must address two major problems: (a) "ensuring equality of opportunity for students now 'locked out' by tracking" and (b) "offering—to all students—a far more fulfilling and satisfying learning experience."[49] In all probability, the solution to the equity-and-excellence and uniformity-versus-diversity issues lies somewhere between the position, on the one hand, that all forms of grouping should be abolished and the same goals and curriculum provided for all, and the position, on the other hand, that there is nothing wrong with grouping since it represents the most effective and efficient way of providing for individual differences.

Over the past seven decades a good deal has been learned about the nature of individual differences among learners and about the consequences of the organizational settings within which instruction takes place. It is clear that learning pace and "ability" are not the only factors affecting what is learned and how. Each learner brings into the classroom or setting certain potentials, aptitudes, values, attitudes, aspirations, perceptions, and other traits and behaviors that affect what is learned and how it is learned. Each individual interacts with the other students, the teachers, the materials, the classroom climate, and other factors of the learning environment. Verbal and/or numerical ability are not the sole determiners of learning. Some individual differences make a difference in learning and instruction and others do not or are less significant.

It has long been clear that there is no such thing as a "homogeneous group." The range of a few differences can be reduced by grouping but on all other variables there continues to be considerable diversity. Moreover, research has established the fact that various forms of grouping have different cognitive and affective outcomes on students of different ability levels in different subject areas. A single, inflexible approach to grouping is, therefore, inappropriate. As Goldberg et al. pointed out, emphasis must be placed on the differentiation and appropriate selection of content and methods of teaching if grouping procedures are to become "effective servants of the curriculum."

There is no question that grouping practices have both cognitive and affective outcomes but, despite the claims of both proponents and opponents, these are neither unidirectionally good nor bad. Those advocates of procedures such as mastery learning, cooperative learning, nongraded classes, new technology, and other techniques as substitutes for grouping add to the alternatives for pedagogical differentiation but do not provide a complete solution to the problems of differentiation any more than does ability grouping.

"Locking out" students from equal access to knowledge is clearly not a practice educators should support in a democratic society. Where grouping institutionalizes expectancies by classifying and labeling students, condemning some to inferior programs and limiting their educational opportunities while encouraging and challenging others, it is clearly an inappropriate practice, both educationally and morally. But grouping is neither the black nor white, good nor bad, right nor wrong practice about which most debates revolve. In our concern for equal access to knowledge, the basic question still remains that of *what knowledge*. Does all schooling consist of common and identical knowledge? Goodlad has argued that:

our increased knowledge of individual differences and individuality demands more creative, sophisticated, professional approaches to engaging learners in common curricula extending beyond elementary education. If knowledge is to be increasingly democratized—that is, extended to larger percentages of the population for longer periods of time—then it simultaneously must be increasingly humanized—that is, rendered in such a way as to be learnable. In effect, increasing the commonality of curricula calls for increasing the uncommonality or diversity of pedagogy.[50]

Increasing diversity of instructional or pedagogical differentiation is obviously necessary. Schools presumably serve a number of functions, including those which the Commission on the Reorganization of Secondary Education called unification and specialization. Can both functions be fulfilled by a common curriculum? Is a common curriculum an identical curriculum for all? Is a common curriculum appropriate for the general education function while a differentiated curriculum is needed to fulfill the specialization function? If a case can be made for a common curriculum with equal access to knowledge for the general education function of schools, it is possible that an equally strong case can be made for a differentiated curriculum with access to different knowledge for the specialization function. The concern for equal access to knowledge must not become the focus for more doctrinaire thinking as has the debate on ability grouping.

Grouping and tracking are organizational procedures intended to facilitate learning and teaching. What is needed is flexibility and more attention to questions like *What kinds of grouping* are needed—together with other elements of curriculum and instruction—to facilitate and enhance learning and teaching? What common knowledge and what different knowledge is needed and what processes contribute to making such knowledge accessible to learners with diverse needs and cognitive and affective characteristics? In asking these kinds of questions, we may come to see the questions regarding grouping and tracking and the impact of these practices on access to knowledge from a different perspective.

FOOTNOTES

1. Committee on Secondary School Studies, *Report of the Committee on Secondary School Studies* (Washington, DC: U.S. Government Printing Office, 1893); Commission on the Reorganization of Secondary Education, *Cardinal Principles of Secondary Education*, Bulletin 1918, No. 35 (Washington, DC: U.S. Government Printing Office, 1918).

2. Committee on Secondary School Studies, *Report of the Committee on Secondary School Studies*, pp. 52-53.

3. Ibid., p. 17.

4. Ibid.

5. Lawrence A. Cremin, "The Revolution in American Secondary Education, 1893-1918," *Teachers College Record* 56 (March 1955): 301.

6. Commission on the Reorganization of Secondary Education, *Cardinal Principles of Secondary Education*, p. 1.

7. Ibid., p. 20.

8. Ibid., p. 16.

9. Ibid.

10. Lawrence A. Cremin, "The Problem of Curriculum Making: An Historical Perspective," in *What Shall the High Schools Teach?* 1956 Yearbook of the Association for Supervision and Curriculum Development (Washington DC: Association for Supervision and Curriculum Development, 1956), pp. 17-18.

11. Jeannie Oakes, *Keeping Track: How Schools Structure Inequality* (New Haven, CT: Yale University Press, 1985), p. 30.

12. Ibid., p. 31.

13. Ibid., p. 32.

14. Ibid., p. 35.

15. Steven Selden, "Education Policy and Biological Science: Genetics, Eugenics, and the College Textbook c. 1908-1931," *Teachers College Record* 87 (Fall 1985): 35-51.

16. Lewis M. Terman, *The Measurement of Intelligence*, cited in Samuel Bowles and Herbert Gintis, *Schooling in Capitalist America* (New York: Basic Books, 1976), p. 123.

17. A. Harry Passow, "Enrichment of Education for the Gifted," in *Education for the Gifted*, ed. Nelson B. Henry, Fifty-seventh Yearbook of the National Society for the Study of Education, Part 1 (Chicago: University of Chicago Press, 1958), p. 204.

18. Alfred Yates, ed., *Grouping in Education* (New York: John Wiley and Sons, 1966), p. 20.

19. Roy O. Billett, *Provisions for Individual Differences, Marking, and Promotion*, Bulletin 1932, No. 17, National Survey of Education Monograph No. 13 (Washington, DC: U.S. Government Printing Office, 1933), p. 11.

20. Henry Harap, "Differentiation of Curriculum Practices and Instruction in Elementary Schools," in *The Grouping of Pupils*, ed. Guy M. Whipple, Thirty-fifth Yearbook of the National Society for the Study of Education, Part 1 (Bloomington, IL: Public School Publishing Co., 1936), p. 163.

21. Guy M. Whipple, "Editor's Preface," in *The Grouping of Pupils*, ed. Whipple, p. ix.

22. Ethel L. Cornell, "Effects of Ability Grouping Determinable from Published Studies," in *The Grouping of Pupils*, ed. Whipple, p. 304.

23. Robert T. Rock, Jr., *A Critical Study of Current Practices in Ability Grouping*, *Educational Research Bulletins* 4, nos. 5, 6 (1929): 125.

24. Miriam L. Goldberg, A. Harry Passow, and Joseph Justman, *The Effects of Ability Grouping* (New York: Teachers College Press, 1966), p. 154.

25. Ibid., p. 168.

26. Ibid., p. 169.

27. A. Harry Passow, "The Maze of the Research on Ability Grouping," *Educational Forum* 26 (March 1962): 281-288.

28. Chen-Lin Kulik and James A. Kulik, "Effects of Ability Grouping on Secondary School Students: A Meta-Analysis of Evaluation Findings," *American Educational Research Journal* 19 (Fall 1982): 425.

29. Ibid., p. 426.

30. Robert E. Slavin, *Ability Grouping and Student Achievement in Elementary Schools: A Best-Evidence Synthesis* (Baltimore, MD: Center for Research on Elementary and Middle Schools, Johns Hopkins University, 1986), p. 74.

31. Ibid., p. 76.

32. Walter E. Schafer and Carol Olexa, *Tracking and Opportunity: The Locking-Out Process and Beyond* (Scranton, PA: Chandler Publishing Co., 1971), p. 10.

33. Jeannie Oakes, *Keeping Track*, pp. 6-7.

34. Dominick Esposito, "Homogeneous and Heterogeneous Ability Grouping: Principal Findings and Implications for Evaluating and Designing More Effective Educational Environments," *Review of Educational Research* 43 (Spring 1973): 166.

35. Schafer and Olexa, *Tracking and Opportunity*, pp. 11-14.

36. James B. Conant, *The American High School Today* (New York: McGraw-Hill, 1959), p. 49.

37. Ibid.

38. Mortimer Adler, *The Paideia Proposal: An Educational Manifesto* (New York: Macmillan, 1982), p. 43.

39. Ibid., p. 44.

40. John I. Goodlad, *A Place Called School* (New York: McGraw-Hill, 1984); Ernest L. Boyer, *High School: A Report on Secondary Education in America* (New York: Harper and Row, 1983).

41. Boyer, *High School*, p. 79.

42. Ibid., pp. 79-80.

43. Ibid., p. 81.

44. Goodlad, *A Place Called School*, p. 165.

45. Ibid., p. 297.

46. Ibid.

47. Gary D Fenstermacher, "Introduction," in *Individual Differences and the Common Curriculum*, ed. Gary D Fenstermacher and John I. Goodlad, Eighty-second Yearbook of the National Society for the Study of Education, Part 1 (Chicago: University of Chicago Press, 1983), p. 1.

48. Ibid., p. 3.

49. Schafer and Olexa, *Tracking and Opportunity*, p. 73.

50. John I. Goodlad, "Individuality, Commonality, and Curricular Practice," in *Individual Differences and the Common Curriculum*, ed. Fenstermacher and Goodlad, p. 304.

CHAPTER X

Issues of Access to Knowledge: Dropping Out of School

MURRY R. NELSON

"There can be no 'Dropout Curriculum'—even a curriculum for 'Potential Dropouts' often affronts both principles and sensitivity and is considered 'second class.' "[1] So wrote William H. Bristow in 1964, who added that "no self-respecting dropout wants to be *so* identified, or *so* labeled or handled."[2] For Bristow, the best hope for dealing with the dropout problem was a good curriculum—for all children. That is substantially the thesis on which this chapter is based: by following approved educational practices rather than encouraging students who do not do well to leave school we can reduce dropouts. Heterogeneous grouping, clarity of instruction, a life-related curriculum, and help for children who cannot keep up with the class are some characteristics of programs where children remain in school.

The idea that the school's holding power is related to what is taught and how it is taught is hardly new. Before World War I, proponents of the junior high school argued that if programs provided the opportunity for election of courses in accord with students' interests and aptitudes, students would be held through the period when most dropping out took place—the period from ages twelve through fifteen. General exploratory courses in the junior high school were intended to reveal to the students the possibilities of a general field of knowledge (such as science) and to whet the appetite for more. These courses were to be life related. According to Thomas H. Briggs, the junior high school was the outcome of criticism from the public, "as it has been unable to keep in the high schools its children, who have neither succeeded nor been satisfied with the traditional offerings."[3]

Briggs knew well that administrative reorganization does not bring about changes in methods of instruction. "Reorganization offers an opportunity rather than assures an ideal."[4] The results would depend on whether the ideal was clear on the part of teachers and administrators, on whether they believed in it, and on the education and supervision of teachers. This is no less true today.

Our forebears were concerned with increasing the "holding power" of the school so that students who left after the eighth grade would stay until the ninth or tenth grade. Today because of the general view that the public school should educate everyone through high school, we are concerned about the "dropout problem." The difference is more than semantic; there has been a subtle shift from the school to the child as the problem. Briggs's generation attempted to improve the school's holding power by developing a diversified curriculum that met a wide range of interests and levels of talent, that offered an effective program of vocational education and academic studies, keeping the lines between the areas of study fluid. Today, dropping out is all too frequently viewed as a problem in the functioning of the individual; he or she must improve, not the curriculum. In the words of the New York State task force on minority dropouts:

The programs seem to be based on blaming the victim while letting teachers and administrators go on with whatever they've been doing. There is no focus on changing teachers' or administrators' attitudes or teaching styles. *There is no suggestion of curriculum revision or creation of new instructional materials.*[5]

Every so often we view the dropout as a problem; the last time was in the Johnson administration with its short-lived War on Poverty. In my view, if teachers continually encouraged young people to remain in school and the encouragement was supported by the way learning experiences were handled, then dropout projects would be unnecessary. In our lifetime we have all seen numerous projects and programs of various kinds inaugurated, only to see them give way to the next real or imagined educational crisis. In the 1960s, the School Dropout Project of the National Education Association suffered this fate.

Curriculum workers and teachers should always seek materials and methods that make the school day more attractive as well as more genuinely educational. Curriculum improvement should be ongoing, not a response to one of the innumerable crises that give rise to educational reform movements. The alternative is that someone's needs will be put on the back burner, and all too often it is those of the child with the habit of failure and frustration—the potential dropout. How should the curriculum be modified to decrease the likelihood of dropping out? What are the cautions and cues for curriculum workers? This chapter addresses these problems.

What Is a Dropout?

At first glance the answer to this question is obvious: a dropout is anyone who leaves school before graduating. Quay and Allen note that it is not a simple matter to determine the extent of dropping out and, since the definition is not universal, "practices differ from district to district or even from school to school within a district, and by the accuracy with which data are collected and transmitted to central authorities."[6] Thus, much latitude is left to the local reporters, who are often school principals. Depending on *their* views, leaving school to marry because of pregnancy, to join the armed forces, or to transfer to evening school may or *may not* be called dropping out. "Stopping out" may be identified as dropping out, although some data identify "stopouts" as 10 percent of the dropout total, most of whom go on to postsecondary education.[7]

Kaeser identifies two common methods for counting dropouts. One method—an incidence count—is to count the number of students who leave school in a certain year. A second method, the cohort survival method, gives the proportion of students who entered the group but did not make it to graduation with their peers.[8]

In many places students who are too young to leave school *legally* are counted as truants when they have dropped out. The writer can easily identify with such "manipulation," having taught in schools where students who accumulated over fifty consecutive days of absence were still kept on the rolls.

In Illinois a study by Arnold suggested that 25 percent of Hispanic and black sophomores eventually dropped out.[9] Over half were female, one-third of whom had one or more children. Arnold's data on 1,950 Illinois sophomores along with national data are shown in table 1.

The 1982 U.S. Census dropout data that McDill, Natriello, and Pallas used estimated that Hispanic males have a dropout rate of 44 percent, Hispanic females 29 percent, with both rates rising annually. For blacks, the rate was 18.9 percent for males, 19.7 percent for females and getting lower. For whites, the rate was 18 percent for males and 13 percent for females, with little change over previous years.[10]

TABLE 1
DROPOUT RATE IN 1984, IN PERCENT

	ILLINOIS	U.S.
Females	10.7	12.6
Males	14.2	14.7
Whites	10.2	12.2
Blacks	24.8	17.0
Hispanics	25.9	18.0
Native Americans	15.2	29.2
All	13.2	13.6

SOURCE: *A Profile of Illinois Dropouts* (Springfield, IL: Illinois State Board of Education, Department of Planning, Research, and Evaluation, 1985). ERIC ED 262 314.

Dropout rates in Ohio, North Carolina, and California are comparable to those found in Illinois. The high school graduation rates for states are highest in Minnesota, Iowa, North Dakota, Wisconsin, and South Dakota, where the rates range from 88.2 to 82.7 percent. The lowest graduation rates are in the District of Columbia, followed by California, Florida, Mississippi, Louisiana, and South Carolina, with rates ranging from 56.9 to 62.6.[11]

Who Drops Out and Why?

A picture that has already begun to emerge is reinforced over and over. A typical dropout is poor, usually a person of color, below average in achievement, often behind chronological peers in grade level, has less educated parents, is easily discouraged, has poor attendance records, and is seen by teachers as uncooperative.

In 1974 the Children's Defense Fund (CDF) issued a report entitled *Children Out of School in America*. In a nine-state study of over 6,500 families in 505 districts, many conclusions regarding dropouts and potential dropouts were drawn. CDF determined that most of the children not in school were poor. Many of them were "allowed" out, "counseled" out, "pushed" out, or "encouraged" to drop out. CDF concluded that whatever the term the result is the same—exclusion from school. Denial of access to the curriculum makes it more likely that "children will grow up to be illiterate, unemployed, delinquent, rebellious, and dependent."[12] CDF regarded dropping out as tantamount to exclusion from school.

When CDF asked children out of school (or their parents) the reasons for their leaving school, the most frequently reported response

was that the children "did not like school." The response was believed
to mask the real reasons: "We found that children may not like school
if they cannot read well and are not given appropriate instruction or
materials in school. They may not like school if they are of average
intelligence but are incorrectly labeled and placed in a special class for
slow learners."[13] McDill, Natriello, and Pallas also found that many
students dropped out because of poor grades or because they felt that
school was "not for them."[14]

Unemployed dropouts interviewed by Miller claimed that they
did not leave school voluntarily but were pushed out and often in
quite a direct way. Although "unemployable," these dropouts had
positive attitudes toward school, thought the teachers were fair, and
missed school for social reasons—such as meeting friends during the
day.[15] Miller's observations match those made by the Children's
Defense Fund and by others made even more recently. He noted that
many of the dropouts saw school as negative and boring. They had to
get away and the school, in turn, *wanted* them away.

Many studies have developed the idea of mutual rejection, but, for
the most part, this theme has not been addressed directly. In North
Carolina, a study of that state's dropouts observed that dropouts,
besides being poor, generally enter school with no direction, have low
levels of achievement, and do poorly early in their careers. In
interviewing dropouts, the researchers ascertained that these entering
characteristics manifested themselves in (a) a general dislike for school,
(b) poor academic performance, and (c) discipline problems. Almost
half cited English as the subject that had given them the most
trouble.[16] A study of schools in Columbus (Ohio) by the Ohio State
Department of Education reinforces most of the general characteristics
of dropouts observed earlier. These include a feeling of rejection, a
high rate of truancy or absenteeism, discipline problems in school, a
lack of definite educational goals, low academic achievement,
enrollment in general courses rather than college preparatory or
vocational education courses, more difficulty in mathematics and
reading, and more failures.[17]

Marsha Hirano-Nakanishi found that 40 percent of all Hispanic
dropouts left school before grade ten, mostly at junior high school.
Hispanic youth, she asserted, were delayed from normal educational
progress during most of their elementary years in much greater
numbers than non-Hispanics, so they tended to drop out at an earlier
grade level. Many of the studies on dropouts do not give attention to

pre-high-school years, so many Hispanic dropouts may go unnoticed or may be seen as truants.[18]

A number of studies have gone right to the source, the dropouts themselves, asking them why they dropped out. Jordan-Davis interviewed ninety-five dropouts in their homes and noted that school-related issues were most commonly mentioned, with inadequate academic preparation, especially in reading and writing, mentioned as the primary reason for such inadequacy.[19]

Wagner also drew on interviews and observations to find out "why poor kids quit attending school." Not only can they not compete with their peers financially (for example, for clothing, curricular and extracurricular materials), but the curriculum is not geared toward the needs and interests of children. For example, the "real" writing of letters, memos, or committee minutes was not taught.[20]

The Children's Defense Fund identified a number of barriers to attendance that included poverty, language, and pregnancy. In trying to prevent dropouts, educators now must deal with even younger girls who are becoming pregnant even more frequently. In New York City, for example, the rate of pregnancy among fifteen to nineteen year olds has remained steady over the past five years, while the rate among younger girls continues to rise. No longer does New York City "force" students to leave their school, although the system has for sixteen years had a School for Pregnant Teens which is now at five sites in the city. "The head of the Board of Education's dropout prevention program, Victor Herbert, said he believed that many of the girls lead such uninspiring lives that becoming pregnant was a way of adding some interest."[21]

Other pushouts-dropouts include expelled or suspended students, children who cannot afford textbook fees, migrant children, and others who are not expected to achieve and are not taught well.

In a unique attempt to combat potential crime, the Dade County Grand Jury investigated the dropout problem in inner-city Miami. Through a questionnaire administered to 264 dropouts and potential dropouts (144 dropouts, 120 still in school), the grand jury found that alienation was the strongest predictor of dropping out of school. The top four reasons for dropping out were: didn't like school, 37 percent; wanted to work, 14 percent; expelled or suspended, 13 percent; drugs, rebellious, arrested, 9 percent.[22] Despite ostensible desires to work, 60 percent of the dropouts were unemployed and not enrolled in any vocational or academic program. Most of those employed were earning the minimum wage.

The grand jury went on to create a not surprising pattern. Failure in school leads to a failure to finish school. This is more likely in poor neighborhoods where elementary teacher expectations are less for Hispanics, much less for blacks, and where teachers see these groups as more likely to become delinquents. In Dade County, most delinquents had dropped out and had lower reading scores.[23]

The grand jury thus identified a key argument for trying to prevent potential dropouts from leaving school: they are likely to cost the county more in terms of costs of crimes committed, incarceration, trials, rehabilitation, and training than the costs of providing better training before students drop out.

Kaeser speaks of what are termed "unquantifiable costs"—higher incidence of alienation, negative psychological effects, less political involvement, fewer opportunities for upward ability.[24] She sees the dropout issue as one of equity. McDill et al. see it as one of both equity and excellence,[25] the latter issue flowing from the impetus of the recent reports on the reform of education. To provide equity and excellence, the school curriculum, both what is taught and how, must more legitimately meet the needs of the "at risk" population of potential dropouts.

Reducing the Dropout Rate

What changes can help to reduce the dropout rate? The first step is a better recognition of the problem that is being faced. Donald Smith has noted that the National Commission on Excellence in Education was not at all concerned with dropouts in its report, *A Nation at Risk*. In New York State the Regents plan did not even mention the word "dropouts." McDill et al. observed that many educational critics cite this as a major problem of omission.[26] The problem of dropping out must be faced squarely, not just nationally but locally as well. C. Fred Bateman, Superintendent of the Chesapeake (Virginia) Public Schools, stresses that the issue of dropouts must be kept before the public and suggests a recognition program for staff involved with dropout prevention in order that the public and school employees know of the commitment to "holding power" and excellence.[27] Bateman suggests that this commitment to holding power be part of stated school policy and that it be regarded as part of the principal's job to see that the policy is implemented.

Almost all researchers and practitioners who work with dropouts agree that early identification is vital to dropout prevention. It is generally agreed that the seeds of dropout prevention must be sown early and that potential dropouts can be identified in elementary school, even in the primary grades.

What are teachers to look for? Background items include a low educational level of the parents, a sibling or parent who dropped out of school, the absence of the father from the home, and an excessively stressful home life. In school, students often exhibit a lack of basic skills, at least one grade failure, disruptive behavior, and a low level of self-esteem. "The best way to avoid dropping out in high school," writes Mann, "is to make the elementary school more successful."[28]

TEACHER UNDERSTANDING AND SUPPORT

Many dropouts say that they get no real help from teachers. Indeed, the teacher and the rest of the school staff may seem as eager (if not more so) for students to drop out as to remain in school. Encouraging students to drop out violates their rights to attend school and is in opposition to the welfare of the state, which, as Reutter points out, "is served by the creation of an enlightened citizenry." Indeed, as he notes, "statutes requiring compulsory education of children within certain ages have long formed the backbone of the American educational system."[29] As professionals, teachers must view the dropout problem as a problem, then work to correct it in a variety of flexible ways. Kaeser points out that schools that are effective with marginal students make it their *policy* to be effective.[30]

Most researchers believe that most of the students in question have the mental ability to succeed. Bloom's work on learning, for example, supports that notion unequivocally. "Most individuals," he concludes, "could learn what the schools had to teach *if* they were provided with the time and help they needed."[31]

How can teachers make successful programs? Nauman's research found that common characteristics of successful dropout prevention programs included the following: teacher power to control the curriculum and commensurate teaching methods, the treatment of students as individuals, the relative independence of teachers from administrative restraints, and a view of the curriculum as a way to enhance student self-worth rather than accentuating content exclusively.[32]

There is often considerable difference between learning experiences as conceived in the minds of the teacher and the curriculum worker and how the student perceives them in the classroom. It is difficult for teachers to know what the youngster is thinking and recent research suggests that the teacher should ask him or her. This practice not only can clear up problems in understanding the work but conveys the teacher's concern. Not all children who have difficulty understanding are potential dropouts, but all have the right to access the knowledge, which often boils down to the seemingly mundane (for the uninitiated) problem of the clarity of teachers' explanations.

Educational research done on related problems offers guidance to curriculum workers, even though the research may not deal directly with the dropout problem. The research conducted by Bloom on alterable variables, such as teacher interaction with students, is helpful, as is Brookover's work on school climate.[33] Research on children's thinking, such as the work done by Peterson and Swing, offers teachers some useful ideas for preventing dysfunctional thinking (worry).[34]

There is no need to reinvent the educational wheel where the dropout problem is concerned. As with other educational problems, we must use and build on what we already know. Work by the National Education Association's Project on School Dropouts in the 1960s suggests many ideas for the curriculum worker, as does other work done in this period on achievement motivation.

SUCCESSFUL CURRICULUM PRACTICES

If a school faculty believes that most children have the ability to succeed, what must be done for that success to be achieved? The faculty must then make a second commitment: to provide equal access to the curriculum through instruction that is sensitive to individual needs. Access is opened when students are heterogeneously grouped for instruction, as was suggested by John Goodlad in his large-scale study of schooling. Since the Goodlad study, a number of schools have adopted this practice in some or all curriculum areas. An interesting example is the California Demonstration Program in Reading and Humanities at Willard Junior High School in Berkeley, California.

Students are grouped heterogeneously (from the 2nd to the 99th percentile) in each core English and History class and there is no retracking inside the classroom. At Willard, heterogeneity is not random; it is planned and organized from April until the following fall when school resumes. All students participate in group discussion.

Adolescent novels are used to teach vocabulary, critical thinking, and independent reading. There is tutoring in or near each classroom. Instruction on a novel begins a week earlier for those students who need extra time. Students role-play adolescent and adult problems. Other instructional techniques include cross-curricular writing (the core curriculum organization lends itself to this) and cooperative learning.

Willard is a feeder school for Berkeley High School and the holding power of the Willard cohort at Berkeley High School has increased by more than 50 percent since the program was inaugurated five years ago. More than 90 percent of pupils who entered grade ten in 1983 graduated three years later. There is more than meets the eye here; these pupils moved to a tracked situation in Berkeley High School and have succeeded when placed in the higher tracks. Not only have Willard students experienced academic achievement (as measured by district and state testing), but there has been increased cooperation among students, greater respect for differences, and a marked decline in negative behavior.[35]

Curriculum materials are of critical importance in whether students stay in school. In recent years, the use of workbooks and xeroxed pages from workbooks has increased enormously. In the 1960s researchers on the dropout problem frequently pointed to a connection between dropping out of school and the overuse of workbooks and other boring materials. Writers warned that workbooks were a teacher's crutch and not a substitute for teaching that was sensitive to individual needs. This is still true today. No mechanical form of instruction can substitute for classroom interactions. It is even more deadly today for potential dropouts, for they frequently are treated as a separate species who must be fed on a diet of dull, often stupid, rote materials. As Wilbur Brookover has cautioned, equality of opportunity is not facilitated by differentiated materials and methods based on the presumed differences between children. A common curriculum with common materials is associated with an open society.[36] The heavy use of Skinnerian technology with poorer students and Deweyan approaches with more able students will only create more dropouts, just as it has been doing. It is also a violation of educators' commitment to equal access to the curriculum.

Moreover, as Daniel Tanner pointed out in his chapter in this yearbook, research does not support the idea that students who have never really become interested in learning do best with a system of learning that relies on workbooks, preprogrammed instruction, drills, and tests (instruction delivered one piece at a time). Indeed, such students prefer discovery approaches. Rote instructional procedures will not keep secondary school students in school.

A number of curriculum practices seem to be effective in the design of a curriculum to prevent dropping out. In North Carolina, for example, these include an extended school day, which permits more individual teacher-pupil interaction; help for students with learning problems so that they accumulate positive experience and develop a positive attitude toward school; work-study programs; special vocational programs; job placement centers; school-within-a-school (for example, teen pregnancy programs, alternative learning centers, special tutoring); alternative programs or optional schools located on or off campus.[37]

ALTERNATIVE PROGRAMS

The alternative program (AP) provides more individualized instruction, reduced student-teacher ratios, more guidance, cooperative on-the-job training, as well as social and vocational counseling. There is disagreement about the usefulness of AP's in dropout prevention. Some critics have noted that in some places alternative schools are used as "dumping grounds" for unruly students, a transitional step before suspension or before the student sees no alternative but to drop out.

Alternative schools recall Briggs's observation that organizational change does not automatically lead to curriculum improvement. Thus, alternative schools are usually smaller than the mainstream high school and provide opportunities for personal contact, support, and varied instruction to meet individual needs. They have the potential to make a significant impact on the dropout problem. But there are trade-offs involved that may not be readily apparent and about which curriculum workers should be forewarned. For example, only in large schools can diversified curricula be offered. Ceilings in alternative schools are low where expectations are concerned (both teachers' expectations of students and students' expectations of themselves) because of the homogeneous low-track nature of the student body.

Moreover, alternative schools seem to be subject to the same constraints as other schools where testing is concerned; the mandated tests still drive the curriculum. In the case of alternative schools, the result may be even more dismaying; an already narrow curriculum becomes a set of machinery aimed at meeting requirements for a

Graduate Equivalency Diploma. That is what has happened in some continuation (alternative) high schools in California.

Since 1919, nearly every school district in California is required by law to provide an adjustment-type continuation program for pupils with severe attendance or behavior problems so that they can complete the requirements for high school graduation. Continuation schools tend to be small and originally they could function with a minimum of regulations. Teachers could be constructors of the curriculum, the instructional program was often multigraded, and students were permitted to work at their own rate. As a result, students who were never successful in school often became motivated to do a great deal of work for the first time.

Whereas the original purpose of the continuation school was to provide opportunities for high school graduation, it is now generally viewed by administrators as supplying students with an individualized program to improve their fundamental skills. The purpose is to prepare students to pass tests of proficiency in reading, writing, and mathematics in order to qualify for a Graduate Equivalency Diploma. Teachers are under pressure to teach to the test as scores on the California Assessment Program are made public. There is an absence of advanced course offerings, so when students pass the minimum or proficiency test, they quit mathematics. Nor would they be inspired to go on, for they become bored with fundamental skills that are repeated and mechanical. As one student said when questioned, "It's the same old stuff, over and over."

At continuation schools, world geography and U.S. history tend to be taught by packet reading; students are assigned individual packets of work—workbooks that are xeroxed and categorized into packets. The students complete the packet, get it corrected by the teacher, then study for a follow-up test. Discussion and interaction is at a minimum. Teachers at continuation schools—as in any school—*could* work together as a team. World geography *could* be combined with U.S. history when studying the origin of road systems and transportation. Geography would center on map-reading concepts. Whatever the state mandates, the curriculum still depends on the teacher. But if teachers are to exploit the opportunities offered by their commitment (which they still have) to the individualized program of study to support student success, they need leadership for curriculum improvement.

According to Foley and Crull, the characteristics of alternative programs that seem to increase the school's holding power include diversified teachers' roles including that of curriculum developer; a curriculum grounded in the reality of the students' lives, intellectual needs, and school system requirements; strong academic leaders; student participation in admissions, course evaluation, and classes; few, but agreed upon, rules of conduct.[38]

Even without an alternative program, Foley and Crull see some ideas that could fit into the existing system, including redesigning the traditional high school to fit the alternative model, putting first-semester high school students in especially motivating classes with expert teachers, and getting all students involved in some school activity. This, of course, seems to fly in the face of recent education commission reports, but "completion of the kinds of core curriculum recommended by recent commission reports appears to do little to improve the performance of students with low GPA's, the very students most likely to be potential dropouts."[39]

VOCATIONAL PROGRAMS

Many successful dropout prevention programs are geared toward the world of work. The typical school curriculum is often seen by potential dropouts as meaningless, removed from life experiences, and affording no linkage with the future. "Since work is seen as the hallmark of adulthood and since the best preparation for work is work itself, the school must offer work experiences for such youths."[40] Many of the students who drop out are in general curriculums preparing them for nothing. Those who drop out have difficulty finding a job, particularly one that pays more than a minimum wage. Vocational education may not only hold them in school, but if they leave, they may have had some training in job skills. Weber and Silvani-Lacey drew this not very surprising conclusion: "Where some specialized vocational training was provided to dropouts, the data suggest that dropouts who receive vocational training generally experience higher employment rates and higher average annual earnings than dropouts who do not receive such training."[41]

Studies of large urban school systems found that the holding power of school systems without separate vocational high schools exceeded that of systems with such schools. Moreover, the holding power of all high schools exceeded the rates of separate vocational schools."[42] While it is possible for school systems to reduce dropping out by making changes in teaching practices, there are limits to the reductions in tracked situations, which is essentially what we have with separate vocational schools.[43]

According to Weber and Silvani-Lacey, vocational education programs aimed at minimizing dropping out should include a paid work experience that relates job to school and vice versa; alternative programming with flexible scheduling; linkage with government-sponsored programs (like the former CETA programs, now the Job Training Partnership Act); strong support services such as guidance; staff cooperation and collaboration (particularly between content area and vocational teachers); student involvement in extracurricular school activities.[44]

Dropouts participate infrequently in the extracurricular life of the school. Recent studies have shown that student involvement in extracurricular activities increases student feeling of "ownership" of the school which, in turn, increases the likelihood of staying in school. This does not just mean band or athletics; it can be student curricular committees, student government, school newspapers, or clubs. In order to avoid further temporal constraints on students, these activities should not all be done after school. School hours and scheduling must become more flexible.

Foley and Crull suggest that the traditional high school, and the junior high and middle school as well, should be redesigned to fit the alternative school model of flexibility and smallness. Greater resources should be allocated to high schools to promote flexibility, which may not be cost-effective in the short run, but will be in the years ahead.[45] But making additional resources available is not enough: changes are called for in the curriculum including teacher expectations, interactions with students, and what is taught.

Local businesses and the citizenry must understand about, and be involved in, the effort to prevent dropouts. In Ohio, an effort has been developed and implemented consisting of problem identification, the identification of community resources, selection of appropriate approaches incorporating resources, incorporation of various approaches into the staff development process, and the establishment of an information clearinghouse. Included in the program is an evaluation of the dropout approaches.[46]

Byerly, too, found the use of community resources useful in retaining students, while Kaeser regards a school that works to involve the community and gain its support as a key element in dropout prevention.[47]

Common Elements of Effective Programs

Effective dropout programs in Wisconsin have in common (a) small size and autonomy, (b) teacher caring and responsibility as well as high expectations, (c) collegial teacher culture and supportive peer culture of students, and (d) an individualized curriculum that emphasizes real-life problem solving.[48]

Successful programs in Ohio include counseling, increasing the participation of students in school activities, parent involvement, and special vocational programs.[49] Success factors in programs considered effective by the North Carolina Department of Public Instruction were the deep commitment of teachers and administrators, early identification of students, and highly flexible schedules in a day extended to 8:00 P.M. Successful programs reduced the dropout rate by as much as 25 percent.[50]

Other successful programs have grown out of the adopt-a-school program, which encourages community and corporate involvement with local education. In East Los Angeles, for example, Coca Cola has provided over $100,000 to help keep Hispanics in the two high schools with the largest populations of Hispanics. The program, the Coca Cola Hispanic Education Fund, begins prior to high school with the early identification of potential dropouts, early counseling, orientation to high school, tutoring, and buddy systems linking teachers with students in need.[51]

If schools are to look for corporate help in the dropout problem, the businesses that are solicited must be local and must have some input into the program. That input can be in planning, placement, and/or evaluation of dropout prevention in the local area. Be that as it may, the responsibility of the school remains that of developing the full potential of each student. Roles of education and industry can only be viewed in this light.

In many ways, dropout prevention is simply following approved educational practices. Basic skills are taught through application. Research on the dropout, as on the curriculum for all students, favors the use of a variety of teacher approaches, life-related content, and a diversified curriculum without tracking. It emphasizes the importance of an individualized approach to instruction. Students need to be known and recognized by staff and be able to gain recognition easily for their accomplishments. But then this is true of all students.

The idea that I hope has come through in this chapter is that the best dropout prevention is a good curriculum for all students. As

Bloom points out, an effective school for all students has three qualities: good teaching, enough time to learn, and remedial help for youngsters as soon as they need it.[52] There are no shortcuts and more of one quality cannot compensate for the absence of another. Time is needed; schools tend to be nervous places. But time will not compensate for poor teaching or for lack of special help for children who fall behind. As one dropout stated: "The teacher didn't show you too much. If you didn't get it the first time, the teacher didn't have much time to show you."

At Willard Junior High School, as at many other schools, in-service education has enhanced the clarity of instruction, with apparently favorable results. It would, of course, be too easy to say that students drop out only because they cannot understand the work. It would be more hopeful to suggest that when schools are finally ready to provide equal access to the curriculum—which includes how to teach as well as what is taught—we will be close to the solution of dropping out.

Footnotes

1. William H. Bristow, "Curriculum Problems of Special Import for Early School Leavers," in *The School Dropout*, ed. Daniel Schreiber (Washington, DC: National Education Association, 1964), p. 144.

2. Ibid.

3. Thomas H. Briggs, *The Junior High School* (Boston: Houghton Mifflin, 1920), p. 3.

4. Ibid., p. 202.

5. *New York Times*, 18 November 1986.

6. Herbert C. Quay and Laurel B. Allen, "Truants and Dropouts," in *Encyclopedia of Educational Research*, 5th ed., ed. Harold E. Mitzel (New York: Free Press, 1982), p. 1959.

7. Dale Mann, "Can We Help Dropouts?" *Teachers College Record* 87 (Spring 1968): 307-323.

8. Susan C. Kaeser, *Citizen Guide to Children Out of School: The Issues, Data, Explanation, and Solutions to Absenteeism, Dropouts, and Disciplinary Exclusion* (Cleveland, Ohio: Citizens' Council for Ohio Schools, September 1984).

9. Gerald Arnold, *A Profile of Illinois Dropouts* (Springfield, IL: Illinois State Board of Education, Department of Planning, Research, and Evaluation, August 1985). ERIC ED 262 314.

10. Edward L. McDill, Gary Natriello, and Aaron M. Pallas, "Raising Standards and Retaining Students: The Impact of Reform Recommendations on Potential Dropouts," *Review of Educational Research* 55 (Winter 1985): 415-433.

11. U.S. Department of Education, Office of Planning, Budget, and Evaluation, 1986. Reported in *Education Week*, 14 May 1986.

242   DROPPING   OUT   OF   SCHOOL

12. Children's Defense Fund, *Children Out of School in America* (Washington, DC: Children's Defense Fund, 1974), p. 6.

13. Ibid., p. 18.

14. McDill, Natriello, and Pallas, "Raising Standards and Retaining Students."

15. S. M. Miller, "Dropouts—A Political Problem," in *Profile of the School Dropout*, ed. Daniel Schreiber (New York: Random House, 1967).

16. North Carolina Department of Public Instruction, *Keeping Students in School: Dropout Data, Research, and Programs* (Raleigh, NC: North Carolina Department of Public Instruction, July, 1985). In a study done in Chicago, Abbott and Breckinridge found that English was not spoken in the homes of the great majority of nonattending children. This in 1917! See Edith Abbott and Sophonisba Breckinridge, *Truancy and Nonattendance in the Chicago Schools* (Chicago: University of Chicago Press, 1917; New York: Arno Press, 1970).

17. Ohio State Department of Education, *Reducing Dropouts in Ohio Schools: Guidelines and Promising Practices* (Columbus, Ohio: Ohio State Department of Education, 1985).

18. Marsha Hirano-Nakanishi, *Hispanic School Dropouts: The Extent and Relevance of Pre-High School Attrition and Delayed Education* (Los Alamitos, CA: Center for Bilingual Research, 1984).

19. Walter E. Jordan-Davis, "The Cry for Help Unheard: Dropout Interviews" (Austin, TX: Office of Research and Evaluation, Austin Independent School District, 1984).

20. Hilmar Wagner, "Why Poor Kids Quit School," *Education* 105 (Winter 1984): 185-188.

21. Jane Perez, "Children with Children: Coping with a Crisis," *New York Times*, 1 December 1986.

22. "The High School Dropout and the Inner-City School" (Miami, FL: Dade County Grand Jury, 1984).

23. Ibid., p. 42.

24. Kaeser, *Citizen Guide to Children Out of School*.

25. McDill, Natriello, and Pallas, "Raising Standards and Retaining Students," p. 415.

26. Donald Smith, as quoted in "The Dropouts Go on Everyone Else's Rolls," *Education Week*, 14 May 1986. See also, McDill, Natriello, and Pallas, "Raising Standards and Retaining Students," p. 415.

27. C. Fred Bateman, "Increase Your School's Holding Power," *American School Board Journal* 172 (October 1985): 39.

28. Mann, "Can We Help Dropouts?" p. 318.

29. E. Edmund Reutter, Jr., *The Law of Public Education*, 3d ed. (Mineola, NY: Foundation Press, 1985), p. 668.

30. Kaeser, *Citizen Guide to Children Out of School*, p. 40.

31. Benjamin S. Bloom, *Human Development and School Learning* (New York: McGraw-Hill, 1976), p. 207.

32. Craig Nauman, "Teacher Culture in Successful Programs for Marginal Students" (Paper presented at the Annual Meeting of the American Educational Research Association, Chicago, 1985).

33. Wilbur B. Brookover et al., *School Social Systems and Student Achievement* (New York: Praeger, 1979).

34. Penelope L. Peterson and Susan R. Swing, "Beyond Time on Task: Students' Reports of Their Thought Processes during Classroom Instruction," *Elementary School Journal* 82 (May 1982): 481-491.

35. A. J. Tudisco, "Why Heterogeneity?" in *Willard Handbook* (Berkeley, CA: Willard Junior High School, n.d.), p. 1.

36. Wilbur B. Brookover, Richard J. Gigliotti, Ronald D. Henderson, Bradley E. Niles, and Jeffrey M. Schneider, "Quality of Educational Attainment Standardized Testing, Assessment, and Accountability," in *Uses of the Sociology of Education*, ed. C. Wayne Gordon, Seventy-third Yearbook of the National Society for the Study of Education, Part 2 (Chicago: University of Chicago Press, 1974), p. 162.

37. North Carolina Department of Public Instruction, *Keeping Students in School.*

38. Eileen Foley and Peggy Crull, "Educating the At-risk Adolescent: More Lessons from Alternative High Schools. A Report" (New York: Public Education Association, 1984).

39. McDill, Natriello, and Pallas, "Raising Standards and Retaining Students."

40. Schreiber, ed., *Profile of the School Dropout*, p. 238.

41. James W. Weber and Cindy Silvani-Lacey, *Building Basic Skills: The Dropout* (Columbus, Ohio: National Center for Research in Vocational Education, 1983).

42. See, for example, Daniel Schreiber, *Holding Power/Large City School Systems* (Washington, DC: National Educational Association, 1964).

43. John I. Goodlad, *A Place Called School* (New York: McGraw-Hill, 1984), pp. 164-6.

44. Weber and Silvani-Lacey, *Building Basic Skills.*

45. Foley and Crull, "Educating the At-risk Adolescent."

46. Weber and Silvani-Lacey, *Building Basic Skills.*

47. Carl L. Byerly, "A School Curriculum for Prevention and Remediation of Deviancy," in *Profile of the School Dropout*, ed. Schreiber; Kaeser, *Citizen Guide to Children Out of School*, p. 41.

48. Stephen Hamilton, "Raising Standards and Reducing Dropout Rates," *Teachers College Record* 55 (Winter 1985): 410-429.

49. Ohio State Department of Education, *Reducing Dropouts in Ohio Schools.*

50. North Carolina Department of Public Instruction, *Keeping Students in School.*

51. Coca Cola Hispanic Education Fund, "Los Angeles Program Description" (Los Angeles: Coca Cola Bottling Co. of Los Angeles, 1984).

52. Bloom, *Human Development and School Learning.*

Section Three:
ISSUES OF LEADERSHIP

CHAPTER XI

Leadership for Curriculum Improvement:
The School Administrator's Role

GARY A. GRIFFIN

Introduction

The role and function of school-level administrators in curriculum improvement provide the focus of this chapter. This emphasis rests on the belief that the school is the logical unit for improvement in terms of planning, implementing, studying, revising, and institutionalizing curriculum change.[1] It also builds from the understanding that the contact between the curriculum and the student takes place in classrooms and in schools. Therefore, although the district level of leadership is important for thinking about policy, providing support for curriculum improvement, ensuring material support for school-level work, and monitoring the process of school change, the work of curriculum change is logically the work of teachers and administrators in schools and classrooms.

The point of view taken here is somewhat different from what has become typical in exhortations for principals, for example, to be "curriculum leaders." The usual claim for such leadership emphasizes curriculum planning skills, knowledge of bodies of curriculum-related literature, maintaining an up-to-date understanding of advances in curriculum materials, and so on. In other words, suggestions about what the principal's role in curriculum improvement ought to be have rested mainly upon knowledge and skill that is inherent in being a curriculum expert.

I take the position in this chapter that the claims for leadership noted above are unrealistic and very wide of the mark in terms of making significant school-level curriculum changes. They are

244

unrealistic because of the competing claims for principals' intellectual, personal, and emotional energy. If the principal is expected to be an expert in curriculum, is it not then also logical that the principal should be an instructional expert, a testing and evaluation expert, a pupil personnel expert, a school-community relations expert, and an expert in the fiscal management of a big business? Clearly, the levels of expertise required across the multiple components of the school as a complex organization can not be located in every principal in every school. And when one makes such claims for expert status in curriculum, one must recognize that there are equally pressing claims for that status in other aspects of the operation of an effective school.

My belief is that the principal must be sensitive and skillful in manipulating a complex environment, one part of which is the curriculum enterprise.[2] Of course, knowledge and skill related to the doing of curriculum development and implementation are important but not sufficient to successful curriculum innovation at the school level. The principal, in this case, should know the rudiments of the curriculum planning process, have a set of criteria against which to make judgments about curriculum-in-use, and be able to engage in curriculum-related discourse and debate. But, he or she need not be the theoretical and technical expert that has often been assumed by those concerned with curriculum improvement.

The persistent belief in the expert status position for school principals derives, in part, from a conception of teaching and schooling wherein principals are "management" and teachers are "labor." In this conception there is a hierarchical system of power and authority, with the concomitant feature that the needed expertise is passed from the manager to the worker. In other words, management needs the knowledge and skill to direct the activities of the workers.[3]

It has become increasingly clear from the past two decades of research on what constitutes effective schools and effective teachers that a conception of schooling quite different from the labor metaphor is consistently associated with outstanding schools and teachers. This emerging set of understandings considers the teacher as a classroom executive, a professional whose responsibilities and functions center on convincing students to learn as a consequence of the exercise of options through complex classroom decision making in an uncertain environment, and who participates in the decision making that affects both the daily activities and future work of the school.[4]

The distinctions between the two metaphors, teachers as workers and teachers as classroom executives, have significant consequences for the ways that principals and teachers interact, for how principals select objects for their work, and for how curriculum improvement, in terms of the purposes of this chapter, is carried forward.

The remainder of this chapter is devoted to an explication of how school principals would promote curriculum work if the metaphor of teacher as classroom executive were used as a basic guide for leadership. Research evidence to support the use of this metaphor is included. The chapter ends with a set of recommendations about how principal preparation programs might be reconceptualized to make the use of the classroom executive metaphor more prevalent in schools.

The Teacher as Classroom Executive and School Leader

The way that a leader conceives of his or her role in relation to colleagues is dramatically influenced by the explicit or implicit view that is held about those colleagues. A school principal who thinks of teachers as subordinate workers will more than likely engage in activities that promote centralized decision making, following rules and regulations, adherence to fairly inflexible expectations for teacher behavior, little widespread inquiry, a top-down evaluation and assessment scheme, and a traditional management orientation to accomplishing the work of the school. There will be little sharing of decision making, few opportunities to collaborate across conventional grade-level or subject boundaries, little variation in teaching in the school, and few rewards for experimentation. This picture is probably more true of schools in the United States than some of us would like to believe.

Of course, other views of teaching and teachers have made modest appearances in the past several decades. During the heyday of the open education movement, teachers were often thought of as "gardeners," people who tilled the academic soil, made certain that the intellectual and affective seeds were planted, and tended to the natural intellectual and social growth that was expected to occur with young people. Another metaphor that was prevalent for a time was what might be considered "teacher as travel guide," someone who took children and youth on journeys of the mind and spirit, pointing out to them the highlights of the cultural panorama while allowing the learning outcomes of the students' contact with the environment to be directed largely by the students themselves.[5]

It should be noted that these two metaphors for the central functions of teachers, as gardeners or as travel guides, emerged from a point of view and a body of knowledge about the nature of childhood. They gained their status from a set of understandings and beliefs about how children and youth learn. In effect, they were responses to what we know, or think we know, about the healthy learning and development of the young in our culture.

However, the most dominant and persistent metaphor, again derived from ways of thinking about learning, was and is teacher as "storyteller." Although the word "storyteller" may suggest somewhat frivolous activity, just the opposite is the case. Because students do not know what they need to know, it is believed, it is the duty and responsibility of the teacher to make present what teachers and other authorities in the culture believe is necessary knowledge and disposition for a satisfying and productive life. In this view, curricula are developed apart from students, modest attention is paid to standardized growth and development patterns, instruction is judged for goodness based upon its efficiency in accomplishing determined objectives, and the teacher is the repository of what is to be presented to and known by children.

Independent of and in contradiction to many aspects of these conceptions is the persistence of the already mentioned teacher-as-worker orientation. Although there have been some significant attempts to restructure schools such that teachers share in the leadership functions with principals and other administrators (the teacher center movement comes to mind) these organizational experiments most often are additions to rather than dramatic changes in schools as organizations.[6] For example, the teacher centers that have been institutionalized around the country are usually the result of an often uneasy agreement between a teachers union and a school district to put together a resource for teachers that is planned and managed by teachers but exists relatively independently from the school workplace. Leadership certainly is vested in the teachers in these instances, but that leadership is exerted away from schools.

Despite a small number of exceptions, schools in general are hierarchical organizations in which the principal and, perhaps, his or her immediate administrative staff are expected to provide leadership and direction while teachers are expected to do the work of teaching such that it "fits" the expectations of the leadership cadre. It is in these very typical school situations that teachers either accept their worker status, often making alterations around the margins of practice, or where they begin to express to themselves and, increasingly, to others their dissatisfaction with what have come to be called "conditions of work."[7]

Too often, I fear, we think of conditions of work in schools solely in terms of the physical environment and student population factors. The phrase conjures up broken windows, graffiti-laden hallways, trash piled up in corners of schoolyards, and other examples of a harsh institutional environment. It also stereotypically brings to mind recalcitrant children and youth who combine the problematic features of reluctance to learn with bringing about through their own misbehavior dangerous conditions for peers and adults alike.

When one moves beyond these stereotypes, however, it becomes sharply apparent that the phrase "conditions of work" refers to a large set of personal and professional variables. It includes teachers' personal feelings of indignity, sometimes outrage, at being excluded from decision making about school practices.[8] It stands for the recognition that preparation for a profession, often a significant human and material investment, often leads only to a job, one that has few institutionalized choice points for taking a path that leads to increased status and greater responsibility. (Teachers, for the most part, must move out of teaching to achieve career advancement within educational organizations.) Also, "conditions of work" refers to the presence or absence of real or ceremonial rewards for exemplary service.

It is not necessary to elaborate further. The present times are witness to calls for major reform in these and other conditions of work. The central theme of the reform agenda seems to me to be paying serious intellectual and practical attention to increasing the status of teachers toward that of true professionals. To some, this movement seems to diminish the role of the principal. A particularly dramatic example of this perception is the confusion surrounding the Carnegie recommendation to establish a "lead teacher" role and the Holmes Group's call for preparation of "career professional teachers," both proposals firmly rooted in a conception of teaching as professional activity that includes expectations and rewards for leadership functions.[9]

These and other professional orientations to teachers and their work suggest that, on the one hand, the teachers can and should be expected to exert considerable authority on life in classrooms, and, on the other, should also be central participants in the life of the school. This *executive* status alters in many major ways how a school functions. At the classroom level, it is assumed that teachers' knowledge and skill, particularly in terms of decision making about relationships between individuals and groups of students and curriculum requirements, can be exerted with minimal external direction. It assumes that the primary external linkage is with technical and intellectual assistance, to be used at the discretion of the teacher because of his or her deep understanding of the chief elements of the learning situation. And, because it assumes that the teacher has been and will continue to be a participant in decisions about evaluation expectations and procedures, the conception of teacher as executive calls for teacher evaluation schemes that question the degree to which the teacher accomplishes those goals that he or she has had a part in determining rather than being rated on whether he or she is responding to the will of others.[10]

We are considerably more knowledgeable than we were a decade or so ago about the uncertainty that is built into the teaching-learning act. Part of our knowledge is rooted in the understanding that, although many classrooms appear to naive observers to be alike, situations are sharply different. Those situational differences require that teachers engage in pedagogy that is very different from "teaching by the numbers." And when we move beyond that simplistic notion of teaching, the issue of how leadership can support a more advanced conception becomes central.

The Executive Teacher, the Principal, and Curriculum Improvement

There is a growing body of research evidence that can give direction to school leaders, principals and teachers, as they create the conditions that support school change, in this instance, curriculum improvement. In contrast to the rather fuzzy notion that principals should be "facilitators," however that term is defined, recent research has uncovered a number of school variables that can be shaped by a thoughtful school leader such that the school demonstrates conventional effectiveness, most often in the forms of student scores on standardized achievement tests, as well as in less conventional measures of success, in the forms of teachers' morale and beliefs about their own efficacy.

Because it is assumed here that teachers will continue to spend the major portion of their professional time with children and youth, it is also assumed that the school principal is the person who can and should take the responsibility for creating an environment, through the manipulation of critical school variables, that supports meaningful curriculum improvement. This view promotes the conception of the school principal as someone who undertakes the responsibility for ensuring that school conditions promote the activity of curriculum development as a school-level focus and who understands that the typical school-level constraints must be reduced or eliminated for this activity to take on current and future meaning. Most importantly, this view distributes responsibility for the curriculum work across the teacher executive cadre rather than reserving it only for administrators.

Although there is a long history to the commonsense rhetoric that "involvement promotes ownership" and "participation guarantees implementation," the instances of these and other slogans taking hold in schools are rare. Most often, teachers are called together to provide advice about textbook selection, for instance, or to develop a curriculum during a summer, work for which they are paid a stipend. It is seldom that the advice can be truly informative rather than impressionistic, given the sporadic nature of the opportunity, or for the curriculum to take hold in schools, given the practice of its development taking place apart from ongoing school situations. Rather, teachers feel betrayed when their advice is not followed by decision makers and, alternately, feel annoyed at having another curriculum guide placed on their library shelf or disappointed that other teachers do not use the products of their summer work. And, because school principals are equivalently separated from these curriculum ventures, they have little vested interest in moving the curriculum into place or in supporting teachers who are frustrated at advice given but not taken.

If, however, we take the view that curriculum improvement is largely a school-level activity, that it is dependent upon broad and deep participation by professionals in the school, and that it must take into account situational variables, then the roles of the teacher and the principal assume sharply different characteristics. For the purposes of this chapter, particular attention is given here to the school principal's contribution to curriculum improvement.

The Principal and the School Context

We are increasingly aware of the complexity of the school as a human organization and that awareness has sharpened our understanding of which school variables can be altered toward accomplishing positive ends.[11] Certain context features appear to be particularly relevant to supporting school change and improvement, including curriculum development. These features, furthermore, appear to be ones over which the school principal has some considerable influence. I have selected for inclusion here those features that seem to me to be conceptually and intuitively realistic in terms of curriculum improvement work in schools.

TEACHER PARTICIPATION IN DECISION MAKING

In the conception of teaching as labor, as noted above, it is not only unimportant but probably heretic to consider that teachers should have major participant roles in decision making about school policy, expectations, practice, and evaluation. If, however, the view of teacher as executive is adopted, it flows naturally that the teacher should be a part of the decision-making process, partly because it is natural for executives to be so, but largely because of the knowledge and disposition the teacher can bring to the process. This view adopts the belief that the teachers' contributions will enrich and sustain decision making and the subsequent events and activities that result from it.

When one examines typical elementary and secondary schools, however, one notes that teachers are most often central participants only about decisions in their own classrooms (and often only on the fringes of curricular issues even there), but are seldom major parties to school-level decision making. It is a common litany among teachers that their voices simply are not heard, that administrative and organizational structures stand between them and opportunities for participation, that they are seldom consulted about major curricular or other alterations in practice, and that, in the end, they feel more like automatons than professionals. (Recent developments in teacher education, particularly those aimed at new teachers, reinforce a dominant view of teaching as paraprofessional activity, something that can be readily taught, easily learned, and quickly remediated if found wanting.)

An imaginative, knowledgeable, and thoughtful principal, however, can bring to the teacher cadre for deliberation and decision making those school-level issues that are considered important at any given time.[12] A typical and long-standing example might be the articulation problems that persist across curricular areas at any point in time and over time. It is seldom that there is smooth or easy transition from grade to grade or from subject to subject, even when the grades and subjects are contained in the same elementary or secondary school. The principal can bring this issue to the attention of the school faculty at large (rather than let it rest as a point of contention within individual teachers), use it as a focus for thinking together, and coordinate the activities and events necessary to its resolution. Rather than dealing in public only with what have come to be termed "administrivia," such as schedules, bulletins from the central office, and the like, the collective professional body deliberates and makes decisions together about issues of major importance to school success and professional expectation.

Although there have been a number of formulations of the process of participation in schools, an appealing one continues to be Bentzen's dialogue, decision making, action, and evaluation.[13] Using the example of curriculum articulation above, the principal would ensure that there was sufficient time to talk together about both perceptions and technical knowledge regarding problems and prospects (dialogue), would work with teacher colleagues toward tentative resolution of the problem (decision), would support and monitor the implementation of the resolution (action), and engage with the faculty in determining the consequences of their work together (evaluation). Naturally, this sequence is not as neatly observed in practice as it is presented here, but the research base is solid and the intuitive appeal of the process is considerable. Further, it is within the realm of a school principal's authority to create the conditions necessary for its introduction into the school organization.

TIME AND SCHEDULES

Schools are busy places, and a good deal of the busyness is regulated by how time is spent and by where people are expected to be. Unfortunately, teachers in the typical school in the United States are controlled by time and schedules that, in extraordinarily lockstep and effective fashion, keep them apart from one another, offer little professional relief from practical activity, and promote the sense of isolation that has received so much attention and so little resolution. The school as an "egg crate," a "cottage industry," and a "2 by 4 by 6" environment will do little to promote widespread curriculum improvement.

There are a number of time and schedule dimensions of school life that principals can orchestrate to bring about the time and space opportunities for the participatory decision making noted above.[14]

Most teachers have as part of their contractual agreements with school systems one or more professional periods each day, time that is expected to be devoted to professional activity. Principals can arrange for these times to coincide for certain groups (for example, teachers in the same subject fields or grade levels) so that opportunities to engage together about curriculum become a reality in the school culture. Principals can act as advocates with district officers to make available professional days for teachers, days in which there can be relatively sustained dialogue. Principals can arrange for substitute teachers so that teachers assigned to the school can observe exemplary curricula in use. Principals can arrange for large-group student events, thereby freeing numbers of teachers to work together toward an improved curriculum.

Interestingly, there are few instances of shifts in time and schedules that can be observed in large numbers of schools. When such shifts are suggested as reasonable ways to create conditions for working on school issues, including curriculum, the problems associated with altering business as usual come to the forefront of attention. And yet, in effective schools, schools where important teaching and learning are taking place, such flexibility is, in fact, a new order of business as usual. This flexibility is essential to promoting school-level deliberation and action that are systematic, ongoing, and developmental.

REWARDS

Although conventional wisdom would have it that teachers' primary preoccupation is with salary, as determined by collective agreements with boards of education, it is increasingly apparent that teachers' conceptions of rewards are considerably more comprehensive and thoughtful than is sometimes believed. Teachers, as is true for most adults in our society, recognize that rewards come in many forms other than the financial.

Rewards for doing well the work of the teacher can be tangible and they can be symbolic.[15] The tangible rewards range from stipends for assuming extra responsibility (a common feature of summer curriculum development work) through access to unconventional or typically unavailable curriculum resources to that most precious of teacher commodities, time. One of the most common teacher litanies is the lack of time to do good work, whether that work is conventional teaching or providing well-tested curriculum proposals for consideration by faculty colleagues. Time is eaten away by the bureaucratic nature of schools and the concomitant need to complete a variety of forms and other paperwork. It is also eroded by the dailiness of schooling, exemplified most dramatically by the notion that teachers are not doing the work of teaching unless they are meeting with students. Although thoughtful teachers and administrators know that teaching involves a wide variety of noninstructional tasks such as planning, evaluating, assessing curriculum materials, reflecting upon one's practice, and others, the time to engage in these important activities is too often unavailable in the stereotypical school day and must be squeezed out of teachers' evenings, weekends, and vacations.

The principal is in a prime position to study and act upon the issue of time and how it is expected to be spent in schools. As noted above, largely in terms of students, time *is* a manipulable variable, at least the expectations for time use. A principal who adopts a school model that has at its heart teacher participation in decision making and decision implementation must alter the conditions of the school such that time for these activities is made available in a systematic fashion. Such a principal would use noninstructional persons to complete the myriad paperwork connected to school recordkeeping, would invest in the computer technology required to minimize data storage and retrieval, would experiment with patterns of large- and small-group instruction, would test a number of flexible scheduling patterns, would work toward the institutionalization of a community and/or parent volunteer cadre of school workers, and would be an advocate of these time-use patterns in negotiations with school system administrators and policymakers.

In terms of symbolic rewards, schools are remarkably barren in this regard. In the same ways that teachers and the public have come to accept, if not believe fully in, the notion of "a teacher is a teacher is a teacher," it is also apparent that this dictum has contributed to the absence of symbolic occasions that suggest that some teachers, or most of the teachers in some schools, are deserving of special recognition for the excellence of their contributions to classrooms and schools. Where are the celebrations of outstanding professional behavior and consequences of that behavior? Where are the recognition points in a teacher's career? Where do teachers who provide curriculum leadership, for example, receive their emotional and intellectual sustenance for continuing to lead?

Only recently, and in connection with various plans for teacher career ladder schemes, have we seen any serious attention paid to

systematic celebration of teachers' important work.[16] The school
principal, because of proximity and ongoing opportunities to observe
and participate with teachers in a building, has ample opportunity to
engage in symbolic rewarding behavior. This might include such
minor events as making sure that all teachers in a school are aware of
the school-level leadership of a few. This can be done publicly and
systematically in both print and oral forms. It might also include the
making available of opportunities for teachers to publish in local or
national outlets the products of their curriculum work. It might also
include the designation of teacher leaders, relatively independent of
principal interaction, who are in full charge of important school
functions. (This last is seen by some as yet another way to coerce
teachers into doing the work of the principal. What is not recognized
in this perception is that a conception of teaching as professional
activity, executive decision making, also calls for teacher leadership.
And, professional teachers are eager to assume that leadership,
providing, of course, that it does not turn into yet another set of
hollow or pro forma ploys to increase involvement without
expectations for real accomplishment.)

STAFF STABILITY

Curriculum improvement is an ongoing, developmental activity. It
requires reasoned deliberation, testing out of ideas in small- and large-
scale ways, a thorough understanding of the institution, the growth of
technical and conceptual skill and understanding, and a continually
deepening sensitivity to what is working and what may need
adaptation or dramatic revision. These elements of curriculum work
can seldom, if ever, be accomplished in a school environment that is
characterized by a revolving door policy or practice, an uncertainty
about which teachers will be there for the next year or, as is true in
some especially difficult schools, even who will be there next month.[17]

The principal can be the key to staff stability. This stability is
partly the consequence of the principal having a clear vision of what
the school is all about, the school's mission, if you will. This
expectation can guide the selection of faculty, can provide absolutely
essential bases for working with those faculty over time, and can give
a teacher candidate the understanding necessary to make a decision to
join or not to join the school. Except in rare cases where faculty
appointments are the responsibility of teachers already in the school,
the principal is the person who has both the most contact with

prospective teachers for the school and the decision-making responsibility to accept and reject from the pool of candidates.

Although it has been widely believed that the principal sets the general "tone" of a school, it is only recently that we have become aware of how this complex set of actions impacts staffing. Teachers will travel many miles each day, seek out and work in schools that have the reputation for being difficult, and go well beyond conventional expectations for performance in schools where the principal has demonstrated sensitive and strong leadership.[18] (And, somewhat counter to the argument for stability but important in terms of aggregating the most effective faculty group, outstanding principals are known to be successful in ensuring that teachers who somehow do not fit the school's mission find other places to teach, even within the constraints of system or union rules and regulations.)

Much of the content of this chapter provides the background against which staff stability is attained and maintained, and the principal is the key agent in realizing these participatory norms and, ultimately, in guaranteeing staff stability for curricular and other school improvement goals.

PROFESSIONAL COLLEGIALITY

An attribute of effective school organizations is that there is a professional atmosphere, a shared understanding that the members are there because of their expectation that they will accomplish the purposes of the organization.[19] This is sharply different from, although not completely contradictory to, a sense of social and personal well-being where people enjoy one another's company because of some nonprofessional affinity.

The principal is a particularly important figure in establishing and sustaining collegial norms that focus on professional activity, interactions, and productivity. He or she, of course, can contribute to the school's more social dimensions as well, but an essential element in making schools work is giving continuous attention to the norm of professional collegiality. This attention is directed toward making certain that the preoccupations of educators in the schools are with the tasks of teaching and schooling, that teacher time is spent well in accomplishing those tasks, and that there are ample opportunities for both formal and informal deliberation around schooling issues, possibilities, and dilemmas.

Curriculum improvement provides an ideal focus for professional collegiality. It brings to the forefront of attention of the partners in the schooling enterprise the content and nature of instruction. It provides a natural forum for deliberations across subject-matter boundaries and age-level assignments. It calls into question the human resources that can be discovered or developed in the school to bring about desired changes in students' behavior. It is a pervasive and deep-seated element of the school culture.[20]

The principal who uses the curriculum as the object of attention, in short, has the opportunity to infuse the school environment with occasions where professional collegiality can be called forth, systematically demonstrated over time, and rewarded. The presence of a professional collegial norm in the school is probably as predictive of school success as any other variable that can be acted upon by a principal.

LINKAGE WITH TECHNICAL ASSISTANCE

It is tempting to believe, in the face of incredible odds against it, that teachers are well-connected with the knowledge and skill required not only to do the work of teaching well but to gain ever more effective control over teaching throughout a career. Unfortunately, such appears not to be the case. Teachers, quite justifiably, are often very insecure in their command over their work and, equally justifiably, resentful of school systems' provision of what are often seen as trivial or meaningless opportunities to grow and develop professionally. The repetition of so-called "in-service days" during which little if anything is learned, the provision of workshops as independent events unconnected to a broad vision of what teaching is, the in-one-day-and-out-the-next visits of so-called experts are quite rightly disdained by teachers as impositions upon their valuable time and energy and as expressions of low expectations for their competence and sense of professional purpose.

A school principal who cares deeply about the work of the school and who respects teachers as growing professionals will, on the one hand, recognize that teachers, even in the best of circumstances, are often isolated from intellectual stimulation and, on the other hand, work to open up windows of opportunity such that the stimulation can occur.[21] He or she will make available new ideas on a regular and sustained basis, ideas that are not presented as prescriptions for practice but for dialogue and deliberation, perhaps even debate. There will not be a sequence of fads of the moment but there will be attention given over time to intellectually and practically sound propositions for alternation of practice. Probably as a consequence of participatory decision making, these propositions will be selected because of their natural relationship to the shifting priorities of the school.

Perhaps in no school arena is it more important to have sustained linkage with technical assistance than in curriculum improvement. Because of the historical dependence upon textbooks for curriculum knowledge and process, teachers are seldom as thoroughly understanding of the complexity of the curriculum development process as is needed for meaningful change to take place. Too often, teachers are exposed only to curriculum planning as a day-to-day event, not as a flow of decisions over periods of months and years.[22] Schools, departments, and colleges of education tend to reserve for graduate programs any deep exploration and understanding of various paradigms of curriculum discourse. (This, of course, fits the teacher-as-worker conception in that it withholds from teacher preparation programs the knowledge and skill believed to be important only for the designated authorities in the system, that is, administrators and supervisors.)

The principal who wants to work with teachers toward curriculum change will need to take very seriously the issue of how the school's capacity for planning and implementing change can be increased. In some cases, technical assistance can be secured from the central office of the school system. But, if the other content of this chapter is taken to heart, the primary purpose of this relationship will be to transfer the knowledge to the school on a permanent basis, implying the need to help one or more teachers become the school-level equivalent of the central office curriculum expert.

TEACHER EVALUATION

One of the most powerful context variables that is subject to principal influence is the evaluation of teachers. Unfortunately, teacher evaluation is often fragmented, lacking in specific focus, and considered by teachers and administrators alike more of an interruption in the business of schooling than as a valued instrument of the school culture.

It is more typical of teacher evaluation for it to be seldom practiced than for it to be a systematic and ongoing feature of the school. New teachers, as a consequence of local and sometimes state regulations, are evaluated more frequently than experienced teachers, many of whom report never being evaluated by their building-level administrators.

Although it may be conventional wisdom that teacher evaluation is a process fraught with anxiety and antagonism between the primary participants, such need not be the case. Teachers, new and experienced, report that, under fair and well-understood conditions, evaluation practices provide a valuable focus for continuing to learn to teach and for understanding their contributions to the school.[23] Rather than resenting evaluation, teachers in general consider it very useful to have a mirror against which to measure their own effectiveness and their perceptions about the consequences of their work. (Naturally, when teacher evaluation appears to be capricious, unconnected to a public understanding of what is valued in teaching, and driven by favoritism rather than fairness, evaluation is perceived to be a negative influence in a school.)

The evaluation of teachers can be an important aspect of promoting teacher growth generally, and of focusing on curriculum work specifically. If the norms of a school, as demonstrated by its mission and its decision-making structure, are centrally concerned with improving the curriculum, the teacher evaluation scheme can include that dimension directly. Too often, teacher evaluation procedures examine only the most stereotypical of teacher behavior, interactions with students. Although these interactions, indeed, make up the heart of teaching activity, it is well known that teachers' work extends well beyond "meeting with students." In the most effective schools, teachers are consistently involved in the goal-setting and decision-making components of school life (see above). And, it is reasonable to assume that a significant number of goals and decisions are directly associated with the school curriculum, in terms of planning, implementation, and evaluation. If such is the case, it is also reasonable to assume that the evaluation of teachers will give considerable emphasis to the teacher's contribution to the school's curriculum enterprise.

Whether for an inexperienced or veteran teacher, it is useful to know how one's work is perceived by one's chief administrator. This knowledge helps to shape decisions about either altering the amount and/or quality of that work as well as to provide information about whether one wishes to remain in a given school. After all, it is certainly possible that a teacher's particular view of schooling or perspective on appropriate pedagogy may not "fit" certain school cultures. This can be revealed in positive as well as negative ways by participation in a well-conceptualized and appropriately conducted evaluation system. If the evaluation procedures focus upon contribution to curriculum improvement and experimentation as a valued aspect of teacher behavior, and a teacher does not believe that this kind of contribution is a worthwhile competitor for other teacher activities, there is the possibility for either renegotiated expectations or for relocation.

Teacher evaluation, then, can support the development and maintenance of school norms related to participation in curriculum work as a consequence of making public expectations for this participation as well as providing ongoing and systematic data regarding its degree of presence. Further, teacher evaluation data can be used as important decision information about necessary and desirable professional development opportunities for teachers and administrators.

PROFESSIONAL GROWTH OPPORTUNITIES

A building-level administrator has explicit responsibility for ensuring that teachers are provided access to and opportunities for professional growth.[24] (This, of course, is also an organizational responsibility of the school system as a whole.) The intensity that the principal brings to this important function, as well as the discrimination regarding its focus, can influence significantly not just the teachers as individual professionals but the school as a social organization.

The recent past has demonstrated the tendency for professional growth to be conceptualized as remediation and be firmly embedded in issues of minimum competence. This stance has resulted in putting in place procedures that reflect a deficit model of typical in-service education, a means less to guarantee excellence than to be certain that teachers do as little harm as possible.[25]

It is intuitively appealing to believe that professional growth opportunities, to be influential upon teachers and upon the workplace, should be pointed toward ambitious rather than minimal goals. At issue for the purpose of this chapter is how to bring together the expectations for staff development as a school convention, the processes of staff development as institutional practices, and the content of staff development as the coherent focus for the processes.

Recent research has identified a set of staff development program variables that are consistently associated with successful outcomes.[26] These variables are ones that are particularly well suited to curriculum improvement in that they accommodate to a high degree the complexity of curriculum work. They can also be manipulated by a school principal through acting upon many of the issues noted already in this chapter.

The variables associated with successful professional development programs are (a) *context-sensitivity* (giving careful attention to curriculum improvement in relation to the nature of a particular school); (b) *knowledge-based* (using appropriate research, theory, proposition, and values in deciding curriculum issues); (c) *ongoing* (recognizing that curriculum work is cumulative over time); (d) *developmental* (ensuring that the curriculum work is not just a set of independent events but, instead, is a consequence of logical and intellectually sound relationships among components); (e) *participatory and collaborative* (involving most, if not all, of the school's professional staff in curriculum improvement activities); (f) *purposeful* (basing the curriculum development firmly in well-articulated and public expectations for learning); and (g) *analytic and reflective* (providing frequent opportunities for participants to think together about their work and to make adjustments as a result of their deliberations).

These staff development program features can be influenced greatly by the manner in which a school principal provides professional growth opportunities for teachers (and, indeed, for school administrators including the principal himself or herself). They also match conceptually the picture of the school culture that is presented in this chapter. Importantly, they are amenable to manipulation by the principal as he or she works with teachers toward reconsideration, alteration, improvement, and assessment of a school's curriculum.

SUMMARY

The view of curriculum work as a schoolwide activity and how that activity can be influenced by building-level administrators has provided the content of this section. This conception of the school as an organization, however, is dependent in large measure upon a reconceptualization of the role of the teacher, a shift from believing and acting as if the teacher is a worker, guided in large part by administrative decisions, to considering the teacher as a school-level executive and professional colleague. This move toward executive status for teachers suggests that principals must involve teachers systematically in school decisions, consider them as partners in program and curriculum planning and implementation, focus evaluation goals and processes on the degree to which the teachers function as participating executive professionals, and identify the school culture variables that must be in place for the vision to be accomplished.

The Dilemma of the Professional Preparation of Principals

The description of the principal as an organizational architect who works primarily on the creation of context conditions that will support curriculum improvement has taken up the bulk of this chapter. This view is validated by research evidence, has intuitive appeal, and is conceptually relevant to thinking of schools as human organizations. Further, this view is consonant with conceptions of curriculum work in regard to complexity, the need for multiple human resources, the requirements of continuity over time, and the belief that the closer one is to the student and teacher populations the more meaningful the curriculum implementation will be.

Unfortunately, this picture of the school principal is seldom reflected in programs designed to prepare people to assume a school administrator role. Typically, a graduate program for principal preparation gives serious attention only to conventional administrative objects of study. A prospective principal usually will be exposed to courses in school law, finance, management techniques, personnel issues, and the like. There might be some attention to teacher supervision and the inclusion of a requirement for a school-based internship of approximately a semester. Seldom is there any systematic and serious study of curriculum or of pedagogy. As problematic, from the perspective taken in this chapter, is the relative absence across graduate programs of disciplined attention to the context variables in schools that have been shown to be influential upon school success, whether success in the form of curriculum improvement or some other valued school activity.

The end result of such principal preparation programs is that school principals are most often unaware of the influence they could have on the school culture and overly dependent upon prescriptions for practice that are firmly based in conventional perceptions of administrative competence. The dominant pattern of school leadership appears to be managerial. Although there are definite aspects of schooling that require skill in management, dependence upon a management orientation for bringing about school improvement, curricular or otherwise, is more than likely insufficient to the task at hand.

What is required to accomplish the relationships, processes, and outcomes described in this chapter is a dramatic shift in how principals are prepared, and, concomitantly, in how the role of the teacher is conceptualized.[27] If teachers are to realize their ambitions for professional status, the work they do and the processes that support that work will be removed from preoccupation with "teacher as worker." Professional teachers will assume much greater responsibility for the life of the school, rather than only assume responsibility for life in a classroom. They will be supported in this and helped to be effective only if building principals have the necessary knowledge and skill to create the contexts for it to happen. And principals will be empowered to be organizational architects largely because of the nature of their preparation.

Principal preparation programs should maintain some measure of preoccupation with conventional topics as noted above. They must also include significantly more attention to curricular issues, paradigms, and dilemmas. They must focus on the nature of teaching as professional activity, including the work of teaching that takes place apart from students and individual classrooms. Preparation programs must attend to conceptions of schools as human organizations, ones that are malleable and susceptible to planned change by thoughtful alterations in business as usual. There is sufficient evidence to support this view over one that promotes management orientations as ways to bring about significant changes in educational institutions.

Conclusion

If schools can be reconsidered as places where everyone learns, students and teachers and administrators, and where learning across the community is a valued and supported activity, many of the goals for schooling that have eluded all but a few schools may have greater chance for realization.[28] For this to happen, I believe strongly that principals must take far more seriously than is typical the curriculum enterprise as a schoolwide focus for professional interaction. They must understand how their own behavior adds to or detracts from that focus, how they contribute through their manipulation of the environment to the development of norms of professional collegiality, participation in valued activity, and investment in the future of the school. Principals, to be successful leaders, must develop the habits of mind and practice that promote interaction over isolation, goal clarity over ambiguity, public rather than private understanding of rewards and sanctions, wise rather than trivial use of time, meaningful rather than incoherent professional development, and linkage with rather than isolation from the assistance that is necessary to engage effectively in schooling.

If we have learned anything during the past two decades of inquiring into schooling practice, we have learned that the power of the school context is extraordinarily strong. And we have learned that the school principal is a primary influence on the school context. This knowledge should be used to support curriculum improvement as a central function of professional educators in schools.

FOOTNOTES

1. John I. Goodlad, "The School as a Workplace," in *Staff Development*, Eighty-second Yearbook of the National Society for the Study of Education, Part 2, ed. Gary A. Griffin (Chicago: University of Chicago Press, 1983): 36-61.

2. Susan J. Rosenholtz and Otto Bassler, *Organizational Conditions of Teacher Learning*, Interim Report to the National Institute of Education, Grant #NIE-G-83-0041, 1983, unpublished manuscript.

3. Talcott Parsons, "General Theory in Sociology," in *Sociology Today*, ed. Robert K. Merton, Leonard Broom, and Leonard S. Cottrell, Jr. (New York: Basic Books, 1959), pp. 3-38.

4. I am grateful to David Berliner who coined this insightful title for the teacher who engages systematically in executive decision making in the complex environment of the classroom. This conception, although not so named, also guided the selection of guidelines contained in Gary A. Griffin and Phillip S. Schlechty, "Recommendations to the Mississippi Department of Education," unpublished manuscript, 1984.

5. Gary A. Griffin and Louise L. Light, *Nutrition Education Curricula: Relevance, Design, and the Problem of Change* (Paris: UNESCO, 1975).

6. Judith Schwartz, "Teacher Directed In-Service: A Model That Works," *Teachers College Record* 86 (Fall 1984): 223-249.

7. Susan J. Rosenholtz, Otto Bassler, and Kathy Hoover-Dempsey, *Elementary School Organization and the Construction of Shared Reality*, Interim Report to the National Institute of Education, Grant #NIE-G-83-0041, 1983, unpublished manuscript.

8. At the inaugural meeting of the Holmes Group in Washington, DC on January 30-February 1, 1987, Albert Shanker and Mary Hatwood Futrell presented a set of views regarding teachers' views of their workplaces that questioned seriously the degree to which schools could improve as a consequence of more rigorous preparation of teachers if the schools where they eventually do their teaching do not become more receptive environments for truly professional practice.

9. The Holmes Group, *Tomorrow's Teachers* (East Lansing, MI: The Holmes Group, 1986); The Carnegie Task Force on Teaching as a Profession, *A Nation Prepared: Teachers for the 21st Century* (New York: Carnegie Corporation, 1986).

10. Arthur Wise, Linda Darling-Hammond, Milbrey McLaughlin, and H. T. Bernstein, *Teacher Evaluation: A Study of Effective Practices* (Santa Monica, CA: Rand Corp., 1984).

11. Ann Lieberman and Lynne Miller, "School Improvement: Themes and Variations," *Teachers College Record* 86 (Fall 1984): 4-19.

12. Judith Warren Little, "Norms of Collegiality and Experimentation: Workplace Conditions of School Success," *American Educational Research Journal* 19 (Fall 1982): 375-40.

13. M. Maxine Bentzen, *Changing Schools: The Magic Feather Principle* (New York: McGraw-Hill, 1974), pp. 77-108.

14. Judith Warren Little, "Professional Development in Schools," address to the Chicago Area School Effectiveness Council, Chicago, February 10, 1987.

15. Phillip C. Schlechty and Ann Walker Joslin, "Images of Schools," *Teachers College Record* 86 (Fall 1984): 156-170.

16. Ibid.

17. Susan J. Rosenholtz, "Workplace Conditions of Teacher Quality and Commitment: Implications for the Design of Teacher Induction Programs," in *The Initial Years of Teaching: Background Papers and Recommendations*, ed. Gary A. Griffin and Suzanne Millies (Chicago: University of Illinois at Chicago, in press).

18. Beatrice A. Ward, "Professional Development of Teachers and School Effectiveness," address to the Chicago Area School Effectiveness Council, Chicago, May 9, 1986.

19. Judith Warren Little, *School Success and Staff Development: The Role of Staff Development in Urban Desegregated Schools* (Boulder, CO: Center for Action Research, 1981).

20. A major curriculum and staff development effort took place in the Yonkers (NY) Public Schools during the period 1978-1983. At first conceived as primarily curriculum development, the work took on the character of a systemwide school improvement strategy as large numbers of teachers participated directly as curriculum writers and less directly as both critics and experimenters as pieces of the new K-12 curriculum became available. The implementation of the new curriculum became the focus of staff development activities for all teachers in the system. In this example, the opportunities for making significant changes in schooling appeared to be the consequence of the complex and continuous interactions between curriculum development and professional growth activities.

21. See, for example, Gary A. Griffin and Susan Barnes, "Using Research Findings to Change School and Classroom Practices: Results of an Experimental Study," *American Educational Research Journal* 23 (Winter 1986): 572-586.

22. Gary A. Griffin, *Student Teaching and the Commonplaces of Schooling* (Austin, TX: Research and Development Center for Teacher Education, The University of Texas at Austin, 1983).

23. Linda Darling-Hammond, "A Proposal for Evaluation in the Teaching Profession," *Elementary School Journal* 86 (March 1986): 531-552.

24. Griffin and Barnes, "Using Research Findings to Change School and Classroom Practices."

25. Examples of the use of minimum standards to guide how teachers are judged can be found in several of the new state-level teacher programs. The consequences of this perspective about teachers seem to be a lowering of expectations, not only by those charged with evaluating teacher competence but by the new teachers themselves. This is discussed in Gary A. Griffin, "The Paraprofessionalization of Teaching" (Paper delivered at the Annual Meeting of the American Educational Research Association, Chicago, 1985).

26. These features were the result of extensive reanalyses of three large-scale studies of teacher education programs. It was found that the successful instances of professional development strategies included these features in interaction. The model that emerged and hypothetical descriptions of how it might appear in practice are found in James V.

Hoffman and Sara A. Edwards, eds., *Reality and Reform in Clinical Teacher Education* (New York: Random House, 1986).

27. An extremely thoughtful picture of the dilemmas and rewards of being a school principal is found in R. Bruce McPherson, Robert L. Crowson, and Nancy J. Pitner, *Managing Uncertainty: Administrative Theory and Practice in Education* (Columbus, OH: Charles E. Merrill, 1986).

28. Susan Rosenholtz reports that in the relatively ineffective schools in her sample, teachers report that it takes approximately one and one-half years to learn to teach. In modestly effective schools, teachers report that it takes about five years to learn to teach. In the most effective schools, teachers report that one never learns how to teach because becoming a teacher is a continuous process. There appears to be a strong relationship between good schools and the context feature of a community of learning.

CHAPTER XII

Progress in Dealing with Curriculum Problems

RALPH W. TYLER

The Long-Term Goal

Current reports on American education frequently fault the school curriculum. This emphasis on inadequacies and weaknesses fails to place the current situation in historical perspective. In order to assess the progress or lack of progress, it is necessary to consider the goal toward which the curriculum should be focused and the evidence of movement toward that goal or lack of such movement.

The most generally accepted goal of American education is to help all young people to learn the attitudes, knowledge, skills, and habits necessary for citizens who are to participate intelligently in the responsibilities of a democratic society. At the time of the American Revolution and a bit later when the Constitution was debated and formulated, our Founding Fathers were well aware of the danger that the new nation would soon perish unless the people participated with understanding of and devotion to its governance. The public schools were established to enable young people to learn what is necessary for intelligent democratic citizenship. As time went on the leaders of American education became increasingly aware of three problems that must be solved in order to reach this goal.

The Requirements of Intelligent Citizenship

The first problem is to identify what young people should learn in order to practice intelligent citizenship. At the time of the American Revolution, Thomas Jefferson emphasized the fact that the new nation was isolated from the rest of the civilized world. In planning for education in Virginia, he emphasized the need for young people to learn to read about the history of civilization, the efforts of Greeks, Romans, and other Europeans to achieve political stability. He stressed the importance of acquainting students with the philosophical discussions that had continued over the centuries. Mathematics was also recommended by some of the leaders as necessary for students to deal with matters of taxation and national defense as well as with the common transactions involved in buying and selling, and in constructing and maintaining household and farm equipment.

As the nation grew and the society became more complex, new conceptions developed about what young people should learn in order to participate intelligently in this changing society. As the rate of social change increased it became evident that this question must be faced anew by each new generation. Hence one aspect of progress in the curriculum must be appraised in terms of the extent to which the curriculum is being developed as a result of continuing study of what citizens in a democratic society need to learn.

Universal Access to Schooling

A second problem is to provide and assure opportunity for all young people to learn what is necessary for intelligent citizenship. At the time of the founding of the new nation, most of the thirteen states did not furnish public education for all the children. Not only was access to schooling denied to slaves; it was also, in most states, denied to the children of indigent parents, and it was often unavailable to all children in sparsely settled rural and frontier regions.

By 1910, approximately 50 percent of American children completed the sixth grade. Since that time, the proportion of young people having access to extended schooling has increased so that about 75 percent of American youth today are reported to have completed high school. However, access to a school does not guarantee access to the learning of what is necessary for intelligent citizenship. The common practice of assigning students to different tracks is found by recent investigations to deny access to students in lower tracks to some of the most important offerings required for intelligent democratic citizenship.

Promoting Student Learning

The third problem is to help all students learn what is required for intelligent democratic citizenship. It is a well-known fact that some students do not learn what the school seeks to teach. The National Assessment of Educational Progress reports that nearly 20 percent of seventeen-year-old Americans cannot read and comprehend simple material like newspaper items. Although a majority of thirteen-year-olds can write interpretable paragraphs of description and exposition, less than a third can write extended organized essays. More than 90 percent of seventeen-year-olds can add, subtract, multiply, and divide accurately with whole numbers, while only 45 percent understand how to use such computation in dealing with practical situations like purchases, figuring sales tax, and the like.

The children who have learned little of what the schools try to teach largely come from homes where the parents have had little or no education. This became so obvious by 1964 that a major recommendation of President Johnson's Task Force on Education was for the federal government to focus funds on the education of what are called "disadvantaged children."

It seems clear that a third aspect that should be assessed in order to appraise the progress made in developing an appropriate and effective curriculum is the extent to which it is helping all students learn what is required for intelligent democratic citizenship.

Continuing Study of What Students Need to Learn

For many centuries prior to 1900 the curriculum discussions of educators and philosophers focused on the presumed educational values of different subjects, and the place of each in the curriculum. For example, the study of geometry was believed to develop the logical faculty of the mind, and the study of Greek and Latin was believed to develop the verbal faculty. The study of any subject that was tightly organized and difficult to master was believed to discipline the mind to think cogently. The discussions of curriculum in the 1890s concerned what subjects should be offered in the high school and how many years of each subject should be required for graduation. There was general agreement about the proper subjects for the curriculum of the elementary school. They were reading, arithmetic, writing, spelling, penmanship, geography, and history.

The typical offerings in the high schools were Latin, a modern foreign language (usually French), English, history, moral philosophy, algebra, plane and solid geometry. There were many differences among the high schools in the length of time devoted to each subject. Four years of Latin were required for graduation in some schools while other schools required only two or three years. In some schools three years of history were required, in others only two. There were many other variations. To establish a uniform standard, the National Education Association appointed a Committee of Ten, chaired by Charles Eliot, president of Harvard. The commission given the committee was to recommend what subjects the high schools should offer and how many years of each subject should be required for graduation. The committee reported in 1893 and the structure it recommended was widely accepted and was followed by American high schools for forty years. The committee viewed this structure, subjects offered and years required, as an adequate specification of the curriculum. It did not outline what students should learn in these subjects.

This view was sharply challenged by the monumental investigations of Edward Lee Thorndike.[1] His studies refuted the long accepted beliefs that the study of the subjects of the school curriculum resulted in the disciplining of the mind, and that particular subjects developed particular faculties of the mind. He demonstrated that students who completed courses in geometry were no better in solving logical problems in fields outside of geometry than were students who had not taken geometry, and that students who completed courses in Latin were no better in their English composition than students who had not taken Latin. These investigations made it clear that the traditional justification for the subjects in the curriculum could no longer be accepted. Thorndike maintained that there must be elements in what was encountered outside of school that are identical with the elements being taught in school in order for students to be able to apply what they were learning in school to these out-of-school contexts. He referred to this as transfer of training.

The effect of these studies was to stimulate those developing public school curricula to examine the situations in which democratic citizenship can be exercised and identify what needs to be learned in order for the students to exercise their citizenship. Curriculum students began to investigate the demands and opportunities in contemporary society for the application of school learning. For example, researchers started looking at the quantitative problems that adults encountered in particular communities in order to select arithmetic topics relevant to those problems. They also studied the kinds of reading and reading materials found in particular towns and cities in order to establish objectives for reading and the materials to be used in the teaching of reading.

Franklin Bobbitt, a professor of education at the University of Chicago, was asked by the Los Angeles school authorities to help them modernize their elementary and secondary school curriculum. He instituted an investigation of the common activities of Angelenos and developed an outline for the curriculum objectives from his findings. In the 1930s, the State of Virginia became a field of inquiry to identify the activities and problems of the citizens of the state as a basis for a sweeping reconstruction of its public school curriculum. Although such wide-scale studies have not been undertaken since the 1930s, in certain states and many localities active inquiries are maintained to identify what students need to learn as social changes continue.

Problems in Curriculum Inquiry

Certain of these studies of what students need to learn are of little or no value because of their failure to distinguish important developments from trivial ones, and because they fail to recognize that human beings are capable of self-directed learning and can formulate and utilize generalizations to guide their activities. As an example of the first, some teachers of English composition have reconstructed their curriculum to focus on "word processing," not recognizing that "word processing" is a particular form of working on a composition and does not involve directly the major principles and problems of writing.

There have been many examples of the second error. Shortly after Thorndike developed the idea of identical elements, curriculum objectives were broken down into tiny specific things to be learned. In Thorndike's psychology of arithmetic, more than 2000 objectives for elementary school arithmetic were listed in such detail that $1+2=3$ is a separate learning objective from $2+1=3$. Pendleton proposed nearly 3000 objectives for secondary school English. Fortunately this practice was discontinued when Charles Judd and his students showed that students could learn to use general principles to guide them and could learn a few dozen general principles in a subject which they could adapt to the hundreds of specific matters they encountered.

I was a student in Judd's class in advanced educational psychology. Each student put the notion of generalized objectives to a practical test. For addition with whole numbers, Thorndike had listed the 100 addition facts obtained when one adds all the combinations from 1 to 10 taken two at a time. I worked with a class of second-grade children. Half of the class practiced all of the 100 combinations, the other half were helped to understand the principle of addition and practiced on only 21 combinations. At the conclusion of the experiment, both groups were given a test in which they had to add the 100 combinations. Both groups did equally well on the test.

Although in the period from 1925-40 curriculum makers formulated generalized educational objectives, there was a resurgence of the statement of minute learning objectives in the 1950s. This grew out of the experience in training employees for war-related activities. Typically an employee would be trained for a small part of a larger assembly task. Trainers learned that the trainees could acquire a few skills quickly if the skills were clearly defined and involved few factors. These training manuals were picked up and recommended to school curriculum groups, without the realization that specific training is not intellectual education. However, this reversal of progress in identifying what needs to be learned by citizens in a democratic society was followed by a wider understanding that democratic citizenship requires self-directed inquiry and problem solving and is inhibited by training in highly specific activities.

Progress in the continuous identification of what students should learn has varied with the school subjects. In reading, writing, and science there has been much recent progress. In mathematics and history much less is evident. In the social studies, much curriculum effort has been devoted to trying to adjudicate the conflicting claims for time in the curriculum made by sociologists, political scientists, anthropologists, economists, geographers, and social psychologists rather than focusing on the question of what is to be learned. There are wide variations in the progress made by different schools. Schools in the United States are greatly decentralized. There are not only widely different practices to be found in different states, but also among different cities within a state and among different schools in the same local district. However, one can identify a group of lead schools that appear to lead in movements to improve their educational effectiveness and they are followed later by a majority of schools which appear to have moved slowly in the same direction as that taken by the lead schools.

There has been progress among the lead schools in making continuing efforts to identify what responsible citizens in a democratic society should learn. Other schools are slowly following. Some seem never to move.

Progress in Providing Universal Access to Schooling

In the early days of this nation, access to the curriculum was largely limited to access to a public school. Not only were sparsely settled areas likely to have few if any schools, but when schools were first made available in these areas a tuition was charged which limited access to those children of families willing and able to pay for the tuition. Access to a curriculum designed for citizens was denied to slaves and to American Indians as well. Northern churches established some schools for Negroes in the South where the public schools did not provide for citizenship education for this group, but the influence of the Civil Rights Movement of the 1960s stimulated the program of access to schools for most of the neglected children and youth. By 1980, more than 95 percent of children six to fourteen years of age were reported to be enrolled in schools, and about 75 percent were reported to have graduated from high school.

However, access to a public school does not guarantee access to a curriculum designed to help students learn what is required for the exercise of citizenship in a democratic society. The practice of grouping and tracking students in the elementary and secondary schools has resulted in large numbers of children being denied access to such a curriculum. The curriculum for students in the lower tracks in most places focuses on memorization rather than on problem solving, on indoctrination rather than on self-directed inquiry. There has been great progress in providing universal access to the public schools, but thus far much less progress in providing access to a curriculum designed to help students learn what is necessary to be a responsible citizen in a democratic society.

Helping All Students Learn

From the establishment of schools until the middle of the twentieth century, the prevailing view was that some young people were educable but many had little potential for education. Intelligence tests and aptitude tests were developed to sort and measure different degrees of educability thought to be characteristic of human beings. As early as 1928, the National Society for the Study of Education produced a yearbook on the influence of nature and nurture upon intelligence.[2] In that volume Lewis Terman and his students reported studies validating the notion that there were wide differences in educability as measured by I.Q., while Frank Freeman and Sewall

Wright reported their study of identical twins raised by different families furnishing different environments. The I.Q.'s of these twins were similar to the I.Q.'s of their foster parents rather than the I.Q.'s of their natural parents.

The Society's Thirty-ninth Yearbook (*Intelligence: Its Nature and Nurture*, 1940)[3] reported the studies of George Stoddard in the University of Iowa Child Welfare Research Station showing not only that identical twins raised in different environments had different I.Q.'s but also that their actual school achievements were related to their home environment and not to the achievement of their parents.

John Dewey had reported in 1906 on his work in the Dewey School in which he found no child who was not learning. He wrote: "The problem is not the educability of the child but the ingenuity of teachers in finding ways to help each child learn." However, the myth of educability persisted until the 1940s when Allison Davis and Kenneth Eells demonstrated that the tests employed to measure intelligence used a vocabulary found in middle-class homes and not in working-class homes. When the test exercises used the wording of the working class, the children of working-class parents increased their test scores by an average of 40 points.

Davis and Eells also found that middle-class parents emphasize to their children the importance of doing well on tests. On the contrary, most working-class parents emphasize to their children "Don't get in trouble," and talk of passivity in school rather than working hard on tests. When working-class children were told that they would get a free ticket to the movies if they made high test scores, their average scores rose 30 points.

It is now the prevailing view among educational leaders that all children can learn and schools need to develop ways of helping all their students learn what the schools are trying to teach. This view was put to the test during the administration of President Lyndon Johnson. Head Start, Follow Through, Title I of the Elementary and Secondary Education Act of 1965 were supported and schools and other agencies were encouraged to obtain funds from the federal government to conduct such programs. The first evaluation of Title I gave disappointing results, but by 1970 more than one-third of the schools in the evaluation sample were getting significant positive results. By 1979, the National Institute of Education reported that a majority of the schools conducting programs focused on educating "disadvantaged children" were obtaining positive results. The recent reports of the National Assessment of Educational Progress show that the only significant improvement in the educational achievements of nine-year-olds and thirteen-year-olds have been made by these "disadvantaged children."

Progress in helping children learn what the schools try to teach has clearly been made in American elementary schools. There is little evidence of widespread progress in the high schools. There are high schools working together in special projects that are making substantial progress, but little or no progress is reported for most schools in the slums and in rural areas enrolling the children of immigrant farm workers.

In Conclusion

This brief commentary on progress of curriculum development and implementation has concentrated on the problems of identifying what needs to be learned to exercise responsible citizenship in a democratic society, on the extent to which universal access to this curriculum has been achieved, and on the progress made in helping all children learn what the schools are expected to teach. There is little reported evidence on the first problem and I have depended on my own reading and my participation in curriculum development activities. My subjective judgment is that slow but significant progress has been made by schools that are widely regarded as leaders.

On the second question, universal access to this curriculum, there are many kinds of available data, particularly from the comprehensive investigation directed by John Goodlad and reported in *A Place Called School*.[4] Far too little progress has been made in providing access to this curriculum. Much progress has been inhibited by the grouping and tracking practices of most schools.

On the third question, I find the reports of Title I, on Follow Through, and the periodic reports of the National Assessment of Educational Progress very helpful. American schools have concentrated their efforts to improve the learning of those students having greatest difficulty in school learning. As a result, the lowest 25 percent in school achievement are about where the middle 50 percent are in the European countries that are participating in the International Evaluation of Educational Achievement.

Yes, there has been progress in dealing with curriculum problems but the progress has not been uniform nor always positive. To understand what progress has been made, one must examine the several major aspects of the school curriculum.

FOOTNOTES

1. Edward L. Thorndike and R. S. Woodworth, "The Influence of Improvement in One Mental Function upon the Efficiency of Other Functions," *Psychological Review* 8 (May, July, November, 1901): 247-261, 384-395, 556-564.

2. *Nature and Nurture: Their Influence Upon Intelligence,* Twenty-seventh Yearbook of the National Society for the Study of Education, Part 1, ed. Guy M. Whipple (Bloomington, IL: Public School Publishing Co., 1928).

3. *Intelligence: Its Nature and Nurture,* Thirty-ninth Yearbook of the National Society for the Study of Education, Parts 1 and 2, ed. Guy M. Whipple (Bloomington, IL: Public School Publishing Co., 1940).

4. John I. Goodlad, *A Place Called School* (New York: McGraw-Hill, 1984).

Name Index

Abbott, Edith, 242
Adler, Mortimer J., 121, 219, 225
Airasian, Peter W., 100, 101, 117, 119, 120
Alioto, Robert, 54
Allen, Laurel B., 228, 241
Anderson, Robert, 2, 43, 60
Angus, I., 118
Anrig, Gregory, 92
Applebee, Arthur N., 146
Arnold, Gerald, 228, 241
Arnold, Matthew, 118, 119
Atkin, J. Myron, 14

Bagley, William C., 123, 145
Barnes, Susan, 265
Bassler, Otto, 264
Bateman, C. Fred, 232, 242
Beck, M.D., 99, 100, 119
Bell, Daniel, 135, 146
Bell, Robert, 118
Bell, Terrel H., 136
Bennett, Albert, 58
Bennett, William J., 139, 140
Bentzen, M. Maxine, 252, 265
Berliner, David, 35, 58, 264
Bernauer, James, S.J., 121
Bernstein, H.T., 264
Bettelheim, Bruno, 136, 146
Billett, Roy O., 224
Bloom, Benjamin S., 9, 91, 101, 117, 120, 121, 233, 234, 241, 242, 243
Bobbitt, Franklin, 18, 19, 20, 21, 33, 270
Boguslaw, Robert, 145
Bowles, Samuel, 224
Boyer, Ernest L., 32, 121, 189, 204, 219, 225
Braun, Robert J., 118, 120
Breckinridge, Sophinisba, 242
Briggs, Thomas H., 226, 227, 236, 241
Bristow, William H., 226, 241
Broadfoot, Patricia, 118
Brookover, Wilbur, 9, 234, 235, 242, 243
Broom, Leonard, 264
Brophy, Jere, 42
Brown, K.P., 109, 120
Bruner, Jerome S., 125, 126, 145

Bryan, William Jennings, 130
Bunzel, John H., 14
Butts, R. Freeman, 82
Byerly, Carl L., 239, 243

Cairns, Dorian, 119
Callahan, Raymond E., 8, 33
Campbell, Donald T., 89, 117
Cardenas, Jose, 120
Carroll, Lewis, 113, 121
Caswell, Hollis L., 132
Chall, Jeanne S., 146
Charters, W.W., 16, 32
Clark, M., 109, 120
Clark, Richard E., 135, 146
Clark, Richard W., 2, 4, 175
Cohen, Clare, 173
Cohen, David K., 32
Colb, Norman, 173
Commager, Henry Steele, 26, 28, 33
Conant, James B., 3, 218, 219, 225
Conard, Sue S., 146
Cornbleth, Catherine, 43, 58
Cornell, Ethel L., 212, 215, 224
Corse, L.B., 119
Cottrell, Leonard S., Jr., 264
Cremin, Lawrence A., 4, 14, 66, 82, 204, 207, 208, 224
Crowson, Robert L., 266
Crull, Peggy, 237, 238, 239, 243
Cruse, Keith L., 110, 117
Cuban, Larry, 188, 204
Cubberley, Ellwood P., 29, 30, 34, 123, 145
Cummings, William K., 118, 119
Cusick, Philip A., 186, 204

Dale, Edgar, 132
Darling-Hammond, Linda, 15, 37, 58, 264, 265
Darrow, Clarence, 130
Davis, Allison, 274
Dewey, John, 6, 15, 21, 22, 23, 24, 25, 26, 33, 38, 43, 47, 58, 74, 134, 146, 177, 221, 274
Dillon-Peterson, Betty, 58

277

Edmonson, J.B., 145
Edwards, Anna Camp, 33
Edwards, Sara A., 266
Eells, Kenneth, 274
Eisner, Elliot, 42, 58
Eliot, Charles, 269
English, Raymond, 134, 146
Esposito, Dominick, 218, 225
Etzioni, Amatai, 204

Fantini, Mario D., 204
Farrar, Eleanor, 32
Feistritzer, C.E., 58
Fenstermacher, Gary D, 203, 220, 225
Ferguson, Thomas, 14
Findley, Warren G., 118
First, Joan McCarty, 120
Fiske, Edward B., 146
Flowers, C.E., 102, 120
Foley, Eileen, 237, 238, 239, 243
Foucault, Michel, 115, 121
Frankel, Charles, 14
Frederiksen, Norman, 121
Freeman, Frank, 273
Futrell, Mary Hatwood, 264

Gage, N.L., 147
Gallup, Alec M., 204
Gayen, A.K., 118
Gernand, Renee, 117
Gigliotti, Richard J., 243
Ginsberg, Rick, 58
Gintis, Herbert, 224
Goldberg, Miriam L., 213, 215, 222, 224
Good, Thomas, 151, 173
Goodlad, John I., 5, 12, 15, 20, 33, 35,
    39, 42, 44, 45, 52, 58, 123, 145, 178,
    188, 190, 196, 203, 204, 219, 220,
    222, 225, 234, 243, 264, 275, 276
Gordon, Peter, 118
Gordon, C. Wayne, 243
Goslin, D.A., 99, 100, 119
Grady, David, 119
Grant, Nigel, 118
Greaney, Vincent, 119
Green, Thomas F., 113, 121
Griffin, Gary A., 6, 173, 244, 264, 265
Grouws, Douglas A., 151, 173

Hall, Gene, 40
Hamilton, Stephen, 243
Hampel, Robert M., 17, 32
Hand, Harold, 132
Haney, Walter, 84, 94, 117, 119
Hanna, Paul, 132

Hansot, Elizabeth, 29, 30, 31, 33, 34
Harap, Henry, 212, 224
Harris, Susan, 146
Harris, William T., 74, 205
Hart, David K., 190, 204
Heisenberg, Werner K., 89
Henderson, Ronald D., 243
Henry, Nelson B., 124, 147, 224
Herbert, Victor, 231
Herrick, Virgil, 45
Herskovits, Melville J., 47, 49, 59
Hirano-Nakanishi, Marsha, 230, 242
Hochman, Arthur, 173
Hoffman, James V., 266
Hofstadter, Richard, 130, 131, 146
Holmes, E.G.A., 118, 119
Homer, Winslow, 72
Honig, Bill, 137
Hoover-Dempsey, Kathy, 264
Hosford, Philip L., 173
Hotyat, F., 118
Howe, Harold, II, 103
Hunter, George, 129
Hunter, Madeline, 77, 173
Husserl, E., 100, 119

Jackson, Philip W., 5, 35, 58, 120
Jacullo-Noto, Joann, 173
Jefferson, Thomas, 267
Johnson, Lyndon B., 274
Jordan-Davis, Walter E., 231, 242
Joslin, Ann Walker, 265
Joyce, Bruce, 46, 58
Judd, Charles, 271
Justman, Joseph, 213, 224

Kaeser, Susan C., 228, 232, 233, 239,
    241, 242
Keenan, P.J., 110, 120
Kelleghan, Thomas, 100, 101, 117, 119,
    120
Kerr, Donna H., 46, 58
Killian, James R., Jr., 126, 145
Kirkland, Marjorie C., 99, 119
Kliebard, Herbert, 6, 13, 16, 45, 62
Koerner, J.D., 118
Kohl, Herbert R., 145
Kuhn, Thomas S., 127, 141, 145
Kulik, Chen-Lin, 215, 216, 224
Kulik, James A., 215, 216, 224

Langer, Judith A., 146
Lawton, Dennis, 118
Leiter, K. C. W., 120

LeMahieu, P.G., 104, 105, 120
Lieberman, Ann, 170, 173, 264
Lieberman, Myron, 3
Light, Louise L., 264
Lightfoot, Sara Lawrence, 186, 204
Linn, Robert, 120
Lipsitz, Joan, 187, 204
Little, Judith Warren, 46, 58, 265
Lortie, Dan, 46, 47, 58, 59, 173
Loucks, Susan, 40
Lumsdaine, A.A., 140, 147
Lynch, John, 59
Lyons, Stewart, 173

Macnamara, John, 118
Madaus, George, 7, 62, 83, 100, 101, 117, 118, 119, 120, 182
Maeroff, Gene I., 59
Mann, Dale, 215, 241, 242
Mann, Horace, 22, 61
Marburger, Carl L., 186, 204
Martin, David S., 196, 204
Mayer, William V., 133, 146
Mayhew, Katherine Camp, 33
McClure, Robert M., 14
McDill, Edward L., 228, 230, 232, 241, 242, 243
McDonald, Frederick, 5
McLaughlin, Milbrey W., 173, 264
McMurry, Charles A., 15
McPherson, R. Bruce, 266
Meier, Deborah, 96, 103
Mendenhall, James E., 132
Merton, Robert K., 116
Miller, Lynne, 170, 264
Miller, S.M., 230, 242
Millies, Suzanne, 265
Millman, Jason, 118
Mitzel, Harold E., 241
Morris, G.C., 90, 118
Morris, Norman, 118
Mukerji, S.N., 118
Mullis, Ina V.S., 146

Natriello, Gary, 228, 230, 241, 242, 243
Nauman, Craig, 233, 242
Nelson, Murry, 7, 226
Newlon, Jesse, 132
Newman, Robert E., Jr., 146
Niles, Bradley F., 243
Nisbet, Robert, 27, 28, 33
Nussbaum, Carole, 173

Oakes, Jeannie, 209, 218, 219, 224, 225
Olexa, Carol, 218, 221, 225

Olson, George, 58
Orwell, George, 90, 91, 93, 118, 119
Orwell, S., 5, 118

Pallas, Aaron M., 228, 230, 241, 242, 243
Parker, Francis W., 74
Parsons, Talcott, 264
Passow, A. Harry, 7, 205, 213, 224
Pedulla, Joseph J., 120
Pendleton, Charles S., 271
Perez, Jane, 242
Pestalozzi, Johann H., 22
Peterson, Paul E., 4, 22, 107
Peterson, Penelope L., 234, 243
Pitner, Nancy J., 51, 59, 266
Polemini, Anthony J., 7, 120
Popham, W. James, 110, 117, 118, 120
Posner, George J., 42, 58
Postman, Neil, 145
Powell, Arthur G., 32
Pratt, David, 82
Preston, Fannie W., 54, 59

Quay, Herbert C., 228, 241

Rafferty, Martin, 118
Rankin, Stuart C., 110, 117
Ravitch, Diane, 46, 58
Rentz, Robert, 95, 119
Resnick, Daniel P., 219
Resnick, Lauren B., 219
Reutter, E. Edmund, Jr., 233, 242
Reynolds, Ann, 58
Richman, C.L., 109, 120
Robey, Ralph, 139
Robinson, Donald W., 146, 147
Rock, R.T., 212, 213, 224
Rogers, Joel, 14
Rosenholtz, Susan J., 264, 265, 266
Rugg, Harold, 131, 139

Sabatini, Anne, 173
Saif, Philip S., 196, 204
Salmon-Cox, Leslie, 100, 119
Sand, Ole, 5, 14
Sandifer, Paul D., 110, 117
Sarason, Seymour B., 24, 26, 33, 52
Saxl, Ellen, 173
Scaros, Barbara, 173
Schafer, Walter E., 218, 221, 225
Schaffarzick, Jon, 145
Schlechty, Phillip S., 264, 265
Schneider, Jeffrey M., 243
Schrader, William B., 119

Schreiber, Daniel, 241, 243
Schwab, Joseph, 42, 44, 48, 49, 51, 58, 59
Schwartz, Henrietta, 5, 35, 46, 58, 59
Schwartz, Judith, 264
Scopes, John T., 129, 130
Scott, William G., 190, 204
Seeley, David S., 186, 204
Selden, Steven, 210, 224
Shanker, Albert, 264
Sharpe, Thomas, 112, 121
Sheed, Wilfred, 95, 119
Shulman, Lee, 39, 41, 58
Silvani-Lacey, Cindy, 238, 239, 243
Simon, John, 121
Sinclair, Robert L., 204
Sizer, T.R., 116, 121
Slavin, Robert E., 216, 217, 225
Smith, Donald, 242
Smith, Eugene, 121
Smith, M.S., 107, 120
Spaulding, Francis T., 90, 112, 117, 121
Sproull, Lee, 99, 119
Srinivasan, J.T., 118
Stedman, L.C., 107, 120
Stetz, Frank P., 99, 100, 119
Stoddard, George, 274
Strayer, George, 30
Swing, Susan R., 234, 243
Sykes, Gary, 145

Taba, Hilda, 45
Tanner, Daniel, 7, 37, 58, 59, 145, 195, 235
Tanner, Laurel, 1, 37, 58, 59, 122, 195
Terman, Lewis M., 210, 224, 273
Thiel, Linda, 196, 204
Thorndike, Edward Lee, 270, 271, 276
Tisher, Richard P., 147
Tlusty, Roger, 32

Tudisco, A.J., 243
Turlington, Ralph D., 120
Turner, Glenn, 90, 118
Tyack, David, 29, 30, 31, 33, 34
Tyler, Ralph W., 4, 9, 45, 97, 116, 117, 118, 119, 121, 267

Unruh, Adolph, 47, 59
Unruh, Glenys G., 47, 59

Vernon, P.E., 119
Vitz, Paul C., 139, 140, 147

Wagner, Hilmar, 231, 242
Ward, Beatrice A., 265
Warming, Eloise O., 140, 145, 147
Weber, James W., 238, 239, 243
Weicker, Lowell P., 139
Weinberg, Alvin M., 145
Weiner, Richard, 173
Weingartner, Charles, 145
Weisskopf, Victor F., 46
Welch, Wayne W., 145
Wells, H.G., 112, 121
Whipple, Guy M., 145, 222, 276
White, Emerson E., 118
White, Richard T., 147
Williams, Paul L., 110, 117
Wise, Arthur E., 10, 11, 15, 264
Wiseman, S., 118
Wittrock, Merlin C., 147
Woodworth, R.S., 276
Wright, Sewall, 274

Yates, Alfred, 211, 224

Zelan, Karen, 136
Zubrow, David, 99, 119
Zumwalt, Karen, 6, 148, 173

Subject Index

Ability grouping: access to knowledge as an issue related to, 222-23; inappropriateness of inflexible approach to, 221-22; issues related to, 212; studies of, 212-17; tracking as a form of, 217-221; types of, 210-11

Access to schooling, effects of grouping and tracking on, 273

"Active system" for curriculum decision making, model of, 191-96

Activity analysis, as basis for curriculum development, 270-71

Administrative personnel, as influencers on curriculum decisions, 186

American Association of University Professors (AAUP), Commission on Academic Freedom and Pre-College Education, 136

American Historical Association, Commission on Social Studies, 131

American Library Association, Newsletter of, 133

A Nation at Risk, 43, 124

Association for Supervision and Curriculum Development, 79, 180

Bayview-Hunters Point Educational Complex, 54-55

Biological Sciences Curriculum Study (BSCS), modular approach of, in text materials, 133-34

Building America series, attacks on, 131-33

California State Board of Education, rejection of textbooks in science and mathematics by, 137, 182

Carnegie Task Force on Teaching as a Profession, 39, 43, 248

Censorship: problem of, in relation to textbook and collateral material, 129-33; "watering down" of curriculum as consequence of, 133

Chicago Mastery Learning Reading Program (CMLR), 105

Children's Defense Fund, report of, on dropouts, 229-31

Citizenship, problems confronted in preparing young people for, 267-69

Coaching of students, for tests: commercial schools for, 94-95; emphasis of, on test-taking skills, 95-96

College Entrance Examination Board (CEEB), 86, 87, 92, 112

Commission on Reorganization of Secondary Education, Report of, on Cardinal Principles of Secondary Education, 207-9, 223

Committee of Ten (1893), 17, 18, 19: challenges to recommendations of, 269-70; recommendations of, regarding curriculum, 206-7

Competition, in classrooms, 73-74

Continuous Achievement Monitoring (CAM), 104

Cultural patterns, application of, to schools, 47-49

Curriculum, controversies over "watering down" of, 134-37

Curriculum change: catalog of human activities as basis for, 19-20, 270-71; central purpose of schooling in relation to, 20-21; four hypotheses regarding cyclical nature of, 16-17, 31-32; impact of social forces on, 27-29; organizational factors in relation to, 21-26; school administration in relation to, 28-31; stages in implementation of, 40

Curriculum improvement: assessment of progress in, 269-75; importance of schoolwide focus in, 250, 263-64; importance of teacher participation in, 251-52; need for technical assistance in, 257-58; need for time to engage in, 252-53; professional collegiality as factor in, 256-57; specificity versus generality of objectives in relation to, 271-72; staff stability as requisite for, 255-56; teacher evaluation in relation to, 258-60

Curriculum issues, crucial characteristics of, 7-14

Curriculum knowledge, application of: barriers to, 39-40, 47; lack of, in classrooms, 35-36; role of curriculum worker in, 51-52

Curriculum worker: importance of organizational unity to, 80-82; need for

281

improved programs for preparation of, 51-52; need to protect time and energies of, 78-80; political pressures on 60-66, 72-77

Decision making, in curriculum development: as a form of policy making, 177; catalog of actors involved in, 180-88; example of school, district, and state-level interaction in, 196-200; importance of building-level action in, 189-91

Dewey's Laboratory School, 6, 24-26, 274

Dropout rates, 226-227

Dropouts: studies of, 229-32; various definitions of, 226

Dropping out, prevention of: alternative programs for, 236-38; common elements of effective programs for, 240-41; curriculum practices for, 234-36; role of teachers in, 233; vocational programs for, 238-39

Drug education, two contrasting scenarios in planning of programs for, 175-76, 200-3

Dual Progress Plan, 211

Education: abiding faith of Americans in, 26-28; goals of, 267; professional and public prerogatives in, 2-3; public opinion in relation to, 4

Educational policy, uses of test results in forming of, 105-10

Educational reforms, effects of conflicting patterns of, on teachers and teaching, 6

Emergent learning, textbooks as useful vehicles for, 129

Evolution, controversies over teaching of, 128, 129-30, 182

External testing: impact of, on administrative practices and school organization, 108; uses of results of, in relation to educational policy matters, 105-7

Florida Task Force on Educational Assessment, 108, 109

Ford Foundation Urban Master of Arts in Teaching Program, 53

General education, definition of, 178-79

Georgia Regents Testing Program, 95

Grouping practices, 74-76

Higher education personnel, as influencers of curriculum decisions, 184-85

High-stakes tests: counterstrategies to diminish negative consequences of, 115-17; examples of, 87-88; influence of, on curricular reform, 92-93; need for study of impact of, 110; symbolic power of, 89

Holmes Group, 39, 171-73, 268

Individual differences in ability and achievement, attempts to provide for, 205, 210-212

Instructional practices, legislative mandates for, 76-77

Interactive Research and Development in Schooling Project (New York City), 155-57

Internal testing programs, effects of, on schools, teachers, and students, 99-105

Job Training Partnership Act, 239

Joplin Plan, 211

Kentucky Essential Skills Test (KEST), 87

Low-stakes tests, 88

Manual training, introduction of, 209

Maximum competency tests, recommendations regarding, in reform reports, 110-14

Measurement-driven instruction: effects of, 84-85; nature of, 84

Media, as influencers of curriculum decisions, 183-84

Minimum competency testing, testimony in hearings on, 96, 108, 109, 114

National Assessment of Educational Progress, 106, 268, 274, 275

National Coalition of Advocates for Students (NCAS), National Board of Inquiry of, 103, 105, 108-9, 113

National Committee for Citizens in Education (NCCE), 180

National Commission on Excellence in Education, 124-25, 232

National Defense Education Act, 98

National Education Association, School Dropout Project of, 225, 234

National Endowment for the Humanities, 184

National Institute of Education, Curriculum Development Task Force of, 128

National Panel on High School and Adolescent Education, 4

National Science Foundation, 125, 126, 184

National Society for the Study of Education, references to prior yearbooks of, 5, 6, 122, 123, 124, 129, 212, 273, 274

National Survey of Secondary Education (1932), 211-212

New York State Regents Examinations, 87, 90, 98, 112

Paideia Proposal, role of testing in, 116

Political leaders, as influencers of curriculum decisions, 181

Political pressures, on curriculum workers: examples of, in support of counterproductive practices, 72-77; illustrative topics that give rise to, 65-66; sources of, 60-64; supervisors' views regarding, 66-69; teachers' views of and responses to, 69-71

Principals: needed changes in programs of preparation for, 262-63; responsibility of, for curriculum improvement, 249-50; role of, in shaping context features that support curriculum improvement, 251-61

Professional organizations, as influencers of curriculum decisions, 185

Public, as influencers of curriculum decisions, 179-80

School culture, effects of, on curricular change, 23-24

Schooling, unchanging character of, 188-89

School surveys, as mechanisms to encourage curriculum change, 30

School-university cooperation, characteristics of productive programs for, 55-56

Society for Curriculum Study, 131-32

Staff development: relation of deliberative view of teaching to, 169-73; variables associated with successful programs for, 260-61

Standardized achievement tests: coaching of students for, 93-95; general principles pertaining to influence of, on curriculum, 88-98; practice of "teaching to," 90-93, 95-97; variables measured by, 85-86; score referents of, 86; symbolic power of, as seen by policymakers, 89; use of, in high-stakes and low-stakes testing programs, 87-88

Student teachers, four cases from follow-up study of, 159-66

Supervision: bureaucratic nature of, 37; limitations of current methods of, 43, 44

Teacher centers, 247

Teacher Corps, 53

Teachers: attitudes of, toward teaching, 155-57; "burnout" of, 50; conception of, as classroom executives, 245, 248-49, 261-62; conception of, as workers, 245, 247-48; curricular conceptions of, 48; impact of school culture on, 45-47; impact of technical conception of teaching on, 155-66, 169; participation of, in decision making, 186-87, 251-52; professional preparation of, 37-39, 41-45; resistance of, to commands, 49; rewards for, 253-54; view of, regarding political pressures, 69-71. See also, Teaching.

Teaching: attitudes of teachers toward, 155-57; "deliberative" approach to, 167-69; technical conception of, 153-54; undermining of, by current trends, 148-52; various conceptions of, 245-49; vision of, as seen in report of the Holmes Group, 172

"Teaching to the test," conditions that encourage, 90-9

Testing: effects of, on goals of schooling, 97; effects of, on teaching practices, 96; increasing attention to, in publications, 84; principles pertaining to influence of, on curriculum, 88-98; recommendations regarding, in education reform reports, 110-11

Testing programs: high-stakes versus low-stakes features of, 88; internal versus external control of, 86-87; use of results of, 87

Test publishers, as influencers of curriculum, 182-83

Textbooks: censorship in relation to, 129-33; decline in expenditures for, 124; importance of, in curriculum reform projects, 125-27; influence of publishers of, on curriculum decisions, 181-82; lack of adequate research on use of, 139-41; need for upgrading of, 124-25; predominance of, as classroom resource, 122-24; recommendations regarding, 141-43

Tracking. See Ability grouping.

Twentieth Century Fund, report of, 107

INFORMATION ABOUT MEMBERSHIP IN THE SOCIETY

Membership in the National Society for the Study of Education is open to all who desire to receive its publications.

There are two categories of membership, Regular and Comprehensive. The Regular Membership (annual dues in 1988, $20) entitles the member to receive both volumes of the yearbook. The Comprehensive Membership (annual dues in 1988, $40) entitles the member to receive the two-volume yearbook and the two current volumes in the Series on Contemporary Educational Issues. For their first year of membership, full-time graduate students pay reduced dues in 1988 as follows: Regular, $16; Comprehensive, $36.

Membership in the Society is for the calendar year. Dues are payable on or before January 1 of each year.

New members are required to pay an entrance fee of $1, in addition to annual dues for the year in which they join.

Members of the Society include professors, researchers, graduate students, and administrators in colleges and universities; teachers, supervisors, curriculum specialists, and administrators in elementary and secondary schools; and a considerable number of persons not formally connected with educational institutions.

All members participate in the nomination and election of the six-member Board of Directors, which is responsible for managing the affairs of the Society, including the authorization of volumes to appear in the yearbook series. All members whose dues are paid for the current year are eligible for election to the Board of Directors.

Each year the Society arranges for meetings to be held in conjunction with the annual conferences of one or more of the major national educational organizations. All members are urged to attend these sessions. Members are also encouraged to submit proposals for future yearbooks or for volumes in the series on Contemporary Educational Issues.

Further information about the Society may be secured by writing to the Secretary-Treasurer, NSSE, 5835 Kimbark Avenue, Chicago, Ill. 60637.

RECENT PUBLICATIONS OF THE NATIONAL SOCIETY FOR THE STUDY OF EDUCATION

1. The Yearbooks

Eighty-seventh Yearbook (1988)
Part 1. *Critical Issues in Curriculum.* Laurel N. Tanner, editor. Cloth.
Part 2. *Cultural Literacy and the Idea of General Education.* Ian Westbury and Alan C. Purves, editors. Cloth.

Eighty-sixth Yearbook (1987)
Part 1. *The Ecology of School Renewal.* John I. Goodlad, editor. Cloth.
Part 2. *Society as Educator in an Age of Transition.* Kenneth D. Benne and Steven Tozer, editors. Cloth.

Eighty-fifth Yearbook (1986)
Part 1. *Microcomputers and Education.* Jack A. Culbertson and Luvern L. Cunningham, editors. Cloth.
Part 2. *The Teaching of Writing.* Anthony R. Petrosky and David Bartholomae, editors. Cloth.

Eighty-fourth Yearbook (1985)
Part 1. *Education in School and Nonschool Settings.* Mario D. Fantini and Robert Sinclair, editors. Cloth.
Part 2. *Learning and Teaching the Ways of Knowing.* Elliot Eisner, editor. Cloth.

Eighty-third Yearbook (1984)
Part 1. *Becoming Readers in a Complex Society.* Alan C. Purves and Olive S. Niles, editors. Cloth.
Part 2. *The Humanities in Precollegiate Education.* Benjamin Ladner, editor. Paper.

Eighty-second Yearbook (1983)
Part 1. *Individual Differences and the Common Curriculum.* Gary D Fenstermacher and John I. Goodlad, editors. Paper.
Part 2. *Staff Development.* Gary Griffin, editor. Paper.

Eighty-first Yearbook (1982)
Part 1. *Policy Making in Education.* Ann Lieberman and Milbrey W. McLaughlin, editors. Cloth.
Part 2. *Education and Work.* Harry F. Silberman, editor. Cloth.

Eightieth Yearbook (1981)
Part 1. *Philosophy and Education.* Jonas P. Soltis, editor. Cloth.
Part 2. *The Social Studies.* Howard D. Mehlinger and O. L. Davis, Jr., editors. Cloth.

Seventy-ninth Yearbook (1980)

Part 1. *Toward Adolescence: The Middle School Years.* Mauritz Johnson, editor. Cloth.
Part 2. *Learning a Second Language.* Frank M. Grittner, editor. Cloth.

Seventy-eighth Yearbook (1979)

Part 1. *The Gifted and the Talented: Their Education and Development.* A. Harry Passow, editor. Paper.
Part 2. *Classroom Management.* Daniel L. Duke, editor. Paper.

Seventy-seventh Yearbook (1978)

Part 1. *The Courts and Education.* Clifford B. Hooker, editor. Cloth.

Seventy-sixth Yearbook (1977)

Part 1. *The Teaching of English.* James R. Squire, editor. Cloth.

The above titles in the Society's Yearbook series may be ordered from the University of Chicago Press, Book Order Department, 11030 Langley Ave., Chicago, IL 60628. For a list of earlier titles in the yearbook series still available, write to the Secretary, NSSE, 5835 Kimbark Ave., Chicago, IL 60637.

2. The Series on Contemporary Educational Issues

The following volumes in the Society's Series on Contemporary Educational Issues may be ordered from the McCutchan Publishing Corporation, P.O. Box 774, Berkeley, Calif. 94701.

Case, Charles W., and Matthes, William A., editors. *Colleges of Education: Perspectives on Their Future.* 1985.
Eisner, Elliot, and Vallance, Elizabeth, editors. *Conflicting Conceptions of Curriculum.* 1974.
Erickson, Donald A., and Reller, Theodore L., editors. *The Principal in Metropolitan Schools.* 1979.
Farley, Frank H., and Gordon, Neal J., editors. *Psychology and Education: The State of the Union.* 1981.
Fennema, Elizabeth, and Ayer, M. Jane, editors. *Women and Education: Equity or Equality.* 1984.
Griffiths, Daniel E., Stout, Robert T., and Forsyth, Patrick, editors. *Better Leaders, Better Schools: Perspectives on School Administration.* 1988.
Jackson, Philip W. *Contributing to Educational Change: Perspectives on Research and Practice.* 1988.
Lane, John J., and Walberg, Herbert J., editors. *Effective School Leadership: Policy and Process.* 1987.
Levine, Daniel U., and Havighurst, Robert J., editors. *The Future of Big City Schools: Desegregation Policies and Magnet Alternatives.* 1977.

Lindquist, Mary M., editor. *Selected Issues in Mathematics Education.* 1981.

Peterson, Penelope L., and Walberg, Herbert J., editors. *Research on Teaching: Concepts, Findings, and Implications.* 1979.

Pflaum-Connor, Susanna, editor. *Aspects of Reading Education.* 1978.

Purves, Alan, and Levine, Daniel U., editors. *Educational Policy and International Assessment: Implications of the IEA Assessment of Achievement.* 1975.

Sinclair, Robert L., and Ghory, Ward. *Reaching Marginal Students: A Prime Concern for School Renewal.* 1987.

Spodek, Bernard, and Walberg, Herbert J., editors. *Early Childhood Education: Issues and Insights.* 1977.

Talmage, Harriet, editor. *Systems of Individualized Education.* 1975.

Tomlinson, Tommy M., and Walberg, Herbert J., editors. *Academic Work and Educational Excellence: Raising Student Productivity.* 1986.

Tyler, Ralph W., editor. *From Youth to Constructive Adult Life: The Role of the Public School.* 1978.

Tyler, Ralph W., and Wolf, Richard M., editors. *Crucial Issues in Testing.* 1974.

Walberg, Herbert J., editor. *Educational Environments and Effects: Evaluation, Policy, and Productivity.* 1979.

Walberg, Herbert J., editor. *Improving Educational Standards and Productivity: The Research Basis for Policy.* 1982.

Wang, Margaret C., and Walberg, Herbert J., editors. *Adapting Instruction to Student Differences.* 1985.

Warren, Donald R., editor. *History, Education, and Public Policy: Recovering the American Educational Past.* 1978.